Second Australian Edition

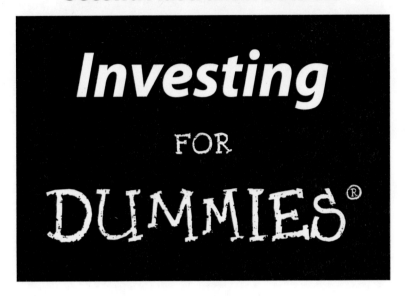

Investing

FOR

DUMMIES®

by James Kirby
and
Barbara Drury

WILEY

Wiley Publishing Australia Pty Ltd

Investing For Dummies®

Second Australian Edition published by
Wiley Publishing Australia Pty Ltd
42 McDougall Street
Milton, Qld 4064
www.dummies.com

Copyright © 2009 Wiley Publishing Australia Pty Ltd

The moral rights of the authors have been asserted.

National Library of Australia Cataloguing-in-Publication data:

Author:	Kirby, James.
Title:	Investing For Dummies/James Kirby and Barbara Drury.
Edition:	2nd Australian ed.
ISBN:	978 1 7421 6851 7 (pbk.)
Subjects:	Investments.
Other Authors:	Drury, Barbara.
Dewey Number:	332.632

Cover image: © Stockbyte

Typeset by diacriTech, Chennai, India

About the Authors

James Kirby has held senior positions on the *Australian Financial Review*, the *Australian*, *Business and Finance* in Dublin and the *South China Morning Post* in Hong Kong. A veteran of reporting on and analysing Australian corporations, he wrote for *Business Review Weekly* before co-founding *Eureka Report*. He has written several business books, including biographies of Janine Allis, Gerry Harvey and Richard Pratt, and was a contributor to *Investing for Australians All-in-One For Dummies*. James is also a columnist on the *Sunday Age*.

Barbara Drury is a personal finance and business writer for publications in Australia and overseas. She is a regular contributor to the *Sydney Morning Herald* and the *Age*, and writes for a number of financial newsletters and corporate publications. She is the author of *Personal Finance For Dummies* and *Sorting Out Your Finances For Dummies*, Australian Edition, a contributor to *Investing for Australians All-in-One For Dummies* and co-author of *The Fairfax Experience: What the Management Texts Didn't Teach Me* with Fred Hilmer, also published by Wiley. Barbara began her career in journalism more than 20 years ago as a staff writer for publications including the *Australian Financial Review*, the *Australian* and the *Sun* newspaper in Sydney. These days Barbara works from her home office on the New South Wales north coast. When she's not writing, she can be spotted on the sidelines at junior soccer or being dragged along the beach by a hyperactive labrador.

Dedication from the First Edition

To Adam Ryan. Since I came to Australia, Adam has always offered excellent advice. Many people can hold forth on the investment markets but few can communicate life's investing lessons so effectively.

Authors' Acknowledgements

From James, for the first edition: Thanks first to Jane Ogilvie, publisher at Wiley Publishing Australia. The best publisher is someone who can see exactly where a writer is coming from and yet remain a publisher first and foremost — hats off to you, Jane. Nicole McKenzie, project editor, for her fine work putting this large book together with an unfailing sense of humour. Thanks also Nicole for volunteering to do work that could easily have fallen back to me without your efficiency. Robi van Nooten (calm and collected at all times), thanks for your careful editing.

At Fairfax Business Publications, I want to thank my editor at *BRW*, Neil Shoebridge, who conceded to my working part-time at the magazine while writing this book. Thanks also to Robin Bowerman and Mike Dobbie at *Personal Investor*, and Tony Featherstone at *Shares* for advice and permission to use various facilities at their magazines. Throughout the book I warn that the investment world yields nothing for free. Yet, a string of people helped me with this book — several reading entire chapters in draft form — without asking for anything in return. Thanks a million to Adam Ryan and Marc Cini at Adamco for their observations (always delivered with zeal!) on the property market. Scott Walters at HSBC for his advice on the changing nature of the stock market, Brendan Donahue at Bank of Ireland Asset Management for his advice on everything from bonds to superannuation, Neil Crawford at Heffernan Crawford for his advice on the realities of investing in managed funds and Roger McIlroy at Christie's for his advice on the art market. Also, Gervase Green at the ASX, Simon Morgan and Doug Sumner at Norwich Union, Tony Kaye at Standard & Poor's, Prabhu Sivabalan and Zoltan Matolcsy at University of Technology, Sydney, and everyone else who helped in any way.

In writing any book you need encouragement from others who have been through the process. So, once again, I wish to thank my fellow non-fiction writers Gideon Haigh and Adrian Tame for saying the right things at the right times.

Finally, I want to thank my partner Mary O'Brien for her help and patience throughout the year I put this book together.

From Barbara, for the second edition: Many thanks to James Kirby, author of the first edition of *Investing For Dummies*, for entrusting the second edition of his book to me. The investment landscape has changed enormously in the seven years since the first edition was published, and James' work has stood the test of time.

This is my fourth major project for Wiley, so thanks also to acquisitions editor Charlotte Duff for her continued faith in me, and to project editor Kerry Davies for her unfailing attention to detail. On a book as broad in scope and as detailed as this one, it is often difficult to tell where the author's work ends and the editor's begins.

I would also like to acknowledge the generous contribution of James Frost, author of *Online Share Investing For Dummies*, for lending his time and expertise to the section on online networking in Chapter 11. Many people helped me with the research for this edition, but I would especially like to thank Phillip Gray, editorial and communications manager at Morningstar, who is unfailingly gracious with his time.

Publisher's Acknowledgements

We're proud of this book; please send us your comments through our online registration form located at www.dummies.com/register/.

Some of the people who helped bring this book to market include the following:

Acquisitions, Editorial and Media Development

Project Editor: Kerry Davies

Acquisitions Editor: Charlotte Duff

Editorial Manager: Gabrielle Packman

Production

Graphics: Wiley Art Studio

Cartoons: Glenn Lumsden

Proofreader: Pamela Dunne

Indexer: Karen Gillen

The authors and publisher would like to thank the following copyright holders, organisations and individuals for their permission to reproduce copyright material in this book: APRA, Australian Securities Exchange Limited, E*TRADE, MLC, Morningstar Australia, Real Estate Institute of Australia, Reserve Bank of Australia. Every effort has been made to trace the ownership of copyright material. Information that will enable the publisher to rectify any error or omission in subsequent editions will be welcome. In such cases, please contact the Permissions Section of John Wiley & Sons Australia, Ltd.

Contents at a Glance

Table of Contents

Introduction

· ·

*J*ames was sitting at his desk writing one of the first chapters of the first edition of *Investing For Dummies* one beautiful spring morning when there was a knock at the door. Being up since dawn meant he went straight to work without glancing at a newspaper or talking to anybody else. Freda, his gardening consultant, was at the door with some of her colleagues to draw plans for a new garden. James stepped out and greeted his visitors with a cheery 'Good morning,' then he looked at their grim faces. 'Isn't it awful what's happened in America? All those people killed,' said Freda, standing on the lawn that fateful day — 11 September 2001.

Looking back on the events, James knew almost immediately that 11 September would create a conservative climate for some time to come. Indeed, the investment markets of the early 2000s were very sober compared to the excitement of the 1990s or the 1980s.

Fast forward seven years to late 2008, when James and Barbara prepared the second edition of *Investing For Dummies*. Another completely unexpected event — the global credit squeeze and the unprecedented financial crisis that followed — was demolishing financial markets even more savagely than the terrorist attack of 11 September 2001.

The message we gained from these events is that investment doesn't occur in a vacuum. You can read every investment book ever written but you must also be alert to the mood and circumstances surrounding your investment. Property is a very reliable investment, with enormous evidence to suggest that it's one of the safest investments you can make. But, if an oversupply of apartments exists in your city, then apartment investing can't be a good investment in that location. In other words, be aware of the bigger picture.

For example, if we had had to choose between shares in a bank and shares in a biotechnology company in late 2007, we might have decided the future of the banking industry was safer than an investment in the risky business of biotechnology. One year later, one of Wall Street's biggest investment banks, Lehman Brothers, had collapsed and others had been rescued by the US government, the UK had nationalised its ailing banks and the Australian government was forced to guarantee bank deposits of up to $1 million to prevent a run on the banks. Amid this turmoil, blood serum group CSL went from strength to strength, one of the few bright spots on the Australian sharemarket.

Investing For Dummies, Second Australian Edition, is a basic road map to help you navigate the investment markets and, although the book can't foresee the circumstances in which you're going to invest, you can use the book as a guide to help you to make those choices.

This book is primarily about investing and we don't spend too much time advising on how to manage your personal finances. You must put your personal finances in good shape, though, before you can become a successful investor. (The basic steps towards managing your money sufficiently to allow yourself the resources to invest are dealt with in Part I, especially in Chapter 3.)

Using This Book

You can read this book from start to finish and we hope it gives you a 'helicopter view' of how to become a successful investor. Just as easily, you can refer to the sections individually as you require information in those areas.

Throughout the book we mention various financial institutions by name. Generally, institutions are mentioned not because they're the best in a certain area, but rather because they have the biggest presence in a certain area, which is a very different criterion. You can also see how some very well known institutions perform badly and little-known institutions perform well. Remember, every time you see a financial institution advertising, they're incurring an expense that they deduct from your returns if you have money with them.

The book can be used as an ideal central reference point. For example, if you're preparing to invest in managed funds, then familiarise yourself with managed funds through the information in this book and then begin to contact the fund managers themselves.

When you go out and deal with the investment market, keep in mind the lessons of the book. Whether you're on the phone, on a website or sitting in someone's office, remember that they're trying to sell you something. You're doing them a favour by considering their services.

One real improvement in recent years is the amount of information about financial products and their performance history on the websites of financial institutions. Use this option as often as you like to gather information at no cost, because this service is one of the few ways in which you can really improve your investment skills for free.

As financial journalists for more than 50 years between us, we still find interesting the fact that the people in financial institutions love to hide behind a smokescreen of financial language. The more you know this language, the better deal you can get from a bank, a fund manager, a stockbroker or an insurer. Sometimes the language is unavoidable because of the diversity of products around these days. But, if you concentrate on what matters to you — the cost of the investment, the return you can expect and the portion of the return that ends up in your bank account — you can do well.

Getting the Most from This Book

Using this book as your bedrock, no-nonsense, no-frills guide to the investment markets is the way forward. When you look at the table of contents carefully, you can see that it's divided into clearly defined parts and then further into specific chapters.

Part I: Investing Fundamentals

In this part we take you through the basic steps of preparing to become an investor, coming to terms with the idea of risk and the different approaches available to you when you enter the market. We also look at managing your money and seeking financial advice.

Part II: The Markets

Here we examine the wonderful world of the stock market. Everything you want to know about 'the market' with its stocks, brokers, floats and rights issues. We also take a look at the flourishing world of online trading, where all sorts of opportunities are opening up for investors like you.

Part III: Managed Funds, Bonds and Cash

Managed funds are becoming more popular every year because you can invest in a whole range of stocks or even stock markets with just one fund. Here we show you how to pick a managed fund, and how to select what you want inside any fund. We also explain what you need to know about cash and bonds.

Part IV: Property and Collectibles

Property is a great money-making machine for many Australians, but the lessons to learn about buying a home and buying a property to rent are very different. Here we look at the entire property market from houses and apartments to industrial land and property trusts. We also provide a chapter on investing in the intriguing art, wine and collectibles sector.

Part V: Your Nest Egg: Superannuation

Superannuation is your opportunity to save for your own financial freedom in later life. Superannuation is a system that you have to learn and understand. Learning the basics of superannuation isn't difficult and is well worth the effort. Here we deal with superannuation saving, tax advantages and the choices you may face inside the industry in the coming years.

Part VI: The Part of Tens

In this final part we deal with our all-time favourite lists when it comes to investing. We list the most important investing lessons you can get and also give you the lowdown on dealing with a financial adviser who can be your major ally in building future wealth.

Glossary

We've included a helpful glossary to define terms that riddle the investment world.

Conventions Used in This Book

We want to help you get the information you need as fast as possible. To help you, we use several conventions:

- ✔ Monofont is used to signal a web address.

    When this book was printed, some web addresses may have needed to break across two lines of text. If that happened, rest assured that there aren't any extra characters (such as hyphens or spaces) to indicate the break. So, when using one of these web addresses, just type in exactly what you see in this book, pretending that the line break doesn't exist.

- ✔ *Italics* signal that a word is a unique and important term for investors.
- ✔ **Bold** words make the key terms and phrases in bulleted and numbered lists jump out and grab your attention.
- ✔ Sidebars, text separated from the rest of the type in grey boxes, are interesting but slightly tangential to the subject at hand. Sidebars are generally fun and optional reading. You won't miss anything critical if you skip the sidebars. If you choose to read the sidebars, though, we think you'll be glad you did.

Getting to Know the Icons

The worst thing about other investment books is a great big slab of writing where all the best points and suggestions get buried. In *Investing For Dummies*, Second Australian Edition, we try to highlight many of the juiciest tips, warnings and recommendations for you. Here's a guide to the icons:

A tip is a very specific piece of advice on a particular topic. For example, in Chapter 17, 'Buying Your Home, Paying for It and Selling It', there's a tip about the First Home Owner Grant.

This is for basic rules, information to file away in your memory. For example, in Chapter 22, 'Getting the Best From Superannuation', we mention the possibility of working longer than you may have planned, and that even two more years in the workforce gives your super a boost.

Here's the stuff that may be a bit technical; you don't really need to know it but you may find it interesting. If you really want to know how an investing concept works, read the information next to this icon; if you don't, you can continue on regardless. For example, in Chapter 12, 'How Do You Do? Getting to Know Fund Managers', there's a paragraph on spreads. It's a bit technical but you may find it interesting. If you don't, you can skip it, as the rest of the section tells you enough.

A warning is just what the word says — a caution. For example, in Chapter 18, 'So You Want to Be a Landlord?', you'll see this warning against a very cautionary tale — about pets. The warning symbol indicates a pitfall, so best to read it.

The financial markets are a great source of smart comments usually made by those who have outsmarted everybody else, like legendary US investor Warren Buffett. We drop in many of these comments for your entertainment and to give you some wider perspective about the material covered in the relevant chapters.

Part I
Investing Fundamentals

Glenn Lumsden

'Money and I have only ever been passing acquaintances. This time I'm interested in a serious relationship.'

In this part ...

Getting your grip on the investment world is the first step on an exciting adventure — and it all starts with this part. Here, we explain risk in all its dimensions, the keys to becoming an investor, how you can get to know the investment markets and, most importantly, how to keep away from the sharks and get the best possible advice.

Chapter 1

Pack Your Bags for the Financial Journey

*L*ucky you! The smartest thing you may have done today is to pick up this book. We wish we'd picked up something like it back in 1987 when we were both establishing our careers and had some disposable income to play with.

Think about James' story: In September 1987, soon after arriving in Australia, he was not only renting an apartment, but he was also too lazy to go and buy some furniture. So he rented a television, a fridge, a lounge suite and a bed.

He estimates now that he was paying about $10 a week for the bed alone — about $500 a year. If he'd never hired the bed and saved the rent money instead, two things could have happened. He could have slept every night in a sleeping bag and had more space in his room! More importantly, after 12 months, he could have put the saved $500 into a conservative investment such as Westpac shares.

Back then, Westpac shares were each worth about $4. Today they're worth about $16, so James' $500 investment would today be worth at least $2,000, even if he'd spent every dividend the bank sent him, which would have happened twice a year for more than two decades.

Our point? Investment over time is easy money — you don't actually earn it by the hour or by the week. You earn the money by making ever-larger profits on the investment markets over an extended period.

In the end, making profits comes down to sensible decisions, and making decisions involves a lot more than just picking shares.

In this chapter, we talk about what you can do to get started in investing — organising your own lifestyle around a better financial system (no more renting beds!), understanding your options and getting to know how you fit into the investment markets.

The Five-Cent Description of Investing

'Investment', says the advertising industry, 'is all about making your money work for you.' This slogan is a very good one; we can't really improve on it. But, like all slogans, this one fails to say a few important things.

When you invest, you're doing something more than saving your money. Investing is making that saved, or non-spent, money create returns for you that are better than what you may expect if you stick the money in a local bank.

Being careful with your money is a useful practice, but don't get the concept of being thrifty mixed up with that of investing successfully. For example, you may drive across the city every morning to save $3 a week on parking fees. But, if it means you take an extra half-hour to get to the office, does the $3 saving make sense?

Now imagine spending that half-hour every day researching and investing in financial markets. And this exercise, for example, earns you the most modest of rewards ... maybe an extra $1,000 a year. Well, using the obscure car park only saves you about $150 a year. So now you're ahead by more than $800. You can probably make even more money next year, because investing is a skill, and the more experienced you are, the more you can be rewarded.

Why Should I Bother Investing?

The best answer to this question is ... to see if you have a talent you haven't already discovered. Seriously, like a lot of life's most enjoyable pursuits, investing becomes more interesting the deeper you get into it. Investing is a truly rewarding activity in theory and in practice!

Here are the key reasons why you can choose to get involved in investing:

- ✔ **You need to:** Unless you want to work until you drop, you're going to need investment earnings to finance your lifestyle, especially when you get older. A baby boy born in Australia today can expect to live to 79; a baby girl can look forward to reaching 84.

- ✔ **You want to:** Everyone has goals in life. Maybe you want to see Paris (and stay in a decent hotel when you get there). Or perhaps you want your kids to go to a private school. Very few people ever achieve these goals by simply earning a salary.

- ✔ **The government wants you to:** The social welfare system that our parents knew is disappearing fast in Australia. Each year Australia is getting more like the United States, where the rich get richer and the poor get poorer. The privatisation of almost every government-owned utility can have a price in the long term. The term *user pays* means those who can't pay can't get the service.

- ✔ **You can't avoid inflation:** Every couple of years the economists think inflation is dead and gone. Then, like a virus, inflation comes back again. Every year, inflation eats away at your savings, unless you invest wisely. Even low levels of inflation can sap the life from your savings, especially if you invest in low-risk products.

Every investor is different. Some people invest so they can be as rich as possible; some people invest so they are never a burden to their families in old age. These two contrasting investors are motivated differently and so have a very different appetite for risk. Decide now what type of investor you want to be and let that decision guide you in your forays into the world of investing.

Just What Are My Investing Options?

One great thing about investing these days is that the whole process has become so easy. The markets have become user friendly! Up until very recently, investment was something of a mystery. At least a lot of the people inside the investment industry tried to make it seem that way (some of them still do).

When we talk about the markets, we mean activities that are key indicators to the health of the economy, such as the stock markets, the bond markets, the commodity markets and the currency markets. The most important indicator in your investment world is the Australian Securities Exchange (ASX).

A number of events over the last decade have changed the way investments are offered to the general public:

- ✔ **Deregulation:** The scrapping of rules that stop foreign investors from competing in Australia on an equal footing opens our markets to competition from around the world. New players make the old players behave better, or so the theory goes. The majority of Australian financial institutions have to start selling you investments rather than behaving as if they're doing you a favour.

- ✔ **Global stock markets:** One of the longest periods of sustained growth seen this century occurred on global stock markets. Booming economies in China, India and other emerging markets carried the rest of the world along with them on a wave of enthusiasm. In Australia, local financial institutions now offer investment opportunities in most developed and developing markets.

- ✔ **Privatisation and demutualisation:** When governments sell state assets on the stock market, and mutual organisations sell shares in themselves to the general public, the process creates a whole new generation of shareholders.

- ✔ **The internet:** Access to the internet has opened up the investment markets like never before. Now, sitting at a computer, any investor has access to a spectacular range of information that even the most resourceful financial adviser previously wasn't able to amass at any one time.

The preceding changes are all for the better — they make becoming a successful investor easier for non-professionals. However, the majority of private investors always need financial advice and, at the very least, they need effective tax advice. (See Chapter 5 for more on financial advisers.)

Although many more changes and innovations are likely to occur in the coming decade, when you analyse the options, the basic range of investments open to you is probably likely to stay the same. Within that basic range, though, your choices can continually expand. We explain the basic range of investments in this section.

Swotting up on the stock market

For you — the early-stage investor — stocks are the most interesting and ultimately the most rewarding investment option available. We go into more detail on the stock market in Part II, but a *stock*, or *share*, is simply a slice of ownership in a company that's publicly traded on the stock market. Australia has a highly developed stock market and Australians' entrepreneurial spirit sees companies taken onto the stock exchange relatively quickly.

Australia has one of the highest rates of share ownership in the world. Figure 1-1 shows Australian share ownership between 1997 and 2006. Even though the number of shareholders decreased slightly between 2004 and 2006, the proportion of Australian shareholders increased from one-third of the adult population to almost half the population in that ten-year period. About 41 per cent of adult Australians directly own shares, down from a peak of 55 per cent in 2004, but still a higher participation rate than most developed countries.

You can choose from a terrific range of shares — more than 2,000 in Australia alone — and some tax benefits are available for those owning shares. On the downside, shares are also the riskiest investment, which is why the returns are so good.

The *equity premium* is the phrase professional investors use for the risk you take with shares. In the 50 years to June 2008, shares returned (after inflation) 7 per cent per year. Government bonds returned 2.5 per cent. The difference (4.5 per cent) is known as the equity premium — your reward for taking on the risks of the stock market. In case you're getting confused, in Australia, the two terms *stocks* and *shares* mean the same thing — ordinary shares.

The stock market is particularly well covered in the media, making information readily available and up-to-date. Likewise, Australian financial institutions such as banks and insurance companies are much better than their stuffy overseas counterparts at explaining their business. Ultimately, this easy access to information helps you, the investor, to make better decisions.

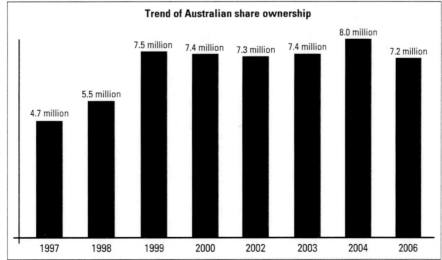

Figure 1-1: Nearly one in two adult Australians invests in the stock market.

So count your blessings, because you have access to a very lively, user-friendly market. In fact, so lively that the Australian Securities Exchange Ltd is on the Australian stock market itself — one of the few stock markets in the world listed on the stock market!

Australians love the stock market and we have a very well regulated (or well-managed) market. But that doesn't mean it's safe or that you won't lose money. It just means that most companies most of the time play by the rules.

Managing your funds

If you're new to the market, then now is the time for getting to know managed funds. The managed-funds industry is the big growth area in local investment markets. Put simply, *managed funds* are blocks of money devoted to a particular investment, like mining stocks or stocks from the Japanese stock market. We get into the nitty-gritty of managed funds in Chapters 12 to 14.

Already you can choose from more than 10,000 managed funds. In December 2007, $950 billion was invested in Australian managed funds, which was almost a fourfold increase on the $269 billion just ten years earlier.

The managed-funds sector is beginning to get as much attention from financial advisers and financial reporters as the stock market sector. Investors can now check the unit prices of funds in the financial press and on financial websites, and can buy managed funds online as readily as shares.

Managed funds are easy to understand and generally less risky than shares. However, because fund managers must be paid substantial fees for their services, managed funds rarely offer returns as high as those offered by shares. What's more, institutional investors such as fund managers are normally more conservative than private investors, who are generally prepared to take higher risks.

As more money pours into managed funds, more investment options become available. This movement is very good news for private investors because certain forms of investment that used to be the exclusive reserve of very rich people willing to invest $100,000 are now accessible to every investor for as little as, say, $2,000.

Inside the managed-funds industry, the hot new areas include private equity, which involves investing in private companies, often just before they arrive on the stock market. Other growth areas in recent years include global property funds (though these fell from grace during 2008), hedge funds and socially responsible investments (SRIs), also known as ethical funds.

Cashing in on fixed-interest investments

Whatever investment options you decide to take, the option of *cash* — putting cash into fixed-interest products that pay a set rate of interest each year — is always an important consideration.

Interest paid on invested money — particularly *compound interest* (where your interest is rolled up into the following year's invested sum, creating an ever larger pool of money) — is the most reliable investment available. Unfortunately, it's also the slowest in terms of growth.

Nevertheless, being aware of what happens with compound interest is important because, if you can't beat the returns from compound interest, then you may as well not be in the investing business at all.

A $1,000 amount invested at 10 per cent interest will only give you $100 the first year. If you don't withdraw the interest earned, then that $1,100 will roll up to $15,000 in 30 years' time. And all you have to do is — nothing!

Pondering over property

You already know quite a bit about the property market. We're sure you know your neighbourhood, your town, where you grew up. The great attraction of this form of investment is the fact that you can feel it, you can walk around it and you can drive past it in your car — all tangible qualities that make understanding property easy.

For many people, property remains the most emotionally satisfying investment because it's physically the most substantial. By comparison, with shares and managed funds, you don't even get a bit of paper anymore because nearly all transactions are held on computer.

Even the most basic property investment — the family home — proves to be a very decent investment in Australia's major cities, returning double figures on an annualised basis for the last two decades. As we write this, residential property values are falling in most capital cities after a lengthy boom, but the falls are likely to be relatively short-lived. Over lengthy periods of ten years or more, investment returns from residential property and real estate investment trusts are second only to shares.

Don't let any financial adviser tell you that the family home isn't an investment. If you've lived in your home for ten years or more, your property has probably grown in value by a significant amount. As well, if you sell the property, you don't have to pay capital gains tax (see Chapter 5 for more on CGT). You also have the security and peace of mind of living in the property — all in all, a pretty good investment.

The rise of the managed-funds industry also opens a new way for small investors to get into the property market without actually owning a building. Many of the biggest names in the property market now run managed funds for property investors.

In Chapter 16, we give you more information about directly investing in property. If you want to know more about investing in property through managed funds, see Chapter 19.

Cleaning up with collectibles

For many people, collectibles are the most *interesting* form of investment. However, while collectibles are interesting, they're rarely interesting *investments*. More often than not, they're dud investments.

For example, James' aunt has a painting in her living room by a famous 19th-century Irish painter who always fetches big prices on the international art market, especially for his landscapes. The painting is a portrait of her grandfather, a prosperous cattle dealer, who had commissioned the artist to do his portrait on his 40th birthday.

The entire Kirby family is very proud to have such a collectible in the family circle. Every time the family visits the house, they're always ushered into the living room for a peek at the painting — a grand piece featuring a severe-looking chap with a big moustache and a face like a battleship!

One night at a party, James met an art dealer and mentioned his aunt's painting. He enquired as to how much it might be worth.

'Is it a man?' he asked somewhat airily. 'Yes,' said James. 'What, a commissioned portrait of a businessman?' he asked. 'Well ... a farmer businessman,' said James, clutching at straws. 'Oh, how dreadful — nobody wants the men. There's loads of them because he did them for cash. They're valued at about 20 per cent of what you get for the landscapes. And that's if you can find a buyer,' he said.

Sure, the dealer may have been exaggerating, but what he said was more or less true. James never has had the heart to tell his aunt; the portrait remains on the wall in her living room, appreciated as an interesting collectible in one house at least. Of course, if she's read this book ...

The problem with antiques, art and collectibles is that you really have to know the market before you invest. If you're prepared to put in the time to thoroughly study the market for a chosen collectible — such as antique French wall clocks — then you may have a chance of making a successful investment. Check out Chapter 20 for more on collectibles as an investment.

If you see investing in collectibles as fun (and the pleasure of owning an antique French clock can surely beat owning 1,000 shares in a mining company) then the traditional investment advice is to invest a very small portion of your portfolio — less than 5 per cent — in this activity.

Don't rule out collectibles as an investment, because ample evidence exists that returns on certain items like paintings or wine can be spectacular, but they are an extremely hit-and-miss investment option. After you build a large diversified portfolio, you can reward yourself with investing in collectibles. Until then, keep away from the antique shops!

Souping up your superannuation

You can't expect to live comfortably on a government pension any longer. Whether you like it or not, society has become a lot meaner about social welfare. The other problem is that, although you can probably expect to live longer than your mother or father, so can everyone else you went to school with. As a result, Australia is going to be looking fairly long in the tooth by the middle of this century.

Economists estimate that one in four people in Australia in 2051 will be older than the current retirement age of 65; today, only about one in ten people are over 65. What does this mean? Well, you can forget about Australia taking away a whole load of medals at the 2052 Olympics for a start — a quarter of Australians will need walking sticks!

If one in four people is going to be among the retirees, no government, Liberal or Labor, can afford to fund the age pension at current levels. Successive governments have made superannuation one of the great tax breaks available today to every investor in order to encourage everybody to make provision for their retirement.

A well-funded superannuation nest egg is absolutely essential if you want to become a successful investor. Just like the managed-funds industry, the superannuation industry is growing strongly each year. The introduction of choice of fund, the government co-contribution and transition-to-retirement pensions have made super an even more attractive home for your savings. What's more, strong competition between industry funds and commercial funds, and the growing popularity of self-managed super funds, is likely to drive further innovation in the products and services on offer. We devote the whole of Part V to examining super.

Finding Your Place in the Investment Landscape

How are you going to fit into this huge investment industry? Becoming an investor from scratch can feel like you're arriving on a busy beach on Sunday afternoon. At first the beach appears to have no room for any more people; however, after a while you see spaces all over the place, and find a spot just perfect for you.

Think of the investment markets the same way — yours for the taking. You just have to decide what your role is going to be.

In establishing that role for yourself, taking stock of who you are and what type of characteristics you have that can help or hinder your quest is important for investment success. Are you practical? Are you comfortable with risk? Do you mind losing money every now and again? Chapter 2 will help you answer these questions.

As you get more familiar with the market, you can start to feel more comfortable with the investment options offered by various financial institutions (see Chapter 4). You may also feel more confident in talking to an investment adviser or a tax adviser about the steps you plan to take.

Neutral advice on investing is incredibly rare. Absolutely nothing comes without a price and that includes 'free' investment guides, newsletters or seminars. In Chapter 5, we tell you the main safeguards to follow when dealing with investment advisers and financial planners.

Understanding your own investment profile is the second most important thing you must do after understanding the investment markets and how they work. You have to fit into these markets, and the more you know them, the more comfortable your place in them becomes.

Chapter 2

Taking Risk by the Horns

. . . .

In This Chapter

▶ Understanding investment risk and return

▶ Mixing risk within your portfolio

▶ Understanding the principles of managing your risk

. . . .

*D*on't be fooled by glossy reports, expensive suits and high-rise office towers. At the end of the day, nobody knows what's going to happen next in the financial markets — especially spotty-faced research analysts straight out of college. If they can really see into the future, then what are they doing sitting inside a bank?

Stockbroker research reports often go into great detail about a company's business plans two to three years ahead and discuss at length various scenarios for the company in the future. They predict the revenues, costs and profits for the company in one year's time, two years' time, even three years' time. As you plough through the detail, reality strikes like a flash of lightning — the whole report is a piece of fiction. The report can be nothing else because it deals with the future. Nobody knows what's going to happen next week, not to mention next year.

When you read a stockbroker's report about any company, the one bit of information that always seems to be missing is an admission by the authors that they're guessing about the future. The report maps out educated and well-researched guessing, perhaps, but it's guessing all the same. Given the way financial markets operate, the authors of the report probably won't be in the same position in five years' time. But that hardly matters, because many of the people in the company being reported on won't be in the same position either. But you — the wise long-term investor — may well be still holding your shares in the company.

The fact that brokers and economists get it so wrong so often just isn't funny, and at the end of the day you must evaluate your own risk with any investment.

This chapter explains the concept of risk, how you can decide what level of risk is right for you and how to minimise risk within your portfolio.

Getting Risqué with Risk

Every time a major downturn on the stock market occurs — such as in September 1987, April 2000 or most of 2008 — you always get people merrily holding forth about how they 'aren't in the stock market'.

But everybody is in the stock market whether they like it or not. If you work for a public or private business, that company is affected by events in the markets. If you're insured, your insurance company can be greatly affected by changes in the markets. The same goes for any superannuation you may have — that money is out in the markets somewhere, and if those markets fall, then your superannuation goes down too.

Even putting your money under the mattress means you risk losing pace with inflation. Putting your money in a bank account means you face a risk that the bank may collapse. (A bank collapse is extremely unlikely in Australia, but a bank could 'get into trouble', tying up your money for a long time.) Until 2008, money in Australian banks was not 'explicitly' guaranteed by the state, but there was a long-held 'implicit' guarantee — no modern government in Australia has let a bank fail. In 2008, the Australian government was forced to guarantee bank deposits up to $1 million to bolster confidence in the banking system.

Accept the fact that you can't keep your money 100 per cent safe. To invest means to take a risk. To understand investing you have to understand risk.

Balancing risk and return

A link between risk and reward exists in every investment situation. The easiest way to see this *risk–reward ratio* in action is to think about how much value you might place on risk if you had to make a choice.

Suppose that two friends come to ask you for a $1,000 loan. You're willing to give both of them a loan, but the risk involved in giving out a loan is very different between these two borrowers.

- ✔ The first borrower is a very sober chap who drives a ten-year-old station wagon. This guy has held the same well-paid position in a local funeral home for the last decade.

- ✔ The second borrower is a notorious gambler and drinker. He has a different job every few months. He's coming to you because no credit card company wants to deal with him. (While arranging the loan, he also asks for a loan of your gas barbeque because his own 'blew up' during a celebration party after a recent football match.)

Do you impose the same conditions on both these borrowers? Of course you don't. You price your risk appropriately. You're likely to impose severe conditions on your rambling, gambling friend. You can ask this borrower to pay you interest at 2 per cent more than your funeral home buddy — and you can also ask for the money back sooner.

All investment markets work on the same principle of risk–reward ratios. If you take very little risk, don't expect much of a reward in return. If you buy shares in supermarkets and transport companies, you can reasonably expect a reasonable return. If you invest in technology companies led by charismatic (and sometimes highly volatile) entrepreneurs, you're taking a bigger risk and you can reasonably expect a better-than-average return.

Finding out how risky is too risky

Establishing the right level of risk for you can eventually come automatically after some trial and error. No hard-and-fast rules apply in the game of risk. How much risk you're willing to take on can broadly match your investment profile. The younger you are, the more risks you can take. As people approach retirement, they generally begin to reduce their risk levels, putting more and more of their money into products that guarantee a certain return and putting less into the stock market.

If your hands tremble and your heart flutters when you check stock prices, then the thing to do is to begin with very conservative investments. Maybe you should put the lot in a cash-management trust!

Conservative doesn't mean slow, sleepy or too careful. In the investment market, to be conservative is always important — you can be conservative and aggressive at the same time. For example, you might decide to buy biotechnology stocks, but not without a thorough analysis of both the science and the financial numbers presented by the companies you favour.

Risking, not gambling

The more risk you take with your portfolio, the less you're able to accurately manage its outcomes.

Check out the very manageable end of the investment market. For fixed-rate products, such as bonds that pay 7 per cent, you can estimate your investment return fairly easily. You only have to calculate what 7 per cent of your principal is to estimate what annual interest payments you may expect, at a minimum, from this bond (assuming you didn't reinvest the interest payments). For more on bonds, see Chapter 15.

Write your own risk-taking rules

A good way to get a grip on the concept of risk and reward inside investment markets is to have your own classification system for any investment product. Every investment decision you may ever face fits into one of these three categories:

✔ **Low risk:** Fixed-return products such as bank savings accounts, cash-management accounts and government bonds; fixed-return managed funds; prime property on long-term leases.

A low-risk investor seeks to have a conservative, debt-free portfolio of investments. The investments are long term and most likely concentrated in local markets where the investor can monitor the portfolio very closely. A low-risk investor has a high portion of cash in their portfolio at any given time and avoids companies that don't have a five-year record of profitability.

✔ **Medium risk:** *Blue-chip stocks* (stocks that have the ability to weather good times as well as the bad times and create a predictable income level for you); low-risk managed funds in local and overseas markets; residential and commercial property in established locations.

A medium-risk investor has a mix of investments that combines a reliable income stream with the prospect of occasional very high returns. The portfolio is managed with a view to achieving medium-term three–five-year targets. Local stocks are the most popular investments, with some exposure to overseas markets, probably through managed funds. The investor may occasionally purchase an option in a stock if that stock seems an exceptional value at the time.

✔ **High risk:** Mining stocks; technology stocks; options and warrants; hedge funds; speculative property developments.

A high-risk investor most likely doesn't depend on the income from the portfolio on the basis that the income is likely to be volatile. This investor is willing to borrow money to finance investments and is also actively trading stocks and options. Either individually or through a managed fund, the investor also uses other *derivatives* (or spin-offs from ordinary shares like options or warrants) to access investment markets. This investor is out to make money anywhere possible.

Similarly, blue-chip stocks can return dividends that are very close to forecasts. A blue-chip company often indicates its future dividend policy, which simply means that the chairman says the company has no problem retaining the same level of dividends in the next reporting season. From these types of forecasts, a reasonable prediction of what you may expect from dividends in the short term from blue-chip shares is possible.

Likewise, property income can be very predictable, especially on longer term leases. Say you buy a warehouse with a ten-year lease to IBM with a built-in two-year rent review. Your minimum income from that tenant is very easy to estimate. (For more on commercial property, see Chapter 19.)

Risk is not the same as *gambling*. If you want to gamble, head for the racecourse — it can be more exciting and, if you win, you don't have to worry about tax. Investment markets, on the other hand, can guarantee some returns and can reasonably forecast, or guess, a certain range of returns from a large number of other investment options. Of course, unlike the racecourse, you'll be expected to pay tax on your improved fortunes.

Virtually all investment market advice is underpinned by one golden rule — to minimise risk you must diversify your investments. Diversifying means splitting things up. Don't have all your eggs in one basket. Make sure your investments are mixed, and you're not exposed to only one market, one stock or one investment institution. Check out Figure 2-1, which gives a good idea of where Australians place their money.

Of course, your investments may not be able to reflect the break-up of the graph in Figure 2-1 until you have a large portfolio but, with the help of managed funds, private investors are now able to have a much wider range of investments if they're prepared to pay fund managers' fees.

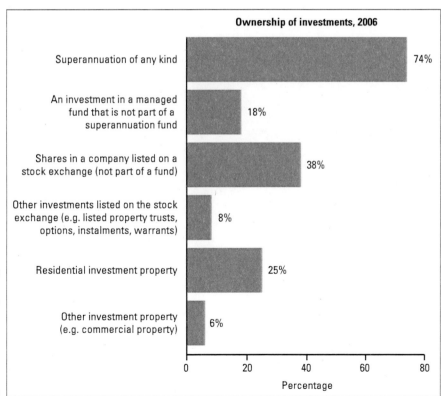

Figure 2-1: How Australians invest: Share of total investments.

Your average, everyday risks

The term *risk* covers a wide range of possible threats to your investment plans. Here are some of the most common risks you can face:

- **Market risk:** Wherever you put your money, the investment markets influence your investments. Markets can rise and fall in dramatic fashion — as do your investments.

- **Inflation risk:** Inflation is above the Reserve Bank's target band of 2–3 per cent at the time of writing, running at more than 4 per cent a year in 2008. But you must always remember that a 4 per cent rate of inflation means your genuine return from an investment must include the subtraction of the inflation rate. For example, if your stocks returned 10 per cent last year, the genuine or net figure is 6 per cent (that is, 10 per cent minus 4 per cent inflation).

- **Interest rate risk:** An increase in interest rates has an impact right across the economy and across investment markets. Investors most immediately affected (and better off) are those depending on fixed-rate investment products, such as pensioners. Almost everyone else becomes worse off, particularly property investors, property developers and builders, who want rates to be as low as possible.

- **Timing risk:** For short-term investors (that is, those with a timeframe of less than one year), timing is an important factor. Markets move in cycles. If you come in at the top of a cycle and sell at a lower point in the cycle, you end up being disappointed. Investors unlucky enough to buy technology stocks in early 2000, before the technology market headed into a year-long nosedive, aren't likely to forget this lesson. Long-term investors are less interested in or exposed to investment cycles. They believe that, if they invest in good companies, the investments look after themselves.

- **Regulation risk:** Legislation in financial markets is rarely retrospective. In other words, the government rarely makes changes that affect decisions you've already made with your money. However, tax and other legal regulations in the financial markets are changing all the time. If you invest to take advantage of a particular feature of government regulation — like an aspect of family trust legislation — then you carry the risk that the laws may change.

- **Political risk:** This form of risk is rarely a problem in Australia, with its stable democracy. However, political risk is a major issue for overseas investors. Perhaps the best example of how politics can change investment conditions is in Papua New Guinea, where the mining giant Rio Tinto lost millions on a gold and copper mine at Bougainville after separatist rebels began attacking the mine in 1989. A decade later, Rio Tinto pulled out of the operation completely. Today ASX-listed gold miner Lihir is back, mining gold successfully in Papua New Guinea.

The risky country

Compared with other economies, such as Switzerland, Germany or Holland, Australia has a long history of highly speculative investment markets. Maybe this boom-and-bust tradition was triggered by our ancestors in the great gold rushes of the 18th century. Whatever the explanation, Australia is seen as a speculative market throughout the globe. The great mining companies that traditionally dominated the former Australian Stock Exchange (now the Australian Securities Exchange, or ASX) — BHP, CRA, MIM and Western Mining — underpinned this reputation. The stock prices of mining companies tend to roll up and down in tandem with commodity prices for items like coal and iron ore.

As a result, the operational performance of a mining company was not the dominant factor in its share price. This exposure of big mining stocks — and consequently the entire ASX (represented by the All Ordinaries Index) — to commodity prices left the local market open to speculators. This perception is still a concern in Australian markets today. The Australian dollar regularly comes under attack from international currency speculators, who try to guess where commodity prices are going and what effect those prices may have on the Australian dollar.

Local investors are also very keen speculators on *penny dreadfuls* — cheap stocks that offer the prospect of big gains. The great resources boom of the 1960s, typified by the spectacular rise and subsequent crash of the nickel miner Poseidon, marked Australia as a gamblers' market. More than 40 years later, another resources boom is being driven by economic development in countries such as China and India, reigniting the penny dreadfuls as well as heavyweight miners such as BHP Billiton and Rio Tinto.

The Australian stock market, too, is still very capable of producing shock incidents where corporations can collapse with the minimum of warning. The 1980s saw the spectacular collapse of empires like the Bond Corporation and the Qintex group (led by Christopher Skase).

More recently, in 2008, the sudden fall from grace of RAMS Home Loans, childcare provider ABC Learning Centres, investment manager MFS Group and property trust Centro Properties Group once again shows our local market can be risky territory. The cause was different — rapid growth underpinned by unsustainable levels of debt — but the song remained the same.

Choosing a Mix of Risks for You

Whenever you invest, you must decide the mix of risk you want to retain in your portfolio. You can have everything you own in $100 notes and hide them around the house. That would be fairly risk-free from a short-term investment perspective — but pretty silly from every other point of view. Likewise, you can put everything you have on an option for a wind technology stock — perhaps a once-in-a-lifetime opportunity — but that too is a foolish move in anyone's book.

To help you decide on the right mix for you, check out the risk levels of the following key investments:

- **Cash:** Nothing is risk-free, although cash, in the short term, comes pretty close. By investing in cash, we mean putting money in a bank-based savings account or a cash-management trust. The best thing about investing in cash is that your capital is safe and you have instant access to your funds. However, this type of investment offers no protection from inflation and, because interest rates are low, you barely keep ahead of inflation. The real cost of cash is the *opportunity cost* — the price of not investing in better investments.

- **Fixed-interest bonds:** When you invest in fixed-interest bonds, the advantage is that risk is very low. *Liquidity* — the ability to sell the investments quickly — is good, and you know what your minimum returns are going to be in advance. The weakness of fixed interest is that, again, inflation is a concern and low interest rates mean your returns remain low.

- **Shares:** Shares have continually out-performed most classes of rival investments over the long term and are well able to exceed the inflation rate in normal circumstances. Shares can also fall more dramatically than other asset classes in the short term. In 2008, Australian shares fell by 43 per cent. Historically, shares return, on average, between 5 and 7 per cent above the rate of inflation. Figure 2-2 shows the annual return of Australian shares since 1900.

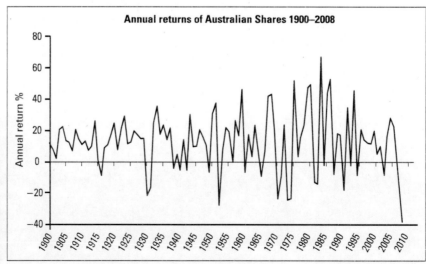

Figure 2-2: The annual returns of Australian shares since 1900 have been strong.

© MLC.

✔ **Managed funds:** Managed funds offer a diverse range of investments as well as tax benefits. The additional advantage of managed funds is that the risk is managed by professionals who understand the investment markets better than you do — though this is by no means guaranteed. With more than 10,000 managed funds on offer, the industry is beginning to mirror the range of investment risk traditionally offered only by shares. Managed funds are also quite liquid — but liquidity can evaporate during a market panic. In 2008, many top-flight mortgage funds temporarily froze redemptions in response to panic selling by investors who wanted to shift their savings into risk-free, government-guaranteed bank deposits.

✔ **Property:** Property has traditionally been used as the best proof against inflation, because property prices tend to keep pace with other price rises across the economy. Property prices can and do fall, however, as they did in parts of Australia in the aftermath of the global credit crunch of 2007–08. For the investor, rent is a predictable form of income, but investors in residential property experience a wide variation with the rate of return. Property is also notoriously *illiquid* (meaning you don't have the ability to sell these investments quickly). Investing in property represents a medium to high risk.

How to Invest without Going Insane (or Broke)

Investment markets are alive with buzzwords. If you want to have fun and stay sane at the same time, then this section is for you. Terms like *diversification* or *asset allocation* don't have strict definitions. They mean different things to a fund manager than they mean to a Mafia boss hiding money around the world. For your purposes, here's a handy guide.

Splitting it up nicely — diversification

Diversification is making sure your selection of investments is mixed and you're not exposed to one market or one group of stocks (such as technology or mining).

Traditionally, financial advisers used to say the best way to break up a small investment portfolio was to split it in three. This breakdown is by no means a golden rule, but it may work as a good option for the first-time investor. Here's how:

✔ **One-third in stocks:** This third gives you the exposure to lively markets where returns exceed all other investment categories over time.

✔ **One-third in property:** This third offers exposure to a market where income is reliable and where the possibility of strong capital gain exists. You can enter the property market with small amounts of money (for example, $1,000 invested in a real estate investment trust, or REIT).

✔ **One-third in fixed-interest securities:** This third allows you to receive an absolutely reliable return from one portion of your investment assets.

After you've managed to get investments up and running in the three key areas of the investment markets (stocks, property and fixed interest), you can then aspire to creating a fully diversified portfolio.

Spreading it around — asset allocation

Splitting your portfolio between different asset classes, such as cash, shares, managed funds and property, makes sense — it's known as *asset allocation*. But spreading your investment around the market, especially to different finance houses, makes *very* good sense.

We are in the golden age of the 'financial supermarket' where major banks and insurance companies now offer absolutely everything you may want, from life insurance to personal loans to mortgages.

The convenience of these 'complete financial package' services is hard to resist. But the first problem with these packages is that they are invariably of very different standards. The home loan may be good, but the insurance may be very poor — or vice versa.

The second problem is that if your chosen financial institution gets into trouble, or begins to fade in prominence, your investments go with it. Don't put all your eggs in one basket — or anyone else's basket either. Spread it around!

Making sure you can sell it — liquidity

The *liquidity* — or saleability — of different assets can vary enormously. Cash is the most liquid asset; property is the most illiquid asset. In between cash and property investments is a wide range of liquidity levels between shares and managed funds. For shares, most *blue chips*, or companies that are among the biggest in the market, have good liquidity. In contrast, shares in very small companies, in the mining, technology or biotechnology sectors, can be very hard to sell, especially if every other investor has the same idea.

In the managed-fund market, the more adventurous and exotic funds tend to have a smaller total value and have more liquidity risk for the individual investor. The risk may be represented by a simple factor such as the fund holding on to your money longer.

For example, at Colonial First State Managed Funds — one of the biggest fund managers in Australia — the Diversified Fund had a fund size of $1,204 million in June 2008; in contrast, the Global Health and Biotechnology Fund had a fund size of $22 million at the same time. Not surprisingly, distributions from the Diversified Fund, which invests in shares, property and cash, were every three months. However, distributions from the Global Health and Biotechnology Fund were only twice a year.

Ensuring investments are safe — security

Investing carries with it a balance between risk and reward. By definition, the safer your investment is, then the less the reward you can expect. But you can take on board methods of improving your security at any time.

Using a reputable adviser or financial institution is the first step towards ensuring financial security (see Chapter 5). Restraining your own desire to succeed very quickly or to chase suspiciously high returns is also important.

Many investment institutions now offer various forms of insurance against poor performance. While the cost to you is that your investment grows more slowly than unprotected products, you do have a choice to insure against dramatic drops in value.

Making sure you understand — analysis

The more you're able to analyse and understand your investments, the less risk you end up taking. This may simply mean understanding what your financial adviser is saying, or what the financial institutions are saying to you in their various reports, brochures and websites.

On a more sophisticated level, analysing your investments can mean being able to thoroughly understand what a chief executive is talking about at an annual general meeting and being able to get the key information you need from an annual report or from a stockbroker's report on a company. The more you read books like this one, the better educated you become.

The higher the reward, the higher the risk. If you see companies or products that offer dramatically higher returns than everybody else in the market, alarm bells ought to be ringing, especially if these companies are not among the better known financial brands in Australia.

Investments that look too good to be true usually are

At the peak of the 1990s boom, the investments regulator ASIC (the Australian Securities and Investments Commission) created a fake internet investment site for a company it called Millennium Bug Insurance, which promised to triple investors' money in 15 months.

The concept of tripling an investment in 15 months should have struck any seasoned investor as being too good to be true. But investors chase the prospect of low risk and high returns as surely as dogs always chase seagulls on the beach.

Millennium Bug Insurance placed plenty of advertisements, but it didn't even bother to register as a company. And guess what? Seven hundred Australian investors sent in requests for information.

Worse still, 230 investors signed up to invest more than $4 million in this government-sanctioned scam designed to educate unwary investors. (Canny investors may have noticed that the scheme was launched on April Fool's Day.)

Using a website specially designed for the purpose, Millennium Bug Insurance claimed it was able to make incredibly high returns because it was offering blue-chip companies insurance against losses for the year 2000 Millennium Bug. The high insurance risk for the blue chip was supposed to create a high level of income for the insurance company and an equally high rate of return for investors.

In total, more than 10,000 investors visited the Millennium Bug Insurance website and, of those, 230 investors signed on to invest between $10,000 and $50,000 in the scheme. After ASIC told each participant the scheme was a scam, they sent their money back to them. What a close shave for those investors! How many more scams like this catch people every year?

In 2008, a Who's Who of international investors lost US$50 billion in funds operated by Wall Street hedge fund manager Bernard Madoff. See Chapter 23 for more on Madoff and the never-ending appeal of high-risk, high-return investment schemes.

Chapter 3

Ready, Set, Invest!

*Y*ou can be a hard worker and maybe a high earner too. But are you an investor?

A neighbour of James recently came to him with a problem. Matthew was approaching retirement; he wanted some investment advice. A lawyer for most of his life, Matthew had built quite a large business dealing mostly with real estate issues. He always drove a luxury car, wore expensive clothes (seven days a week) and took holidays around the world.

No doubt about it, Matthew was a high earner. James had often wondered whether he was a good investor or whether his business produced enough money to completely bankroll his enviable lifestyle. Matthew gave the impression he was a seasoned investor because he was always keen to talk about the fortunes of leading companies or property prices in his area.

Well, James was half right. As Matthew began talking about his need to finance his retirement lifestyle, James discovered he had always made plenty of money from his business — that explained the high-flying lifestyle. But to James' disbelief he had no history of investing whatsoever. He had bought his house 30 years earlier and that was his one and only investment. He was a big earner and a big spender but he had never been an investor.

At 63, Matthew is now an investor, not by choice, but through necessity. Taking full advantage of the markets at this late stage isn't really an option for him, but he has little choice other than to begin an investment plan because his savings aren't sufficient to finance a comfortable retirement. Luckily, he owns his own house and is able to extract a modest amount of cash from his business.

We come across lots of self-employed men and women like Matthew; and not all of them own their own houses or even their own cars. Investing is something everyone must learn — even high earners. This chapter shows you the first steps to becoming an investor; that is, laying a good foundation so that you review your existing financial patterns, don't waste money, keep your existing assets as safe as possible and educate yourself about inherent market hurdles so you can build your own investment strategy.

What Do I Want for My Money?

Every investor has different objectives, and the investment markets in Australia are now sophisticated enough to deal with almost every conceivable investment demand. To become an investor you must first take stock of your position in this market. How much money do you have? What's your overall earning power? Do you spend more than you earn?

These questions are the hoary old chestnuts of personal finance, but you absolutely must sort these issues out before becoming an investor. What's the point in trying to make money from the investment markets if you're already wasting money each week on credit card charges or rent on an apartment that you could easily own?

Put this challenge another way: Don't bother with the sailing race until you're sure that your boat isn't leaking.

Successful investing depends on you working from a sound personal financial base with clear objectives. Take some time to jot down what your short-, medium- and long-term investment goals are. Here's an example of how your investment targets can look:

- **Short term (less than 12 months):** A new personal computer, an overseas holiday, a new car, a new front fence.

- **Medium term (one to five years):** A home extension, a one-year career break, a swimming pool, an investment property.

- **Long term (five years or more):** A private education for your children, a well-funded retirement, a portfolio of investment properties.

Getting Down to Some Serious Saving

Take a wide-angle look at your personal finances. Are you wasting money anywhere? Are there any regular payments you make that can be made smaller or less frequently? You invariably discover that financial arrangements you made some time ago no longer make sense.

If you make very big changes to your lifestyle, your financial plans may also need to change. The best example we can think of is divorce. No matter how wealthy you may be, divorce means your material lifestyle is about to be cut dramatically, and your previous financial arrangements need to be reviewed accordingly. Becoming a successful investor involves a lot more than making simple investment decisions in isolation; sometimes it means changing how you live your life.

What's the old saying? A penny saved is a penny earned. It's true! Before you start making big efforts to make money, don't ignore opportunities to save money that might be just under your nose. The following sections hold a few suggestions.

To buy or not to buy ... housing

Unless you're lucky enough to own your house, then housing yourself or your family is probably going to be your biggest expense. People are always asking us whether they're better off renting or buying their accommodation. The answer, of course, is ... it depends. But, in the majority of circumstances, our feeling is that you try to buy your own place if it makes sense.

Renting makes sense if you're not staying long in any one place. It can also make sense if you're an excellent investor and can make after-tax returns on your investment portfolio that greatly exceed property price increases. On the other hand, renting the same apartment or house for years on end while lending rates remain historically low and property prices continue to rise doesn't make sense.

Rob from the rich ... rent to the poor.

—*Anonymous property developer*
(with apologies to Robin Hood)

If you have a mortgage, reviewing your mortgage rate against other mortgage rates to ensure you're not paying too much is a worthwhile exercise. Lending institutions have introduced variations to the traditional variable mortgage rate; some of these products may suit you.

Shopping around for mortgage rates may seem excessive if you're already with a lending institution, but doing so makes good sense. Mortgages are often the biggest financial commitment investors make in their career, so make sure you're getting good value.

Paying off your mortgage can also be a good investment (although this is by no means guaranteed because you can sometimes make better use of your money elsewhere). Your primary residence is one of the few investments that's exempt from capital gains tax, which means the capital gain (profit) you make when you sell is all yours to keep.

If you don't plan to become an active investor and the security of completely owning your own house appeals to you, then consider paying off your mortgage faster than you've planned.

Controlling those credit cards

Here's the nub of the situation. The financial pages may be saying that official lending rates are more than 7 per cent, but the lending rate on your credit or charge card may be around 20 per cent. First off, credit and charge cards have a few differences:

- ✔ MasterCard and Visa are *credit cards*; you pay them off monthly and pay interest-rate-based charges on the amount outstanding. You can roll over that amount into the following month if you continue to pay the interest. Credit cards have a pre-set spending limit.

- ✔ American Express and Diners Club are *charge cards*; you settle your account at the end of every month. If your account is paid late, you face a flat fee. Charge cards carry no pre-set spending limits.

You don't have to go so far as cutting up credit or charge cards (though we're sure snipping the little critters would be a very interesting experiment in most households). But use them carefully and don't let the payments ever run late. If you ever need a loan for short-term purposes, the rates from banks on what are called personal loans are invariably much lower. While credit card rates were at up to 20 per cent (in 2008), personal loan rates were running at around 14 per cent for amounts in excess of $2,000.

The number that matters most on your credit card statement — after your bill — is the APR (annual percentage rate). APR is the amount you pay in interest per month calculated on an annual basis. Understanding how much interest you're paying is much easier when you get the APR because most people only ever think of interest as an annual percentage.

Credit cards can create a very severe debt trap, and the infuriating fact for many people is that the original amount owed may have been only a couple of thousand dollars. Still, people leave that amount unpaid for months on end paying hundreds of dollars in interest for, effectively, a loan they never wanted in the first place.

Paying some bills — like retail merchandise or groceries — with *EFTPOS* (electronic funds transfer at point of sale) allows you the convenience of paying by 'card', yet you avoid the prospect of high interest rates and the possibility of higher-than-expected credit card bills.

Saving to pay off an overdue credit card bill is probably one of the most lucrative investments you can ever make. Think about it ... you no longer need to pay those interest fees. Money saved is money earned. What's more, this money is earned tax-free.

Setting up your super

After the family home, the other great tax shelter for every Australian is superannuation. Surely, one of the main things you invest for is a comfortable retirement.

With superannuation, you can invest in a tax-efficient manner. Your investments inside a superannuation fund are only taxed at 15 per cent, whereas your returns from other non-superannuation investments can be taxed as high as 46.5 per cent.

Also, if you salary-sacrifice (that is, place some of your pre-tax salary directly into superannuation), you can make investments in superannuation on a pre-tax basis. (See Chapter 22 for more information on salary sacrifice.)

Estimates vary on the ideal amount you need in order to live comfortably in your retirement but tend to range between 65 per cent and 70 per cent of your current income. If you estimate 70 per cent of your annual income and put that against what you may get from a government pension at the moment, we guarantee you the news goads you into action — a bit like smokers getting to see a video of a smoker's lungs. Terror is a great incentive!

Here's the bad news. At the moment, the age pension is about $274 a week for singles and $229 for each member of a couple. The majority of Australian retirees are currently living on less than $20,000 a year.

Look at superannuation this way — if your income is currently $70,000 a year, economists estimate that you need about $50,000 a year to live comfortably. (On the government pension, assuming you were a swinging — if elderly — single, you're entitled to about $14,217 a year!) Presume that you have superannuation from other sources but no more than the national average. All up, you can manage a retirement income of $20,000 a year.

The problem is that almost $30,000 a year is missing from that simple piece of mathematics. If you wish to live 'comfortably', ask yourself where the shortfall's going to come from.

Understanding how our tax system works (yeah, right!)

One essential thing to know about tax is that the Australian Taxation Office (ATO) charges you different levels of tax as your income goes higher. These tax bands are changing all the time. Successive governments are always trying to lower tax rates, but, after a certain level of income, you start paying fairly hefty amounts of tax right up to the top level.

The tax system in Australia is very complex. In Hong Kong, an individual pays 17 per cent income tax at most, which more or less sums up the entire income tax system there. The tax system offers no concessions, no deductions and no rebates — just a simple flat tax. In the United States, the tax system consists of five tax bands, and the highest band is 35 per cent — applying when you make above US$357,700 a year! In Australia there are also five bands; the difference is that the highest band kicks in at only $180,001.

Without years of study, nobody can be expected to have a comprehensive grasp of the bizarre logic that dominates Australia's tax system. But knowing the basics makes sense so that you don't go wasting money. Understanding the tax considerations that apply with almost any choice of investment activity can give you an edge. (We talk about getting tax advice in Chapter 5.)

Your marginal rate of tax is the rate of tax that you pay on the portion of your salary that falls into the highest tax band. In Australia, the top marginal rate of the tax under the current system is 45 per cent and is applied to any income you make over $180,000. In addition, you must add the Medicare levy of 1.5 per cent, which brings the effective top marginal rate to 46.5 per cent. Table 3-1 shows current (2009) rates of tax payable.

Table 3-1	ATO Income Tax Rates, 2008–09
Taxable Income	*Tax on This Income*
$0–6,000	Nil
$6,001–34,000	15c for each $1 over $6,000
$34,001–80,000	$4,200 plus 30c for each $1 over $34,000
$80,001–180,000	$18,000 plus 40c for each $1 over $80,000
$180,001+	$58,000 plus 45c for each $1 over $180,000

Note: The above rates do not include the Medicare levy of 1.5 per cent.

Playing It Safe — Securing Your Finances

Taking steps to secure personal wealth is vitally important for any investor. Securing your assets can be as simple as locking your house when you go on a daytrip, or as complex as taking out income-protection insurance. Either way, you're attempting to minimise any possible losses.

Times of high danger can include when you're moving house, or for any reason your daily life is upset by a major routine-breaking development. Although these developments can be negative (poor health) or positive (an extension to your home), the main objective for you is to protect your assets. We talk about how to safeguard your personal fortune in this section.

Insuring your health

Make sure you have a comprehensive policy with a reputable health insurance company that covers the full range of likely health issues. Don't penny pinch on this particular insurance. Getting through your working life without at least one major trauma is highly unlikely.

In 1999, the Howard government introduced both a carrot and a stick to relieve the burden on Medicare. The carrot came in the form of a tax rebate worth 30 per cent of the cost of health insurance premiums. The stick was a little sharper. If you earn more than $70,000 a year ($140,000 for couples) and you don't have private hospital cover, you have to pay a 1 per cent Medicare levy surcharge. This surcharge is imposed on top of the 1.5 per cent Medicare levy.

Insuring your home

Get home building and contents insurance and review it every year when your premiums fall due. The big mistake most people make is that they don't fully value their home and contents, and, if they're robbed, the insurance compensation is not even close to what they need to replace stolen or damaged goods. This happens either because most houses are improved slowly over the years and the owner 'forgets' to upgrade the insurance cover, or because the owner doesn't understand the full financial implications of underinsuring. (For example, you take an unnecessary risk if you insure your contents for only 80 per cent of full value because, in the event of a claim, you're only compensated an amount that accords with what that 80 per cent represents.) Your insurance cover calculations need to include any improvements — such as a new television, a new personal computer — that you have invested in over the previous 12 months.

Don't forget to pay attention to the people you let through your front door. Leaving anyone working alone in your home when you're not there is a big risk if you don't know the contractor. If someone has access past your front door and robs your house, you're unlikely to get a dollar of compensation from any insurance company because such a situation doesn't qualify as a 'break-in'.

Facing the facts of life insurance

The topic of life insurance is grim stuff indeed. But we're all going to die sooner or later. With life insurance, other people avoid being left behind in a big financial mess when you finally depart for the pearly gates. Think of life insurance as an essential item, because arranging this type of cover really means investing in 'insurance for the rest of your family'.

Ignore narrow-focus accidental-death policies that come rolling through the door with your junk mail. Statistically, few of us die accidentally; as a result, the insurer incurs little risk, which is why your credit card company is always offering accidental-death insurance. (Ask them to insure your 19-year-old, motorcycle-owning son and see how they react!)

Consider taking out comprehensive life insurance — if money is tight, you can arrange cover through your superannuation fund and the premiums will be deducted from your account balance.

Money on hand

Emergency money need not be kept in your local bank. You can put the money in a cash-management account that pays a higher interest rate than a standard bank account. The minimum amount for a cash-management account tends to be around $5,000, and you can withdraw the money at short notice, usually around 24 hours. Internet-based, high-yield accounts have no minimum amounts.

Putting money into very *liquid* — easily sold — assets such as blue-chip stocks that trade in large volumes on the stock exchange is also a feasible option.

Financial planners consider any of the top 50 Australian stocks as a liquid asset. However, this type of investment reduces your possibility of getting cash immediately. Even if you choose online trading, getting the actual cash can still take a few days and, if you sell within 12 months of purchase, you pay capital gains tax (CGT) on any profits at your full marginal tax rate.

Where there's a will ...

Do you think there's a taboo around making a will? Just do it; it can't kill you. Even the simplest document that says something like 'Split everything equally between everyone who's left standing after I'm gone' is better than nothing.

What's more, think of the thrill you'll feel in beating one of the great items for procrastination in the western world.

Whenever you have any significant investments, or your family affairs become complex, ensure that changes to your will are overseen by a lawyer.

Making sure you're cashed up

Always have some cash in the bank. Though you can focus hard on investing your money in the most lucrative manner, you still need cash on hand for emergencies. If you manage your finances so finely that you have no spare cash, you have no choice but to get a loan if anything goes wrong.

And things can go wrong! For example, say you and your partner each have a car covered by a combined insurance contract. One Sunday afternoon — avoiding your partner's cat — you reverse your trend-setting, soft-top sports car into your partner's very sensible steel-framed station wagon. You immediately need $5,000 to get your car back on the road. If you don't have the cash on hand, then you have to take out a loan. If you take out a loan, this unfortunate accident (why did you park the car there anyway?) can cost you even more than you expected.

Working out how much cash you decide to keep on hand depends on your lifestyle. Lachlan Murdoch may keep a little more in cash than the rest of us, but financial advisers generally suggest the amount should be three months' income of the highest earning member of the family. In our opinion, two months' income is a suitable amount for most people.

Creating Your Personal Investment Strategy

If you've read this far in this chapter, you've already set the old brain machinery churning. Now it's time to focus: Do you understand your personal finance demands? You should be able to answer these questions in fewer than ten minutes:

- ✔ What rate of interest do you pay on your mortgage?
- ✔ What are your repayments on your mortgage each week?
- ✔ How often are those payments made?
- ✔ What's the annual rate of interest charged on your credit card?
- ✔ What's the tax rate that your superannuation fund pays on income?
- ✔ When you renewed your home and contents insurance policy last year, did you update your cover?
- ✔ If you're hit with a $5,000 bill tomorrow, can you pay it in cash?
- ✔ If you died tomorrow, in what manner is your personal wealth going to be divided?

Nothing like a few hard questions to focus the mind!

Investing, especially those first cautious steps, is a bit like jogging round the park. You don't look like you're having a lot of fun at the time, but you sure feel better afterwards!

A few aspects of becoming an investor can disappoint you. Unless you're very lucky, you may be wrong about certain investments, and they may not work out. Or you may well have very bad timing in one or two investments, which can take years to work itself out.

Don't take short cuts. James was coming home in a taxi one night a few years ago, and the taxi driver was talking about how he was going to become an investor. James asked him whether he had started shopping around among the big financial institutions and reading the financial press.

'Oh, I don't need that stuff,' he said. 'I'm working off a special plan you can't get from local papers. I had to send away for it on the radio. It cost me about $500 to get this package that I have at home.'

What a hopeless way to enter the investment market — wasting $500 on some investment 'do-it-yourself' package! For only $200, this guy is able to buy himself a subscription to a financial publication and a few good investment guides (like this one!). And with the $300 left over, he can underpin his first share or managed-fund investment. The way to successful investing isn't via taking short cuts. In this section, we talk about why you have to have a strategic approach, especially in the early days of becoming an investor.

Ultimately — when you've digested this book — you have to decide what that strategic approach will be. In the early days, the mix will most likely include shares and managed funds. When you've accumulated enough funds, then it will be time to consider property. Throughout your life, whatever approach you're following, you should be ensuring that your superannuation is accumulating steadily, regardless of the progress of your other investments.

Slow and steady wins the race

Getting into your stride with investing can seem so slow at first. Unless you hit the jackpot and your first share or managed fund takes off like a rocket, you need to call on all your patience before the investment process pays rewards.

But hang in there, because the beauty in the reward comes from watching your investment grow faster and faster.

Look at the most basic example of all, compound interest. If you invest $1,000 at 10 per cent, almost nothing happens in the first year — by the end of that first year you make $100 for the total amount at risk of $1,000. However, without ever touching or even thinking about this money, at the end of the fifth year the total worth is now more than $1,600. By the end of the eighth year you've doubled your money and the total is at more than $2,100. If you can wait until the end of 25 years without touching the money, the reward for waiting becomes worth more than $10,000. The growth result is guaranteed.

The steady accumulation of dividends reinvested in stocks, or profits reinvested in managed funds, perform in a similar fashion. As the financial institutions never tire of telling us, investing is about making your money work for you.

Diversifying takes time and money

Everyone tells you to diversify, but splitting your investments up when you don't have that much money in the market is tricky. Accept that diversification is not always possible in the early days. The best way to diversify with small amounts of money is through managed funds. As soon as you have investments totalling more than around $20,000, you can really start to diversify your portfolio to include shares and funds.

Paying regularly into anything can be a trap

Many investment plans — especially those offered by banks and insurance companies — operate on the basis that you pay a certain amount, such as $200 each month, into a certain product such as a managed fund. The theory is that you always make money because, when stock prices are up, you're enjoying a rising market and, when prices go down, you get the stocks that make up the fund more cheaply. This theory doesn't hold water. When the market is falling — as it did for much of 2008 — sometimes the best solution is to do nothing and stay out of the stock market altogether. Regular investing is a good discipline for anyone, but make sure you don't find yourself investing when it clearly doesn't make sense.

Having a choice doesn't come cheap

The less money you have to invest, the fewer options you have about what to invest in. Many managed funds that specialise in anything other than a very predictable range of Australian or international shares have a minimum entry level of $20,000.

Financial institutions make 90 per cent of their revenue from 10 per cent of their customers. Smaller 'low net worth' customers are not very profitable. Low net worth customers are those with less than $100,000 to invest. Don't expect great service from the big end of town until you get to this level. Instead, take the best services you can find — 'cherry pick' the market to suit your own purposes.

A penny for your stocks

Speculators love to talk about *penny stocks* — very cheap stocks often in the mining or technology sectors that have the potential to show great growth. But penny stocks are only cheap on paper — if you invest $500 in something, whether you get ten shares or a thousand shares doesn't matter. Instead, you need to view the investment in terms of a $500 amount only.

The attraction of very cheap stocks is that they can make dramatic increases. After all, a stock that goes from two cents to four cents has just lifted by 100 per cent.

But if you're thinking you can put $40 on a single stock, forget it. Under the rules of the ASX, brokers can only deal in 'minimum parcels' of $500 or more. So, with a minimum parcel and stockbroker fees, the least amount you could possibly spend to buy a piece of stock market action is probably around $520.

Investing in penny stocks is always more risky than blue chips. Nothing's wrong with investing in very small stocks with good growth potential. Just remember these stocks are more risky than blue chips; that's one of the main reasons they're cheap.

Chapter 4

Finding Your Feet in the Investment Markets

In This Chapter

▶ Understanding your position in the markets

▶ Gauging how the market works

▶ Avoiding common investment mistakes

*W*hen you think of the investment markets, think of a forest. You're the hunter–gatherer, and the best fruit sits at the top of the tallest trees. You have to get a handle on the lay of the land. You need to know where you are in this forest, the main areas of growth, the clearings, the ravines and the soggy, boggy areas where nothing ever grows and many people lose their way.

Now, if you were to fly in a helicopter over this area, many things become clear. One of the most important discoveries for you to make is that certain obstacles in the forest can't be overcome. You may also find areas that are simply not worth exploring. More importantly, you may find certain things in the forest that are beyond your control.

In this chapter, we look at some of the areas in the investment markets that you need to recognise and come to terms with. We explain the difference between inside traders and market-movers, and we check out exotic investing instruments such as derivatives and hedge funds. When you understand some of the powerful forces that move the markets, you can begin to minimise your inevitable investment mistakes. And this chapter explains a few of those investment potholes.

Cliquing Into the Investment Scene

When you read the stock market prices in your daily newspaper, they reflect exactly what happened in the markets a day earlier. The prices move up or down or sideways thanks to the buying and selling of millions of people trading shares. But not everyone plays the same game. Individual investors, like you, may have very different strategies from those of a trader in a bank or a powerful billionaire. We may surprise you with this odd-sounding remark, but not everyone wants stock prices to rise.

For example, just after you buy stocks in a company, an overseas trader may want the stock to drop because the trader has recently decided that her bank (her client) should quit Australia. Although this decision may be the wrong decision, that trader is selling large amounts of stock in your chosen company. These events can push the price down.

On the other hand, you may be lucky. In the hours after you buy the stock, the market may discover that a rival company has been accumulating funds for a takeover and the stock you just bought is a takeover target. Or maybe one of the world's best-known investors is revealed to be behind one of the investment companies holding stock in the company over recent months. Such news can push the stock price up.

Movements of stock often have very little to do with the day-to-day operations of the company; they hinge on stock market activity. (When we talk about *stocks*, we mean ordinary shares or common stock — in Australia, the two terms mean the same thing.)

Eventually, though, the financial performance of a company will always dictate the long-term trend of any stock price.

A range of factors can influence the movement of stock prices, some of which you never find out about. If an investor could know everything about a stock — including what everyone else is planning — no element of risk would exist.

Investing in the stock market is not for the short term. The range of factors that can move a share price in the short term is beyond anybody's grasp. In contrast, you can make reasonable predictions about longer term investing. Put simply, over the long term you'll be rewarded for investing in the best companies.

Tricks and Tricksters of the Trade

The Art of War, an ancient Chinese fighting manual, is a favourite desktop ornament among financiers. This guide to dealing with enemies has some useful advice for investors at any level. One of the key rules of the book is never to attack your enemies head on.

Trying to beat the giants of the stock market at their own game rarely makes sense. To know what they're doing, however — or what they're capable of doing — always makes sense.

Insider information

For all the hype about insider information, only a handful of convictions for insider trading of shares have transpired.

The term *insider trading* has an exact legal meaning — people using information on stocks to their advantage, before the information is disclosed to the stock exchange and made public.

To a degree, all markets work on the basis of insider-style information. James worked for a few years in the early 1980s as a reporter on the Irish Stock Exchange. At that time, the entire Dublin market consisted of about 80 stocks! In his innocence he asked a senior stockbroker if any insider trading occurred in Dublin. 'You mean to say, "Is there anything else?"' he said with a wicked grin.

People work very long hours inside broking companies and banks to get the edge in terms of information. Banking analysts, for example, know every tiny thing about the big four banks (Commonwealth Bank, NAB, ANZ and Westpac). If one analyst gets a piece of information that makes a difference to a bank stock, they make sure that their clients benefit first. They let the rest of the world know later. Although this type of first-hand information is not insider trading, information in itself is power in the stock market — a fact that's never going to change.

As a private investor, you never get to hear the snippets of information passing around the market between professionals. If the information is very important, it eventually passes into the public domain through the media, but by that time the stock price has almost always increased or decreased, depending on the news. Again, if you're a long-term investor, you can accommodate all these issues because, over an extended period, the best companies turn in the best performance.

Market-movers

Inside any stock market are very big players who can literally move the market or move a single stock price. In Australia, buying and selling by the Packer family or Murdoch family can instantly influence stock prices. These family dynasties have enormous power in the Australian market because they have a very strong record of successful investments. Also, these families have huge amounts of money at their disposal. When investors see Murdoch buying or selling, he may well set off a chain reaction. Of course, by the time small investors follow market-movers like Murdoch in, the market-movers may be getting out. In Hong Kong, the name Li Ka-shing is the most influential; in New York, Warren Buffett; and in London, Richard Branson.

Small investors can do little to stop the influence of big players, except to join them. By investing in companies like News Corporation (Rupert Murdoch), investors can take a ride with the tycoons who dominate the market.

Volume trading

Big institutions — like your superannuation fund — have a lot of power in the stock market. Sometimes large organisations can change the outlook for a stock if they decide to buy or sell a large number of shares. This market clout means a big investor can change the fortunes of a small company just by arriving on the scene, especially in small companies, such as those employing less than 100 people.

For example, if the Very Big Insurance Company (VBIC) decides to buy stocks in your favourite technology company, Robot Nuts Ltd, buying just $5,000 worth of stock doesn't make sense because the administrative costs to VBIC can exceed the cost of the shares.

Assume VBIC lives up to its name and is a big player going into everything in a big way. Robot Nuts Ltd may have thousands of small investors supporting the stock and a total value of $100 million on the stock market (that is, the market capitalisation — the total value of all shares of the company on the stock market is $100 million). VBIC may be impressed with Robot Nuts and buy 15 per cent of the stock in one day, which pushes the price upwards.

The problem for you — and for Robot Nuts — is that a small company (by the standards of the stock market) now has a big shareholder. If a new managing director joins VBIC and rules that the company should have no more holdings in technology, VBIC may try to sell its 15 per cent holding in the market. In turn, this aggressive sale creates a huge downward pressure on the share price because most likely more stock is for sale than there are people wanting to buy it.

Consistently following the financial media helps you to become familiar with situations in the stock market when an institutional investor has become a major investor in a small company. Such investments are often trumpeted as very good news for a small company. But not always, especially if the big investor ever wants to sell its shares.

Funny money — derivatives

A *derivative* is any variation on a share that can also be traded. Derivatives include options, warrants, contracts for difference (CFDs) and futures (see Chapter 7). Derivatives allow investors to bet on the future price of the underlying share, or the ordinary share. The best-known derivatives are *options*, where you can buy the right to buy or sell an amount of stock at a set price at or before a future date.

Stocks that have options and warrants affect share price. Most big companies like BHP Billiton or Westpac have options and warrants for traders who want to take bets on whether stocks will rise or fall in the future.

While you're doing your best to understand the basics of the BHP business and how that business reflects its share price, professional investors are playing games with BHP options trying to improve the returns on their total investments in BHP. For these professional investors, the sensible move may be to sell shares in BHP and buy options instead. This strategy may drive down the BHP share price even though these professional investors are supporting the company more strongly than ever.

If you're interested in derivatives investing, a wide range of derivative-based products is now available for retail investors (see Chapter 7). But you really have to understand the sharemarket first. Take time to figure out shares, then you'll have the knowledge to enter the derivatives market.

Hedging your bets — hedge funds

On the esoteric fringe of the stock market are investors employed by hedge funds, who spend the bulk of their time trying to make money from anticipating future movements in stock prices. Hedge funds could not exist without derivatives. But now that the hedge funds have become popular — even with superannuation funds — the derivatives market is boosted further. The whole business is something of a merry-go-round where the companies that underpin the stock market can be almost forgotten.

Nevertheless, perfectly respectable sections of the market use hedging — an attempt to gauge future price movements — as part of their operations. For example, mining companies genuinely need to anticipate prices in the future because that business is heavily based on long-term planning. After all, mines are built in anticipation of future prices of certain commodities.

The business of guessing future movement in market prices, however, has taken on a life of its own. *Hedge funds* make money from making bets on every conceivable stock, bond or currency they can find.

Overall, hedge funds accelerate the speed at which everything happens. Markets now go up and down faster than ever before. If a hedge fund is playing games with investments in your portfolio, you have one of two choices — go along for the ride or sell out of the investment. If the company, bond or currency you support is fundamentally sound, then any price movements driven by the hedge fund are often temporary.

Despite the flood of brokers' reports and investment tips in the market, the majority of investors miss huge success stories. Major companies, too, make fatal mistakes, which most investors don't realise until too late. Nobody knows the future, no matter how plausible a prediction might sound.

Here's a list of market events that caught everybody by surprise:

- ABC Learning Centres, a high-flying childcare centre operator, fell in a heap after the global credit squeeze pulled the rug from under its rapid expansion. The company was forced to restructure when hedge funds *shorted* the stock; that is, they placed bets on the share price plummeting.

- Ansett Australia was Australia's second airline, flying domestically and to destinations in Asia, at its height in 1996. Then, in 2002, Air New Zealand bought the carrier, biting off more than it could chew. At the same time, the Australian government changed the rules and allowed foreign airlines to compete in the domestic market. Short of cash and unable to compete with new low-cost carriers, Ansett was put into liquidation in 2002, 67 years after it was launched by Sir Reginald Ansett.

- The Commonwealth Bank was a sleepy government-owned savings bank that nobody in the stock market took seriously against the strength of ANZ, NAB and Westpac. Then, in the 1990s, the bank was privatised and listed on the ASX. Today, more than a decade later, the Commonwealth Bank is the biggest bank on the stock market in Australia.

✔ In 2008, Western Australian mining entrepreneur Andrew 'Twiggy' Forrest became Australia's richest man — until the sharemarket collapsed. That year, his company, Fortescue Minerals, sent its first shipload of iron ore to China, just three and a half years after drilling proved it had enough iron ore to break the BHP Billiton–Rio Tinto stranglehold on the Australian iron ore trade.

✔ In 1993, the Commonwealth Serum Laboratories was a little known division of the Department of Health that developed products and technologies based on blood. Today, this company, better known as CSL, is one of the leading biotechnology companies in the world and a star of the Australian stock market.

By reviewing this series of market 'surprises' the message is clear. A herd mentality exists in the stock market and very often almost everyone in the market can get it wrong. The market can seriously undervalue or overvalue a company or its chief executive. Eventually, however, the true picture becomes clear to all investors; if you can see the true picture earlier than the rest of the herd (and invest appropriately) you'll be onto a winner.

The man who broke the bank

If you don't fully understand how derivatives trading or hedging actually works, don't worry, very few people do understand — even those who are paid to do so.

When markets are soaring, derivatives trading becomes more popular, as people believe they can make even more money by taking bets on future stock prices. In Asia during the mid-1990s, the combination of a soaring stock market, a gambling culture in local markets and the presence of overseas banks and brokers trying desperately to make money from local markets was always going to mean trouble.

In Singapore, a unit of Barings Bank — a blue-blood, London-based British bank — concentrated on trading and speculating on Asian financial markets. A young trader at the bank, Nick Leeson, was a star performer in the unit. Leeson managed to make very good returns for the bank, trading in increasingly exotic stocks and bonds that few investors clearly understood.

As it turned out, Leeson's senior management back in London were among those who never understood the risks Leeson was taking. However, they were more than happy to share in the returns his unit was sending back to the bank headquarters.

Over time, making these high returns became harder and harder for Leeson, and he started to take ever-more-daring risks with the bank's money. Eventually, in 1995, Leeson's game was up — he lost so much money that the unit got into deep trouble. Eventually the global bank itself was so much in debt it was put up for sale and was bought by the ever-so-sober Dutch bank ING.

Today, Leeson is out of jail but, in the aftermath of the 2008 financial crisis, a new generation of derivatives traders is under investigation. Rogue trader Jerome Kerviel lost US$7 billion in derivative trading for French bank Société Générale before anyone noticed.

Watching Out for Investment Potholes

As you, the new investor, move stealthily and skilfully through the forest of the investment markets, you have to watch for those bear traps, not to mention those 100-year-old mining shafts your entrepreneurial ancestors forgot to fill in.

Your investments won't ever look after themselves. And investment markets change all the time. You don't ever have to be a *daytrader* (an investor who trades shares every day), but you do have to take note of the major issues that may mean you should be buying or selling.

Selling at the wrong time

On the stock market, when it rains it pours. Just when you have the least cash, that's the time when your stocks can be at their lowest. An extended stock market *bull run* — a continuous increase in share prices — means that many people have had little or no experience of downturns in the market. Although being patient when the markets are down is a hard approach to adopt, the important thing is to be patient for long enough to ask the right questions.

The average annual return from Australian shares on the All Ordinaries Index from 1950 to 2007 was 12.8 per cent.

Think hard before you sell stock in good companies that are stuck in a bad market. Among the questions to ask yourself are:

- ✔ Is this stock in temporary trouble, or has this stock had its day?
- ✔ Does the stock represent a good company in a weak industry?
- ✔ Is the sell-off in the stock justified by the earnings of the company?
- ✔ Do I have something better in mind if I sell this stock?

Answering these questions will come down to trusting the figures released by the company and believing the future as outlined by the management. If a company remains a potentially profitable force in a weak situation, you're likely to stick with them. On the other hand, if the company does things that make you lose trust, such as 'restating its figures' or announcing further problems when it earlier said 'the worst is over', then you're likely to seek better investments elsewhere.

Hindsight is a great thing, of course, but, to long-term investors in the mid-1990s, BHP was clearly a great resources company that had made a string of mistakes. The situation was by no means irreversible.

In contrast, ten years later, ABC Learning Centres had also clearly made mistakes that were irreversible. The company had expanded locally and overseas, quickly becoming the world's biggest childcare services provider, on the back of unsustainable levels of debt. When the global credit squeeze took hold, and cheap funds dried up, the music stopped for ABC Learning. The situation was beyond repair.

Buying at the wrong time

If you can see the bandwagon, it's already too late.

—*Anonymous*

Buying profitable, well-managed companies that have a sound strategic plan for extending their success always makes sense.

Buying stocks in a hot sector, however, is another issue entirely. If a certain sector is running hot, then all companies in the sector reflect the optimism of investors for stock in that area.

When the dot-com boom started in Australia, investors were unable to get enough stock in dot-com companies; not enough companies existed to invest in back in 1997 and 1998. Liberty One, the company regarded as Australia's first dot-com company, never had profits, good management or anything like a long-term plan. The company was a great success in the early days of the boom. However, in 2001, Liberty One was one of the first dot-com companies to end up in liquidation.

Stocks must fit your basic buying criteria as a serious investor. Ideally, you want a stock to be a profitable investment over the medium to long term. You'll stay with this stock for a decade if the management keeps making the profits.

On that basis, you want real revenues and real profits — not just promises. If those profits are not possible at this time, then you need to be absolutely convinced they'll be achieved in the near future, say within 12 months.

If you buy stocks for other reasons, you're playing a game of pass-the-parcel, as most Liberty One investors know only too well.

Avoiding dodgy salesfolk

Seek advice in your investments, by all means. But be wary about listening to almost anyone who has a commercial interest in your buying a certain stock, bond or managed fund, as this advice is rarely objective. As you know, in any walk of life, a good salesperson can sell you something you don't really need.

On the investment market, almost any investment is potentially ideal for you. You are, therefore, a salesperson's paradise. Financial sales executives — and we include financial advisers and everyone in the broking and banking industries — can be fabulously well paid if they can sell investments. Just remember they can't be expected to care for your best interests. Only you can look after yourself. A favourite phrase among Wall Street's tough-as-nails investment bankers is: 'We ripped their faces off' — ugh! — and sometimes they're talking about their own customers.

Treat stockbrokers, fund managers, bankers and financial advisers with a degree of cynicism. They're all in the same business — making money from selling you something they know more about than you do.

Professional investors try to minimise their mistakes by using derivatives and other exotic forms of investment. But really, when you think about it, as an early-stage personal investor, if you have a very good basic investment portfolio in the first place, you don't need to depend on derivatives. Any stock investment other than ordinary shares should be left to either the professional investors or very seasoned private investors.

Don't be enticed by well-placed advertisements from respectable banks and brokers that offer derivatives such as options and warrants. If you're not an experienced investor in ordinary shares, you're out of your depth — a bit like someone trying to rent you a Ferrari the day you pass your driving test.

Here are some realities behind the hype of finance industry advertising:

- ✔ The volume of advertising that you see reflects nothing more than the amount of money a company is willing to spend on advertising.
- ✔ Some of the best products in the market are rarely advertised, and some of the worst are advertised so much that you can't escape them.
- ✔ Some advertisers saturate one channel of information — like an easy-listening radio station — but don't appear to be prominent elsewhere. Be exceptionally careful of these companies.
- ✔ Remember that a company can be doing poor business or very little business, yet they can advertise so heavily as to give the impression they dominate the investment world.

Top sectors through history

Here are some hot sectors from recent times:

- ✔ Energy boom (1970s), oil and other resources in high demand.

- ✔ Finance boom (1980s), lighter banking regulations boosted banks and insurers.

- ✔ Japan boom (1980s), Japanese companies emerged as world beaters.

- ✔ Asia boom (1980s), South-East Asian tiger economies held huge promise.

- ✔ Internet boom (1990s), communications technology took a leap forward.

- ✔ Commodities boom (2000s), demand for raw materials from developing nations such as China and India drove up the price of commodities such as iron ore.

The finance industry is riddled with hype and slick advertising. Don't believe the advertisements; believe the returns. The more thoroughly you follow the financial media and the less you look at the adverts, the more familiar you'll become with the real winners in financial services.

Biting off more than you can chew

We've been in financial markets for nearly 50 years between us, and we still feel like beginners. Although we buy shares, options, funds, houses and other investments, we don't go near some derivatives. We don't go near overseas markets that we don't understand, and we never, ever examine investment offerings in small advertisements from box numbers with suburban addresses. (If a company can't even afford the rent downtown, how can it ever make it in the big league!)

The investment markets are huge and complex and great fun. You can always find good companies making good profits. Likewise, you can always find hotspots in the market that can offer exciting opportunities. Don't rush; you're just starting.

James remembers meeting a recently retrenched engineer on the public floor of the old Sydney Stock Exchange. He had received a lump sum from an electricity utility and had set up as a full-time private investor. He dealt with several brokers and talked to the other investors who hung around the stock exchange. As he talked of good tips he had got and unlucky breaks with other stocks, it was clear he simply didn't have a clue what he was doing. He never examined the one thing that was driving his stock market profits — the performance of the companies in his share portfolio. Lucky for him, an extended bull market meant that he was probably going to make money most of the time, regardless of what he bought. The market is very different now, and this guy is the type of investor who will fail in tougher investment markets. Hopefully he now reads books like this one.

The accidental investor

You can know absolutely nothing about the stock market and do well, especially in a bull market. In the four years to June 2007, Australian shares returned an average of 25 per cent a year, the strongest gains since 1987, easily beating the odds in almost any other risk-based activity.

In the mid-1990s, Australia had a rush of privatisations, such as Commonwealth Bank and Qantas. *Demutualisation* also began, in that insurance companies entered the stock market — companies like AMP and NRMA. We discuss demutualisation further in Chapter 7.

Through these ventures — especially demutualisations — millions of Australians entered the stock market for the first time. Sometimes they simply got shares for free in the post.

If you're lucky enough to get free shares in a demutualisation or shares through a privatisation, count your blessings. Remember though, you didn't pick these shares — they picked you. Successfully selecting stocks from a market with more than 2,200 different stocks to choose from is a different business. If you're an accidental investor, be aware that you have a long way to go.

Chapter 5

Listen Up! Finding the Best Advice

. . . .

In This Chapter

▶ Taking advantage of the tax system

▶ Choosing a financial adviser

. . . .

*W*hether your investment skills are junior high school or MBA (Master of Business Administration), you need advice. In the early stages of becoming an investor, you need advice on all aspects of investing. In the later stages, the key advice you need most likely relates to financial planning and all aspects of tax.

Getting neutral financial advice is almost impossible. Absolutely everybody you ask for advice (with the possible exception of your grandmother . . . though she could be scheming too!) has something to gain from it.

Don't be under any illusion — the area of financial advice is a minefield. But, before you set out to negotiate it, you can do some research of your own. In this chapter, we describe how to go about it. We also let you know about some of the best opportunities for tax concessions you need to look for as an investor.

You can only expect so much from financial planners or tax advisers. After all, if they know all the answers, they're more likely to be sitting in the Bahamas — not across from you in their office. Use them to get advice on the rules and regulations you don't have time to understand.

Tracking Down Good Tax Advice

James has a friend who loves having late-night parties at his house. As an experienced party thrower, he has devised a way of clearing his house of unwanted friends early in the morning. He simply puts on a record of a Turkish folk singer who has a superb technical range but a corrosive style, singing songs that run for up to quarter of an hour each. By the end of the first song, everybody is at the front door looking for a taxi!

Talking about tax has the same effect. People's eyes just glaze over. We find this a funny reaction, because, when we talk about tax, we're talking about getting money back.

You must get tax advice every year because the tax system never stops changing. No matter what efforts are made to simplify the ins and outs of tax, the system just gets more and more complicated. If you want to get into further detail on tax matters, check out *Tax for Australians For Dummies*, written by Jimmy B. Prince (Wiley Publishing Australia).

But the trick to tackling tax is to look at the tax system another way. Think of the whole exercise as a treasure hunt where money can be waiting for you in the most unlikely places.

Even if you're a hard-pressed salary earner, some tax advantages are probably available to you. The bulk of these advantages, however, only apply when you're beginning to invest — or, more often, when you borrow to invest.

A broker is someone who invests other people's money until it is all gone.

—*Woody Allen, American comedian*

The two best tax breaks in Australia

While hundreds of tax breaks exist throughout the tax system, they mostly apply at the edges of the system, where very specialised investors are doing very particular things with their money.

Nevertheless, almost everyone under the sun can benefit from two basic tax breaks. In this section we show you how you can benefit from investing in both the family home and superannuation.

Your humble abode

Several reasons exist as to why you shouldn't buy a family home, but nearly all are short term. In the long term, owning your own house is hard to beat as an investment because house prices in Australia rarely go down (see Table 5-1). And, more importantly, while you pay capital gains tax at almost every turn in your daily life, you don't have to pay this tax on the sale of your primary place of residence.

Table 5-1	House Prices in Australia: Percentage Change from Previous Year						
Year	Sydney	Melbourne	Brisbane	Adelaide	Perth	Hobart	Darwin
2007–08	4.4	14.1	14.0	16.2	−0.9	3.0	7.0
2006–07	3.0	11.5	15.7	11.7	15.3	9.7	7.4
2005–06	−0.5	5.5	4.5	7.3	35.4	7.4	18.7

Source: Australian Bureau of Statistics, extracted from House Price Indexes *(6416.0), September 2008.*

If you think about home ownership realistically, you like to keep where you live in good shape; you may even like to make improvements regularly. In rented accommodation, any improvements you make are for someone else. Interestingly, although you may find lots of slick advisers telling you that you don't need to own your house, if you ask them where they live, you're sure to find out that they own their house. Don't be fooled — owning your own house is a very good idea most of the time.

If you want to maximise the tax advantage of owning your own home, stay in it for at least five years before you sell it. This way, you invariably cover any relocation expenses and make a solid capital gain, tax-free!

Capital gains tax (CGT) is the tax applied on profits or the extra value you achieve on the sale of investments. The tax is applied at your marginal tax rate (that is, possibly as high as 46.5 per cent). You only pay CGT on half the gains you make on an investment as long as you're owned the investment for at least 12 months.

Your old-age fund

Taking every opportunity to reduce your tax makes sense. One way, which we sometimes think is too good to be true, is called *salary sacrifice*. Salary sacrifice means putting an extra bit of your salary into your superannuation every week. (We discuss salary sacrifice further in Chapter 22.)

The tax break comes from the fact that you can put the money into your superannuation from your pre-tax salary — the amount on the top line of your pay slip that's always much bigger than the amount you bring home! So, instead of paying tax on your full salary at your marginal income tax rate, when you salary-sacrifice into super, you pay a contributions tax of just 15 per cent.

Better still, as soon as that money is inside the superannuation system, any gains you make are only taxed at 15 per cent.

If you ignore the opportunity to salary-sacrifice and, instead, put some money into an investment each week, the disadvantages are clear:

✔ You pay tax on that money put into another investment.

✔ Any extra income you gain is taxed at your marginal rate.

Behind the generous treatment for superannuation is the fact that too many people are going to be too old for the government to bankroll a decent pension in the near future. Although various restraints exist on how much you can enjoy this tax break, for most people most of the time superannuation is a very good idea.

Opportunities to save on tax

Tax authorities never stop tinkering with the tax system, which means you can never be really sure if you're up to speed with the main tax breaks. However, despite the constancy of tax changes, a number of enduring tax opportunities seem to arise year after year.

Of course, your tax treatment depends a lot on what you do for a living. Small-business owners have very different tax affairs than salaried people. Low-income retirees are in yet another boat.

Here are some of the key opportunities to get money back or save money on your tax bill as an investor:

✔ **Salary-sacrifice to superannuation:** Anything that allows you to pay 15 per cent tax on investments where you may otherwise pay more than 40 per cent sounds good to us.

✔ **Split your super:** If you're one of a couple, examine whether you and your partner are better off having two superannuation accounts. Some very good reasons exist (including a lower individual tax bill) for having two accounts, especially when you retire and you start to live off these savings (see Chapter 22 for more information).

- ✔ **Borrow to invest:** You can get tax deductions if you borrow to invest. Called *gearing*, it's most commonly used for investing in property and shares. However, you should choose your investments and your loan wisely and never borrow for the tax benefits alone. Gearing makes sense when interest rates are low, asset prices are rising and you have sufficient income to meet your repayments. During the 2008 sharemarket collapse, many investors who had borrowed to buy shares were forced to sell stocks at rock-bottom prices to meet their loan repayments.

- ✔ **Offset your losses:** If you make a loss on some investments, consider whether the time is right to sell those investments and set the losses against gains that have to be taxed in your year-end bill from the tax office. Many seasoned investors believe the best thing to do with a loss-making investment is to take a hit by selling out and move on. If you believe a stock is never going to recover within a reasonable timeframe, get out and start again.

- ✔ **Claim your fees:** You can claim the fees charged by your tax adviser.

- ✔ **Claim for reference books:** You can claim a tax deduction for professional publications or investment books (including this one).

- ✔ **Claim for course fees:** If you go as far as taking a course in the investment markets (the Australian Securities Exchange and many third-level institutions offer very good courses), you can claim your course fees.

Here are some of the more sophisticated ways to get money back or save money from tax as an investor:

- ✔ **Franking credits:** By investing in Australian shares that have *franked dividends* (dividends that offer a tax credit), you can reduce your tax bill by claiming the tax credits on your annual income tax return. (We discuss this further in Chapter 10, where we talk about dividend imputation.)

- ✔ **Pre-paid interest:** In a number of investment strategies, such as borrowing to buy shares, you can pay interest 12 months in advance, and then set these payments off against your tax bill.

- ✔ **Section 221D:** This section is an obscure piece of tax legislation and the sort of information you only find out about from a tax adviser. Believe it or not, if you're fairly sure you're going to get a tax refund of, say, $20,800 at the end of the next financial year, you can get the tax office to make a 221D allowance on the $20,800 (or $400 a week) in advance. If you're on a 41.5 per cent tax rate, you don't have to pay tax on that $400 amount, which means you take home more than $160 more each week.

Plenty of other bizarre and wonderful twists and turns in the tax system are waiting for your attention, but you need help to find them, which is why paying a tax adviser is worthwhile.

Don't scrimp on tax adviser fees. How much an adviser can save you on tax is the important outcome. If you're an active investor, simply paying a small flat fee for a tax adviser to run your accounts through a computer in five minutes is a total waste of your time and money.

Finding Someone You Can Trust with Your Money

The bad news is that, despite repeated attempts to brush up its image, the financial-planning industry in Australia is notorious for being riddled with crooks, charlatans and rogues. In the wake of the collapse of the Westpoint Group of companies in 2006, the Australian Securities and Investments Commission banned 20 financial advisers!

Where do you start looking for an adviser? That man with white shoes and clip-on tie at the railway station with a badge that says 'Save money now, ask me how' probably isn't a good place to begin! Unfortunately, designer office suites in skyscraper buildings are often no better an indicator of propriety than that man at the railway station; indeed, they can be worse.

Finding an adviser is perhaps the toughest task you can face in the investment market. One of the most seductive options is to walk into a major bank or financial institution and let the institution's 'independent adviser' take care of all your finances. The big problem here, of course, is that you're walking into a lion's den. A single financial institution may be very good at managed funds but hopeless at stockbroking.

The best financial adviser is independent of any institution and doesn't depend on income from any of the financial institutions that dominate the market.

One of the best ways to assess a financial planner is for you to ask: 'How are you paid?' If the answer means that the adviser charges you by the hour for her time and that this income is the only income she receives from your session, then you're off to a good start.

Who can give you advice?

Financial advice is regulated by the Australian Securities and Investments Commission (ASIC). The only people permitted by law to give personal financial advice are those who hold an Australian Financial Services Licence, or their representatives. Licensed advice covers superannuation, insurance, shares, managed funds and many banking products. Unfortunately, anyone can give advice about loans and real estate, and everyone does. However, a lot of advice, especially from non-professionals, can be well worth hearing. The problem is whether that advice makes as much sense for you as it does for them.

As an early-stage investor, you need top-quality, independent advice. You want someone with a long view of investment opportunities and the intelligence to see what the best opportunities are for you in your situation.

A good place to start your search for a licensed financial adviser is the Financial Planning Association (discussed in the next section), which sets standards for financial planners.

What to demand from a financial planner

You alone have the responsibility to make sure that a financial planner of your choosing has the ability to manage your affairs. Here's a list of the key factors to explore when looking for a financial adviser:

- **Qualifications:** What is the nature of the adviser's qualifications? For example, does the adviser have an accountancy qualification? Or a specific Certified Financial Planner qualification?

- **Licences:** Is the adviser licensed to give advice? You can check if an adviser is licensed, or banned, by going to the ASIC consumer website FIDO (www.fido.gov.au).

- **Payment arrangements:** What is the process for paying this adviser? Can money be handed over to the adviser by anyone other than you? The best possible arrangement is a straight fee from you for the advice and no other payments to the adviser from related parties.

- **Industry relationships:** Has the planner been working for a financial institution in the past and is there a current relationship of any sort with that institution or any other financial companies? The more independent the adviser is from large institutions, the better for you.

✔ **Dispute resolution:** How can you go about sorting out a dispute between you and the adviser? Is the adviser a member of a dispute-resolution scheme? A clear path for dispute resolution will be good for both you and the adviser.

✔ **FPA membership:** Is your adviser a member of the Financial Planning Association (FPA)? The chances are that, if your adviser already meets the preceding criteria, he's already a member. You may find a perfectly good adviser outside the FPA, but the chances of someone fleecing you are also much more likely if he's not an FPA member.

The scary thing about crooked financial advisers is that they can hide behind some of the best brand names in the country. The licensing of financial advice has been tightened up in recent years, but too many advisers still sell products to their clients that feather their own bank balance and leave their clients short-changed.

The Financial Planning Association (FPA)

You may take comfort knowing that the Financial Planning Association (FPA) monitors the standards of financial advisers and planners.

The problem is, however, that not everybody who sets up as an adviser bothers to join this group. Only about one in three financial advisers are estimated to be members of the FPA. The FPA has about 12,000 members; the overall number of advisers in Australia is estimated to be around 40,000.

As a result, the very good work done by the FPA is often irrelevant to the majority of financial advice transactions that take place every day. From within this larger group (that is, the two out of three who aren't members),

come the vast bulk of the scams and swindles that break so many hearts among Australian investors.

An adviser who isn't in the FPA isn't necessarily of a lower standard than a member adviser. However, the vast majority of crooks and charlatans who populate the financial-planning industry haven't been — and are unlikely to become — members of this industry group or any other organisation that seeks to set standards in this industry.

Check out the FPA website at www.fpa.asn.au for more information on how to find a financial planner in your area, and what questions you should ask when choosing an adviser.

What you need to tell an adviser

Dealing with a financial adviser or planner is often akin to dealing with your family doctor — the more you reveal, the better chance your doctor has of making the correct diagnosis.

In the early stages of your relationship, a financial planner can guide you towards sensible 'structures' for becoming an investor. This structure may include getting some basic things done, like attending to your superannuation and your mortgage financing.

As soon as you begin to build an investment portfolio, the adviser is able to steer you through issues relating to the balance of assets inside that portfolio and the tax issues that can affect any moves you may make.

Ideally, a financial adviser helps you to construct a long-term plan around your investment skills and your desired financial targets. Rather than fitting you into an existing plan, the adviser builds a plan for you and your situation.

The amount of personal information about your financial status that you tell an adviser is up to you. Our advice is to tell them absolutely everything (financial, that is) if you want the absolute best value for your money.

The following is a list of documents to take along to a meeting with a financial adviser:

- ✔ Your last pay slip
- ✔ Your most recent tax assessment notice
- ✔ Your last superannuation statement
- ✔ Your most recent mortgage statement
- ✔ An estimate of your spending each week
- ✔ An estimate of how much you wish to save or invest each week

Part II
The Markets

Glenn Lumsden

*'My stockbroker said we should go around
at least a dozen times to get a feel for
the sharemarket.'*

In this part ...

Every day you can hear about *the markets* and they seem to be the central source of news for investors. But *what* are 'the markets'? And *where* are 'the markets'? The biggest problem with investment markets is that they just aren't user friendly. But access to the markets is getting better all the time, and now there are many ways you can use the investment markets to improve your financial position. Here's a little introduction to get you started ...

Chapter 6

The Stock Market and You

*N*ew investors often comment that the sharemarket is more like a casino than a suitable home for hard-earned savings. If you made your first foray into the world of share investing in 2008, then you probably see shares as a gamble you no longer wish to take. In 2008, Australian shares plunged by 43 per cent, the biggest annual loss on record, and US shares fell 34 per cent. Only three sharemarkets posted gains in 2008, in Ghana, Tunisia and Ecuador, and we're guessing you didn't have any money invested in those markets!

Now step back and take a wider view. In the five years leading up to 2008, total returns from Australian shares — that is, capital gains plus dividend income — rose by a staggering 164 per cent. In the short term, share investing involves risk and share prices fluctuate, often without good reason, but, unlike a casino, you can minimise the risk of being wiped out by investing in quality companies and holding on to them for the long haul. In bad years it is tempting to shift all your savings into government-guaranteed bank deposits, but doing so guarantees you'll miss out on the big returns on offer when the sharemarket recovers.

History is peppered with years that investors would like to forget, but it's worth remembering one simple fact: Over the long term, investing in quality companies pays handsomely. In this chapter, we cut through the noise and the hype that make the sharemarket a confusing place for beginners, and steer you safely along the path of successful long-term share investing. We look at the markets of most interest to Australian investors, the ASX and Wall Street, and examine categories of stock and the relative size of companies listed on the stock market, as well as market indices.

To Market, To Market

Think of your local fresh produce market — a noisy and boisterous place where a mixed range of products is for sale at different prices. The market is the place where you (the potential buyer) meet the farmer (the potential seller).

If you buy that pre-packed bag of pears for $3, the chances are the price is accurate — by that we mean you pay no more than anyone else needs to pay for the pears, at that moment in time.

Likewise, if you come back next month and a pear disease is sweeping the country, that bag of pears may cost $6. Alternatively, if the season has produced a bumper pear crop, the pears may cost only $2. The market reacts to supply and demand. The market is always changing, but one constant feature exists — prices are 'accurate', so you're not paying any more than anyone else at that moment in time.

The market never lies.

—Anonymous

The stock exchange reflects prices in the same way as a fresh produce market. This time, you, the investor, are the potential buyer and any listed company — say BHP Billiton — is the potential seller. The stockbroker is the market trader. The price of BHP shares is determined by supply and demand. Say BHP is $38 a share. If you come back to the market in a month and BHP has closed down for three weeks because of a huge strike, the price may have dropped to $32 a share because BHP is now less valuable.

Alternatively, if the price of copper and coal has soared over the last few weeks, you may find BHP is up at $42 a share because the stock has become more valuable. Just like the price of pears in your local market, BHP shares go up or down depending on the activity in the sharemarket. (In Australia, the terms *stocks* and *shares* mean the same thing — ordinary shares.)

When you buy a BHP share, or any other share, in the market, the trade may turn out to be good value or bad value, but, because you buy in the open market, you can always be comfortable that you get the shares at the best price on the day.

Once upon a time ...

Not very long ago there really was a stock market. Raffish-looking gentlemen with sharp suits bought and sold parcels of stock at a place called the stock exchange.

Today you can't really see much at the stock exchange. The stock market gradually became more and more computerised to the point where it's now just a network of electronic screens where buyers and sellers meet to trade stocks.

If you want to see the remnants of the public stock market in action, take a trip to any of the major stock exchanges, such as Bridge Street in Sydney or Collins Street in Melbourne. Here you can see a giant trading screen in the lobby with a panel that details activity across the entire stock market.

Coloured lights make the process pretty easy to follow: The stocks lit up in green lights are going up, the stocks lit up in red lights are going down and the yellow lights mean a stock is steady. Most days you see more green lights than red lights, unless bad news dominates the market.

Under these screens is a little bunch of investors chatting to each other about the market. They come in to swap information and give each other advice ... but don't be fooled by these scenes, because that activity isn't the market.

The real market activity takes place upstairs, in the high-rise trading rooms run by the major banks and stockbroking firms. In these rooms are thousands of professional market traders who sit trading stocks on computer screens all day. These traders are the modern-day 'screen jockeys' — looking at their trading screen, talking on the phone, eating a cheeseburger and reading the newspaper all at the same time!

These noisy claustrophobic trading rooms are found in every big city from Perth to New York. They deal in stocks, bonds, currencies and almost anything else that can be bought and sold — put them all together and you have the markets.

Meeting Two Major Markets

In Australia your main opening to the investment market is through the Australian Securities Exchange (ASX). The ASX is a combination of what was once a string of local exchanges in the major cities. Here are some fascinating facts about the ASX:

- ✔ The vast majority of shares bought and sold in Australia go through the ASX — for all intents and purposes the ASX is 'the market' for Australian shares and related investments.
- ✔ You have more than 2,200 stocks to choose from on the ASX, with about 90 different stockbroking firms offering their services.

✔ Rules and regulations for the exchange are set by the ASX in association with a government agency called the Australian Securities and Investments Commission (ASIC).

✔ When you go to buy or sell any of the 2,200 stocks on the ASX, the exchange ensures that the deal is done efficiently. In the 2007–08 financial year, $1.6 trillion worth of shares, warrants and interest-rate securities traded on the ASX.

✔ Even in this age of computerisation, some old-world aspects to the stock exchange still exist ... such as trading hours. The ASX opens each morning at 10 am (Eastern Standard Time) and closes at 4 pm.

Understanding the movements of the ASX

As you start to follow the markets, you can see that they bounce around for all sorts of unlikely reasons. As the internet and other technologies reduce effective distance from overseas markets — especially the United States — the influences that move our markets are changing rapidly.

Here are some of the key movers on the ASX:

✔ **Economic data:** Key economic data, such as business investment, unemployment or inflation, remain the single most powerful overall influence on the direction of the market. However, only when the data is overwhelmingly positive or negative is the influence of economic data obvious on the market.

✔ **Overseas markets:** Forty years ago the Australian stock market was a world of its own. Today the ASX is totally plugged into the bigger markets around the world. (The ASX rates among the world's top ten stock markets.) When global markets are trending sharply up or down, the ASX nearly always follows.

✔ **Business results:** The ASX can be heavily influenced by news from a single company if that company has a particularly large role in the market, such as the Commonwealth Bank or Woolworths. Major movements up or down in the share price of either of these companies can shift the entire stock market up or down.

Getting street-wise about Wall Street

You may not know a single thing about Wall Street. You may not even know where to find Wall Street exactly. (Actually, this very unimpressive little street squeezes into the very bottom of Manhattan.) Each year, however, Wall Street's power over global stock market trading increases.

Wall Street (which really means the stock market companies that dominate the US economy) is widely seen as the locomotive that drives world markets. To a degree, this influential power play has been true for most of the last 50 years, but, more recently, the influence of Wall Street is becoming more immediate, especially in Australia. Here's why:

- Wall Street, represented by three stock exchanges — the American Stock Exchange, the New York Stock Exchange and the National Association of Securities Dealers Association (NASDAQ) — is the biggest and most powerful stock market in the world.

- Over the last decade, American institutional investors such as pension funds have been allowed to invest more outside the United States. These investors tend to sell out of overseas markets when things are bad and buy back into the foreign markets when trading conditions improve.

- Australian companies are now more active than ever before in the United States. Some companies have moved across to the US markets completely, such as James Hardie. Other companies have substantial US operations, such as News Corporation, Westfield and Foster's Group.

- Australian investors now have more money held in US markets as superannuation and other institutional investors launch international funds that concentrate on the United States. Also, individual investors can now directly buy stocks on the US markets for much lower fees than ever before.

The stock market scenario that happened on Wall Street yesterday often happens on the ASX today — especially if a downturn in the markets occurs. When homeowners in Ohio began defaulting on their loan repayments in 2007, precipitating a credit squeeze on Wall Street, few people guessed the extent of the crisis that would follow. In 2008, the rest of the developed world was swept up in the panic, as credit dried up, debt-laden companies defaulted on their loans and sharemarkets went into freefall. In 2009, the world is looking to the United States for a sign that the worst is over so global markets can begin a long, slow recovery.

Running with the Herd

Just before being finally voted out of office, former Labor Prime Minister Paul Keating, during a major public speech, took a shot at institutional investors, calling them 'donkeys'.

Keating's criticism was about institutional investors acting very much like a group of donkeys in the way they stick stubbornly together on many issues and invest in the same group of companies all the time. By omission, the same investors continually overlook other investments such as renewable energy or biotech companies that can add real value to the Australian economy.

Ample evidence exists to support the sentiment that institutional investors act as a pack. For example, when companies are in favour, they're in favour with just about everybody, and institutional investors move together to buy up stock. On the other hand, as soon as a company falls from grace, the herd sells out at the same time, leaving the company — and smaller investors — utterly bewildered.

The market works this way because only a handful of very powerful expert players exists in any area of the markets, and the rest of the market tends to follow this group.

At one stage in the early 1990s, James worked as a banking correspondent. Every time the annual results of a major bank were due, he did a straw poll of about ten analysts to see what their estimates of the results were. Every time he conducted the poll, the forecasts were strangely similar. For example, if NAB was about to release full-year profits, the range from ten different analysts was between about $1.42 billion and $1.45 billion ... thus clearly showing that nobody inside the herd was ready to take any chances.

Very little has changed. Behind the scenes all the analysts talk to each other on a regular basis. The less experienced (and less expert) analysts follow the numbers that are being circulated by the top analysts. In the end, everyone has more or less the same numbers.

Amazingly, very often everyone is wrong with the forecasts. But that result isn't a big problem inside the herd, because everyone is tarred with the same brush and no single analyst gets their rear kicked. The herd mentality protects itself!

As an investor, you can't do anything about the herd mentality except to be aware of its existence. As soon as you know which way the herd is moving, you can make better investment decisions.

Know that, in the same way institutional investors all end up with the same estimates for bank results, they also move the same way in buying and selling companies. As a result, some companies at certain times seem to be beyond criticism, such as BHP in the 1980s, Lend Lease in the 1990s or Woolworths in the noughties, when analysts all agreed those companies were terrific. On the other hand, when an area of the market is out of fashion — such as listed property after the credit crunch hit home in 2008 — the herd makes sure it stays that way.

Deciphering Financial Gibberish

Perhaps the worst thing for you in getting to know the markets is the jargon that is peppered throughout financial services. Learning new terminology never ends. We've worked as financial journalists in many different markets around the globe and nearly every week we come across another new term.

Apart from mangling the English language, this torrent of terms for financial instruments ensures that financial advisers can always earn a living, if only to translate investment information.

Here is a typical snippet of jargon-filled financial news (with real names changed):

> *James Smith's Unified Press Group has again supported Brisbane-based Perpetual Health Care as a lead investor in its $82 million rights issue. Perpetual said yesterday big investors led by the major banks supported the one-for-two issue to fund further expansion of its Australia-wide healthcare business.*

What does this text mean in plain English? The problem for all investors is that certain information is worded in the language used by the industry, even if the result means the information isn't easy to understand.

Imagine if this same financial news item was written in the following less formal language:

> *The Unified Press Group — that's the company owned by James Smith that owns a lot of the newspapers and magazines in Australia — is investing more money in the Perpetual Health Care group. It's a bit of a mystery why a paper group is putting money into a healthcare company. But Unified Press is not alone in its decision; other investors, according to Perpetual, include the big banks.*
>
> *Perpetual is raising the $82 million through a scheme that creates more shares and offers the shares to existing shareholders under a special arrangement. In this case the arrangement is that for every two shares already held by existing shareholders, Perpetual will allow them to buy one more by sending a cheque straight to the company, and there won't be any stockbroking fees under this arrangement.*

You can see the problem; the plain English version is too long-winded! If everyone in the markets has to explain everything, all the time, quick availability of information may grind to a halt. The main reason that investment markets have a language of their own is efficiency. Unfortunately, some people who work inside the investment markets use financial jargon to confuse investors or to reduce their negotiating power.

In our experience, invariably junior staff and less capable salespeople overdo the jargon inside investment markets. When you deal with very good people at the top levels in business, they usually try to minimise their use of jargon.

Do your best to learn the language of the markets. You'll experience many situations when technical language can't be avoided. But, equally, anyone in the markets who makes information sound more complicated than necessary isn't serving you well.

Learning to understand market jargon is a bit like understanding cricket. James has a French friend who came to understand cricket out of circumstance. In 1997, she was working a late shift throughout the Ashes series and got home from this job each night around 11 pm. With nothing good on TV at this time, out of desperation she began watching the cricket, which was broadcast live from England every night. Slowly she became more interested in the game, and she began to understand how certain terms used by the cricket commentators perfectly describe actions she was already familiar with from her late-night viewing.

You can come to understand investment markets the same way as James' friend (and the markets are so much more exciting than cricket!). Use the glossary at the back of this book or even buy yourself an investment dictionary (or find one online such as Investopedia, www.investopedia. com), read all you can, watch the business news in your nightly news bulletin, attend investment seminars and surf the web.

The Shape of the Australian Stock Market

Like any stock market, the Australian stock market has two key functions:

- ✔ **To allow companies to raise money:** This market is called the *primary market*.
- ✔ **To allow shares in companies to be traded by the general public:** This market is called the *secondary market*.

For most investors the bulk of the action takes place in the secondary market, which is where shares go up or down in price. To help, we take a look at a few basic elements of the ASX design.

Who's who in the Australian market?

First of all, a little more than 2,200 companies are listed on the ASX. The main thing to remember is that most of those companies are very small. So, in pure money terms, the market is dominated by a relatively small group of very big companies.

Almost 40 per cent of the total value of all companies listed on the ASX is taken up by just ten companies.

The companies on the ASX break into two main groups:

- **Industrials:** The dominant group of companies is called the *S&P/ASX Industrials* and includes all the household names of Australian business, such as Telstra, Woolworths, Foster's and Qantas.
- **Resources:** The other important group of companies in the local market is the *mining and oil sector*. Resources still play an extremely valuable role in Australian markets. Mining and oil companies represent around one-third of all companies listed on the ASX. The major mining and oil companies include BHP Billiton, Rio Tinto and Woodside Petroleum.

As soon as you digest these two dominant groups that characterise the Australian sharemarket, you can stand back and look at the market from another angle.

What are the categories of stock?

Standard & Poor's (S&P) classifies all the companies on the ASX in accordance with the Global Industry Classification Standard (GICS), which consists of 10 economic sectors, aggregated from 23 industry groups, 59 industries and 123 sub-industries, currently covering over 14,000 companies globally.

In order to tailor the GICS system to the Australian market, S&P splits the financials sector into two groups: Property Trusts and Financials Excluding Property Trusts. In 2006, Gold, and Metals and Mining were added in recognition of the importance of these sectors to the local market. Table 6-1 shows the resulting global sector indices for Australia.

Table 6-1	ASX Categories as of 2008
Economic Sector	*Example Company*
Consumer Discretionary	Seven Network
Consumer Staples	Woolworths
Energy	Santos
Financials — Property Trusts — Financials Excluding Property Trusts	Westfield Group National Australia Bank
Gold	Lihir
Health Care	CSL
Industrials	Wesfarmers
Information Technology	Computershare
Materials	BHP Billiton
Metals and Mining	BHP Billiton
Telecommunication Services	Telstra
Utilities	AGL Energy

The markets are almost as complex as life itself, and not everything falls into neat categories. In the end, a good company is a good company; categories are just a neat way of helping some investors to focus on certain industries.

Taking Stock of Stock Size

The size of a company is absolutely no guide to the performance you can expect from it. For example, at its peak, Coles grew to include supermarkets, discount stores, department stores, liquor outlets, toy stores, office supplies and discount fuel. But Coles' sheer size was also its downfall.

The Coles name has been synonymous with discount retailing since the early 20th century. The retailer's problems began when it merged with the Myer department store chain in the mid-1980s. In 2006, Coles sold Myer to a private-equity group in order to focus on supermarkets and discount stores, but Coles failed to turn its fortunes around quickly enough. In November 2007, Coles was purchased by Wesfarmers and its name was removed from the ASX list. Alternatively, many small companies can represent very good investments as they grow rapidly from start-up phase to maturity.

Still, the size of a company matters in investment markets. Size affects a company's ability to make money and to attract investors.

Market capitalisation (the total value of a company's shares at current prices, as quoted on the exchange) is the main way of telling the overall worth placed on a company by the investing public. As soon as you know the market capitalisation of a stock, you have some idea of where the stock stands in the pecking order of investment markets.

A simple example is JB Hi-Fi, the electronic retailing company that has about 107 million shares issued to investors. You can work out the market capitalisation of JB Hi-Fi by multiplying the share price by 107 million. This formula of multiplying the share price by the number of shares on issue can be used to get the market capitalisation of any stock.

In September 2008, JB Hi-Fi had a share price of about $12.60. So the company's market capitalisation was $12.60 × 107 million, or roughly $1,348 million.

What does this indicate about JB Hi-Fi? Well, very little unless you look at another company such as Harvey Norman, which sells many of the same products. When you check out the market capitalisation of Harvey Norman, you find it has no less than 1,026 million shares on issue, and those shares were worth about $3.50 in September 2008. So, to get the Harvey Norman market capitalisation, you take $3.50 × 1,026 million, which gives $3,591 million. At a glance, you now see that Harvey Norman is a much bigger company than JB Hi-Fi, despite the fact that JB Hi-Fi has a much higher share price. In fact, Harvey Norman is almost three times the size of its rival.

Although being bigger doesn't mean Harvey Norman is any better value than JB Hi-Fi, its size does, however, indicate the two companies are in different leagues.

Pint-sized small caps

Small caps are stocks that have a relatively small market capitalisation. In Australia a small-cap stock is one where the market capitalisation is less than $100 million.

The vast majority of the 2,200 stocks on the ASX fall into this category. Moreover, this trading category is one of the liveliest on the market. A relatively minor piece of news can put a rocket under a small-cap share price. Say a gold-mining company's shares are worth five cents, and news that its exploration team has found gold hits the market. The stock can easily move to ten cents, creating a 100 per cent profit for investors.

The problem for investors is that, for every small cap that makes a big leap in value, another handful may be treading water. Small caps are where speculators feel most at home, because institutional analysts tend not to spend much time analysing small companies. If you think you have a future as a speculator, start working in the small-cap category.

Some of the big investment companies have unwritten rules about small-cap companies. For example, very often, institutional investors don't buy stocks with a share price of, say, less than $1, because it simply isn't worth the trouble in terms of paperwork and bureaucracy.

Medium-sized mid caps

Mid caps are companies that have a market capitalisation of more than $100 million but are not regarded as major companies or blue-chip stocks.

Some of the best companies in Australia fall into this category. Mid caps are often companies that become the next-generation blue-chip companies. Their significant size means mid-cap stocks are unlikely to double overnight in price like small-cap stocks. On the other hand, mid caps can offer much better returns than blue-chip companies because they're still growing in stature.

The weakness of mid-cap companies is that they rarely offer the speculative excitement of small-cap companies, or the security of blue-chip companies that invariably belong to a dominant group in any one market.

If you want the balance of steady growth and good returns offered by mid caps, and can do without the excitement of small caps or the prestige of blue chips, then try investing in this area of the market.

Top-notch stuff — leading stocks and blue chips

Blue-chip stocks don't have a set definition. According to Reuters's financial glossary, *blue chips* are

> *Stocks of major companies with sound earnings and dividend records and above-average share performance.*

Another more light-hearted definition common in the markets is

> *Any stock that has a five-year track record of profitability, where the company would be unaffected if the chief executive was run over by a bus.*

This latter definition moves to cut out companies heavily associated with one outstanding executive.

James' own definition of blue chips is

> *A big company that has not made a loss in the last five years and is not expected to do so in the near future.*

Between these three definitions you can get quite close to the aura surrounding a blue chip.

If you consider these definitions, you can see why, in the retailing sector, Woolworths is seen as a blue chip. Billabong, a company with a good track record and a charismatic founder, Gordon Merchant, doesn't make the grade. Although Billabong is a worthy competitor to Woolworths, institutional investors often don't feel comfortable investing in a relatively small company heavily identified with one individual.

Unwritten rules about blue chips abound in the market, and the more you get to know the market, the more you start to develop your own definition of blue-chip stocks. Blue chips are for the conservative investor — you won't make a killing on blue chips but you should almost always make a strong return over the longer term.

Technically, blue-chip stocks have a market capitalisation of at least $500 million and are characterised by an enduring ability to make profits and pay dividends.

Indicators and Indices

If you listen to radio news bulletins, you may hear a newsreader tell you something like the following: 'On the stock market the All Ordinaries Index was trading sharply higher at 4,800. Trading was also lively on Wall Street, where the Dow Jones Index was up 2 per cent. However, Tokyo's Nikkei Index continued to struggle, dropping 3 per cent.'

What on earth does this international summary mean? And why does knowing about overseas trading matter to investors in Australia?

Stock market *indices* are the nearest thing you can get to a snapshot of any stock market at a given time. The movement in an index indicates the general price trend across the entire market.

In Australia, the All Ordinaries Index (or the All Ords, as it's fondly known) is made up of a basket of 500 leading stocks that represent 99 per cent of the value of all the stocks — or the total market capitalisation — of the Australian sharemarket.

The ASX started its All Ordinaries Index at a level of 500 on 1 January 1980. After a rocky start, the index was cruising, managing to climb as high as 2,400 until 1987, when it sank dramatically to 1,400 and took almost six years to get back to the 1987 level. In 2007, the index reached another peak of 6,800 and, at the time of writing in late 2008, it is difficult to tell when the index will recover the ground it has lost since then.

You must be following a market very closely before any minor movement in an index makes any sense to you. But, if you make the effort to get to know the level of an index, then you can gain important information from those radio news bulletins. Just like following a soap opera, watching the All Ords regularly means you can easily get hooked!

The other major indices around the world are the Dow Jones Index in the United States, the FT (Financial Times) Index in the United Kingdom — known affectionately as the Footsie — and the Nikkei Index in Tokyo. As a general rule, sharemarket indices are best used as a way of tracking the overall health of a market.

TECHNICAL STUFF

The market that's on the market

The Australian Securities Exchange (ASX) was the first stock market in the world to be listed on the stock market, on 14 October 1998. And, needless to say, the market the ASX decided to join was none other than the ASX!

This curious state of affairs was a big experiment for all concerned. Stock exchanges are normally run like partnerships or clubs — under this arrangement, profit is not the outstanding motivation of the exchange, rather a successful trading environment is provided.

The idea to float the stock exchange itself came at a time when just about everything in sight was being put on the stock market, from AMP to Qantas.

Today the ASX has a market capitalisation of more than $1,345 billion. The ASX float has been copied by the exchanges of Hong Kong, Singapore and London.

The experiment has been a resounding success for Australian investors. As a company, the ASX is doing fine, thank you very much, with revenues of around $615 million annually, but we have concerns as to whether the ASX is as well run as it used to be. During the sub-prime crisis of 2008, the ASX-sanctioned practice of *short-selling* — that is, betting on a share price falling — made a volatile situation even more unstable.

Invest in the ASX? Investing in the ASX is something like investing in a utility like a toll road. A certain level of traffic, or turnover, is assured. The difference with the ASX is that this traffic can be very volatile because activity on the market roars ahead in a strong economy and weakens considerably in a slow economy.

Chapter 7

The World of Stocks and Shares

*W*riting about financial markets for many years has helped us realise that the stock market really is the centre of the action from an investment perspective. Knowing that the hub of the investment markets is the stock market doesn't mean you must ever limit yourself to stocks, but it does mean that understanding stocks is really important.

The wonderful thing about stocks is that they offer you a perfect picture of a company's fortunes at any given moment. You ask your friendly local property agent: 'How strong is the local market for industrial warehouses?' 'Oh, it's going terrific,' he says. 'We're having very strong interest at the moment. Lots of enquiries. Why, just this morning I had a call ...' and so on. You know what to expect from property people.

Understanding what's happening with managed funds is the same as for property. You ask your friendly local fund manager: 'Is this a good time to buy managed funds?' 'Oh, it's a perfect time,' she says. 'Our funds have made very good returns on average over the last five years. Actually, if you invest at the moment, you can take advantage of a new fund that specialises in ...' and so on. You can also guess what to expect from fund managers.

But the stock market is different. If you consider an individual stock, you ask your friendly local broker: 'Is this a good time to buy Telstra?' Funnily enough, he almost certainly says something like: 'Oh, yes, it's an ideal time. We see some very good value at the moment ...' and so on. The difference this time, however, is that you can check the facts quite thoroughly and make an informed decision.

With the property developer, you can't know with accuracy how many units have really sold in your area, the exact price of those units, and the volume and specifications of those transactions. Likewise, with managed funds, because so many layers of 'management' lie between your investment and your return, knowing accurately how your return comes to be calculated is mystifying.

But, with stocks, you can get down with a calculator and figure out a hell of a lot yourself. You can find out how much Telstra is worth on the open market at the exact time of your phone call and how many Telstra shares were bought and sold in the last 24 hours. You can figure out how Telstra's share price relates to its full-year earnings, and how that price looks against the company's expected earnings next year. You can get an amazing amount of information.

But first you have to get a grip on just what constitutes a stock. In this chapter we describe what stocks are, the types of stocks that are available, how public companies list on the stock exchange and how to go about getting stock when new companies enter — or *float* — on the stock market.

What's in the Stockpot?

Think of any company as a bag of sugar (okay, we know this may sound corny, but stick with us). The bag contains millions of granules of sugar. The founders and staff of the company own some of the sugar, institutional investors hold a large amount and individual investors like you hold the rest. (You and your mates are called *retail investors*.)

Maybe you have 10,000 shares. With that holding, you own a piece of the action. But keep thinking of the bag of sugar — in perspective, you have 10,000 granules from a bag of millions.

When we talk about stocks, we mean *ordinary shares*, or common stock. Nothing fancy, just basic granules of ownership in our sharemarket-listed companies. Don't get confused between stocks and shares. In Australia, the two terms mean the same thing — ordinary shares.

When a company is established, it has very few assets to begin with, but the value of the company can always be planned around shares.

You may want to establish a new company tomorrow called Awesome Awnings; maybe you have 1,000 awnings in a small factory. You decide that Awesome Awnings has a notional value of $100,000. To make life easier for all your future investors, you create a company with 100,000 shares. Each share has a value of $1. Your absurdly supportive two best friends each decide to take 25 per cent of the company for which they have to pay $25,000 each. In turn they both hold 25,000 shares in the company.

Every company from Amcor to Qantas had a beginning that was similar to Awesome Awnings. The main point we're making here is that a stock is a tradable slice of ownership in any company. As companies get bigger and create different types of shares and different types of shareholders, things get more complicated, but boil it all down and you come back to this basic structure.

Your Typical Public Company

The public, or *listed*, company is the centre of the universe as far as most investors are concerned. Nothing matters more than public companies because these are the companies where you, the investor, can get a slice of the action.

More importantly, the majority of Australian investors want to see these companies listed on the Australian Securities Exchange (ASX). When BHP took over London-based Billiton in 2001, investors were concerned that BHP might no longer be an Australian-listed company. (In the end, BHP Billiton settled for a dual listing, where the company is listed in Australia and London at the same time.) If a company is publicly listed, the possibilities for investors are endless:

- ✔ You can watch the company grow.
- ✔ You can buy and sell your 'slice' of the company as you see fit.
- ✔ If this company hits the jackpot with a wonder product, you can be in on the action.
- ✔ You, the investor, can put news and information about the company to good use in your investment decisions.

Why can't you read much about Cadbury Schweppes or Microsoft or Ford in the financial pages of your daily newspapers? These companies employ thousands of people in Australia; many people use their products every day. But they're not listed on the Australian stock market, so Australian investors can't get a slice of the action, unless they purchase shares on the US market in US dollars.

Just your ordinary shares

The majority of shares (or stock) in most public companies are called ordinary shares or, to be precise, ordinary fully paid shares. When you hold ordinary shares — or common stock — you have a claim to the ownership of the company and a portion of the profits made by that company.

The main features of ordinary shares that relate to you, the investor, are:

- ✔ **The right to receive dividends:** Dividends are payments of part of the company profits to shareholders.

- ✔ **The right to trade your ownership in the shares and to retain your level of ownership if the company issues more shares:** If you have 1 per cent of the company, you have the right to acquire enough shares to keep your holding at 1 per cent of the expanded company if more shares are issued. This right can be exercised through a *rights issue* (see Chapter 8). The retail investor often doesn't have the individual clout to control the decision by a company to engage in a rights issue, if it seeks to employ new capital.

- ✔ **An entitlement to voting rights within the company:** An ordinary share entitles you to a vote on the key issues facing the company, such as takeovers or the appointment of senior officers, and on other important matters that affect the company.

- ✔ **The right to security from limited liability:** If a company goes belly up and you hold shares in it, the worst thing that can happen is that you lose the entire amount that you invested in its shares. You can't be held responsible for bad management, for example.

- ✔ **The right to a claim on assets:** If the company collapses and has money left over, as a common shareholder you have a limited right to get a return of funds from the liquidator.

  Being realistic, your claim on the assets of a failed listed company is very tenuous indeed. Ordinary shareholders are at the back of the queue if a company is liquidated and its assets sold off.

Fancier types of stocks and shares

Apart from ordinary shares, many other types of stocks and financial instruments are based on stock price activity. As an early-stage investor, you're unlikely to use these types of investments, except perhaps as a way to take an occasional gamble when you believe an exceptional opportunity exists.

Shares or even some of the more exotic spin-offs (or derivatives) like convertible notes, options, warrants, contracts for difference (CFDs) and futures all come under the general classification of *securities*.

We describe these other securities here but, in general, we caution early investors against investing in any type of security other than ordinary shares.

Convertible notes

Professional investors use convertible notes as a way to invest in stocks at a future date. *Convertible notes* are investments that pay a set amount of interest for a set period before investors can convert them into ordinary shares. A convertible preference share is similar except that this type of security is already a 'share' and so the income is actually a dividend.

Options

There are two types of options. *Call options* give you the right — but not the obligation — to buy shares at a certain price on or before a set date in the future. *Put options* give you the right to sell shares at a certain price on or before the options' expiry date. Call options are much more common among individual, or retail, investors.

Look at Awesome Awnings — currently valued at $1 each (and looking very good value at that price, we must say!). A call option at $1.20 with a six-month expiry date allows you to buy a set amount of Awesome Awnings shares at $1.20 any time in the next six months, even if the price goes to $1.80 in that time.

The problem with investing in derivatives such as options is that, although you can make more money faster, you can also lose all — or even more than all — the money you invested.

Warrants

A warrant works something like an option, with *call warrants* (the right to buy) and *put warrants* (the right to sell) both available. Warrants are generally used by professional traders, who tend to use them for trading over a much shorter period than options.

Instalment warrants are more commonly used by long-term investors. *Instalment warrants* allow you to make a downpayment, or an instalment, on an ordinary share and pay the balance at a specified date in the future. One of the benefits of instalment warrants is that the investor has full entitlement to any dividends paid during the life of the instalment for a fraction of the ordinary share price.

Contracts for difference

Contracts for difference (CFDs) are relatively new to Australia and allow investors to punt on the difference between the price of shares today and their price in the future. CFD holders don't own the underlying asset but they do receive all dividend payments.

A CFD is a contract between you and a licensed provider, although these days many CFDs are listed and traded on the ASX. CFDs can be bought on local and international stocks, indices or foreign exchanges for an up-front payment, which is typically 5–10 per cent of the value of shares or 1 per cent for indices. Hence, CFDs hold out the potential to maximise profits, but they can just as easily maximise losses. For example, if you pay $1,000 for $10,000 worth of shares and the share price falls 10 per cent, you will lose your entire outlay. If losses exceed your initial outlay you must top up your investment.

Unlike warrants and options, CFDs have no set expiry date, although in practice most people hold them for weeks rather than months. In other words, they're best left to dedicated traders. And, be warned, you can lose more than you invest in a CFD.

Futures

Like options, an investment in a *futures contract* allows you to buy or sell a certain amount of securities at an agreed price by an agreed date. However, profits and losses can be greatly magnified with futures. Unlike options, you can lose more than you invest in the futures stock through ongoing obligations to the contracts you sign. With an option, the worst thing that can happen is that the option is worthless and you've lost the price of buying it; with a future, you can face extra costs and lose all your money.

Futures may be based on a sharemarket index, currencies or commodities like wool or wheat.

We recommend that you ignore the advertisements about investing in futures or contracts for difference. Don't invest in either as an early-stage investor because you stand to lose more than you put in — for most investors, the risks outweigh the rewards.

The Listed and the Listless

For a few wild and wacky months in 1999 and early 2000, at the height of the dot-com boom, the rules that normally govern a listing on the stock market went out the window. Amazing developments happened; companies with no sales or profits listed on the stock exchange. (In fact, listings of this type are still happening with biotechnology stocks, but this category is a different ball game. Biotechnology companies need to perform research activities for years before they can become profit-making operations. Investors in biotechnology companies must have long-term faith in the ability of the researchers to ultimately hit the jackpot with a wonder drug or unique treatment.)

In an environment such as the dot-com boom, however, entrepreneurs made wild assumptions about their ability to make profits and people simply believed them. Everybody became so enthusiastic about the internet (and so enthusiastic about making easy money) that nobody asked any hard questions.

To get a whiff of just how wild those times were, think about this piece of historic data. In May 2000, the US stock markets were heading into what was to become an extended downturn. Over the next three years, a key US index — the Standard & Poor's 500 — fell 47 per cent, its biggest fall since the Wall Street Crash, when the market lost 80 per cent of its value between 1929 and 1932. The US market recovered between 2003 and 2007, until the global financial crisis ended the party. By the end of 2008, the S&P 500 Index was 51 points below its historic peak at the height of the dot-com boom in 2000.

One positive legacy of the dot-com boom is that entrepreneurs wanting to list companies on the stock market now need a track record. Likewise, investors are more likely to ask searching questions about future revenues and future profits. Even so, history has a nasty habit of repeating itself. Human nature being what it is, even professional investors sometimes let their enthusiasm get the better of them. In 2008, Aussie market darling ABC Learning Centres went into receivership when it became apparent that the company's rapid growth and high levels of borrowing were unsustainable.

In this section, we go into some of the ways a company can list on the stock exchange.

Floating on the stock market

The most common way a company gets to be listed on the stock market is through a *float*, also known as a *listing*.

When a company is floating (or listing) it may also choose to raise money from its new investors. This first-time tapping of stock market investors for new capital is called an *IPO (initial public offering)*. Contrary to popular belief, gaining access to shares in an IPO is not a licence to print money. Table 7-1 shows the early performance of a selection of newly listed companies. Note that many IPOs are worth less at the end of their first day of trading than investors paid for them.

Table 7-1		Float Performance			
Company Name	*ASX Code*	*Quotation Date*	*Issue Price*	*Opening Price*	*Closing Price*
Alamar Resources	ALG	29/7/08	0.20	0.22	0.22
Buru Energy	BRU	1/9/08	0.525	0.26	0.30
Emergent Resources	EMG	4/8/08	0.20	0.225	0.20
Ivanhoe Australia	IVA	6/8/08	2.00	1.60	1.57
Manas Resources	MSR	22/7/08	0.20	0.21	0.20
Mt Isa Metals	MET	22/8/08	0.20	0.20	0.195
Outback Metals	OUM	2/9/08	0.20	0.27	0.185
Riviera Resources	RVE	10/9/08	0.20	0.15	0.20

Source: Compiled from ASX and company data.

A company floats on the stock market by issuing a set number of its shares to private investors for the first time.

Traditionally, before a company can receive the support needed to float on the stock market it has to have

- A five-year track record of increasing revenues and profits.
- A strong management team.
- A dominant position in its field of activity.
- Support from institutional investors like stockbrokers and fund managers.

Now, however, many variations to this rule exist. For instance, in biotechnology, a company may not have profits or even sales, but it may have put five years' work into research and development of a certain drug. This drug may have a real value in the marketplace, and the company can then float on the stock market on the strength of its past research and development, or IP (intellectual property). Similarly, mining-exploration companies may have a series of promising exploration reports.

Privatising

The privatisation boom in Australia is almost over; the majority of the best assets in the country are now on the stock market. Privatisation occurs when a government issues stock in a state company and then sells that stock on the stock market by floating the company. The trend took off in the 1980s when the then Conservative leader of the United Kingdom,

Margaret Thatcher, sold off a string of assets like British Telecom and British Gas. Australia soon followed. Among the most successful privatisations were the Commonwealth Bank and Qantas.

Demutualising

Nothing like an awkward word! *Demutualisation* is the term used for estimating the value of assets in an existing 'mutual society' and then floating those assets on the stock market. A *mutual society* is owned by its members, for the good of its members. Over many generations, the policyholders of the AMP mutual society were the official owners of all AMP assets. In the mid-1990s, spurred on by the privatisation boom, the management of insurance companies decided that their generation was going to be the one to cash in the accumulated assets of many generations.

Few policyholders complained when they got thousands of dollars worth of shares from AMP when it privatised in 1998. For many people, this result is the nearest thing to money for old rope yet seen on the stock market. Other successful demutualisations include Colonial Ltd, which was later taken over by the Commonwealth Bank, and NRMA, now called IAG.

Converting

Conversions occur at financial organisations that are neither state-owned companies nor mutual societies (like AMP used to be; refer to 'Demutualising'). Nonetheless, the management of these organisations want to get the value of the assets sold onto the stock market through a float. Among the best-known conversions are many of the former building societies (though most were eventually taken over in turn by banks). This group includes St.George Bank, Suncorp-Metway, Bendigo Bank and the Australian Securities Exchange.

Sneaking through the 'back door'

This type of listing sounds a bit suspicious, don't you think? A *back-door listing* occurs when a group of entrepreneurs take control of an existing listed company and change it into another company. In effect, the entrepreneurs get a stock market listing for an enterprise that never went through the process of floating on the stock market.

During the dot-com boom, dozens of long-forgotten mining companies that had retained a stock market listing were taken over in this manner and reinvented as technology companies.

Understanding why companies float

Companies float for many reasons. At the top of the food chain, the best companies list to expand their ability to become great companies. At the bottom, companies can sometimes list because nobody else wants them! The markets can be just as easily the last refuge for scoundrels seeking cheap money from innocent investors.

Here's why most companies float:

✔ **Creating a market for the company stock:** After a number of years of making good sales and profits, many companies want to get a bigger spread of investors inside the company. A stock market listing is the optimal way to broaden a company's investor base.

✔ **Raising money cheaply:** By issuing publicly traded shares, a company can raise money for a lot less than going to the banks or issuing securities to professional investors.

✔ **Cashing out:** Company executives can finally get a chance to cash in some of the value built up in a company through a float.

✔ **Enabling takeovers:** A company traded on the stock market can easily use its shares to take over other listed companies.

✔ **Rewarding staff:** Being able to issue staff with shares and options in a company is a great way to reward and encourage staff loyalty.

✔ **Attaining prestige:** A high status is attached to a business that can achieve a listing on the stock market. This type of business is often seen as more professionally managed than a private company because it must be open to public inspection.

If a company has a good enough financial track record, listing on the stock market in the traditional manner usually presents no obstacles. With any back-door listing, however, you have to ask: 'Can this company make it onto the stock market any other way?'

Snooping into Company Secrets

A private company need do almost nothing in terms of providing public information; providing a simple return of estimated annual turnover can do. Interestingly, that return can be sent in late. On the other hand, a public company has to tell everyone — investors and potential investors — a very wide range of information, from trading results to the salaries of top executives.

That's because regulators believe investors in public companies should be protected. On the other hand, the authorities take the view that private-company investors can largely look after themselves.

Your investment in a public company gives you the right to thoroughly check the performance of your company. (And, yes, the company is every bit as much yours as it is for the board of directors who pull in huge fees for attending a few meetings a year.)

While public companies are required to tell investors a lot more than private companies are, endless ways still exist for a public company to pull the wool over investors' eyes. Indeed, you can learn only so much by reading company accounts. A company's stock price is ultimately the best window into any company, because this indicator tells how the entire market rates the company.

The one result that you can demand from a public company is, in a word, performance. We're not saying you can always get top performance, but the chances of a chief executive's useless cousin holding a senior management position are likely to be a lot less than if the company is privately owned.

Over the years, public companies have become very good at appearing to reveal information to investors while actually omitting or concealing the items in the accounts that can make the difference between profit and loss. Nevertheless, you can check some key indicators released by public companies that can guide you towards understanding the performance of any public company.

The key indicators that can give you a guide to a public company's performance include:

- ✔ **The annual report:** Inside the annual report is some of the most important information on any company. The problem is where to find this relevant information. At the very least, an annual report can give you a recent snapshot of how a company is trading in terms of revenues, profits and other key items. Read an annual report from the back. By the time you get to the cheerleading 'spin' from the chief executive at the front, you already know a lot of the real nitty-gritty that matters to any company.

- ✔ **Regular financial statements:** Half-yearly statements and (from bigger companies) quarterly statements offer a detailed guide to the ongoing performance of a company. A number of start-up companies also offer quarterly reports on *cash flow* (a measure that indicates if a company has enough cash to survive).

- ✔ **ASX statements:** Public companies must inform the ASX of all major developments that can affect the share price, such as takeover activity or a change of management. These statements, while once the reserve of brokers and other finance professionals, are now accessible to anyone via the internet. You can see some of the statements for free at www.asx.com.au.

Just because a company is categorised as public doesn't necessarily mean you can poke around company headquarters! However, these companies do make themselves available to the investing public regularly. In the United States, for example, the whole business of visiting public companies is becoming a fine art. Many major companies now have executive reception centres where special staff are employed doing nothing else but informing investors about their activities.

For most investors, however, the best way to get to know a public company is to attend investor presentations. The biggest investor presentation of the year for any company is the annual general meeting (AGM). The 'season' for AGMs is in the July–August period if accounts for the year end on 30 June, or else around January–February if accounts for the year end on 31 December.

The truth about AGMs is that most people who attend them are retired — who else can afford to go to such an event in the middle of a working day? The same bunch of elderly investors tend to ask the same questions every year, and the voting is nearly always a foregone conclusion, because company managers know which way institutional investors are going to vote before they start proceedings. Some institutional investors are beginning to take a stand at AGMs, however, to vote down excessive remuneration packages for executives.

Regardless of the probability of a known outcome, we recommend that you attend at least one AGM — you get an invitation if you're a shareholder — because seeing leading business figures in action is always a worthwhile experience.

If you take the trouble to go to an AGM, make the effort worth your while. Ask questions at the meeting. Alternatively, hang around at the end of the meeting for tea and biscuits and ask company directors that killer question maybe only you want answered: Is the company secure from hacker attacks? Will the company be opening a new factory in your hometown? Has the chairman dyed his hair?

Getting Shares in a Float

A company normally decides to split publicly issued shares between institutional and private investors because doing so creates a lively market for the company.

The good, the bad and the ugly

Your chance of getting shares in a float depends largely on the size of the float and your own relationship with stockbrokers. Your chance of getting stock in a float that makes you money is probably about two to one. Even if you do manage to get your hands on some shares in a new float, you aren't guaranteed to make a killing when the shares list on the ASX (refer to Table 7-1). Sometimes shares make their market debut at a discount to the issue price.

You can easily get shares in a float destined to lose you money.

Shares are hard to get when a float is

- ✔ **A major opportunity for all investors.** The float of CSL in 1994 by the Australian government allowed investors to grab a slice of one of the world's best blood-products companies. The government wanted the float to be a success, and so the float price of CSL was also very reasonable. Everyone wanted stock. Today CSL has a bigger market capitalisation than Qantas.

- ✔ **A clear opportunity for an informed circle of investors.** The float of the domain name registration company Melbourne IT Limited was virtually restricted to former academics of Melbourne University and some well-connected clients of stockbrokers JBWere and CommSec. At the time, in 1999, the float of such a well-connected company in the internet industry was seen as a licence to print money. Investors bought shares in the IPO at the issue price of $2.20 and some of them made a killing selling on the first day of trading on the ASX, when the shares hit a high of $8.80. Again, everyone wanted stock. Nine years later, the company is ranked around fifth in the world as a domain name registrar.

Shares are easy to get when a float is

- ✔ **Too big for the local market.** The planned $2 billion float of telecommunications company Vodafone Pacific was cancelled in 2000 because the float was seen as 'too big' for the Australian market. Not only were Vodafone shares viewed as being easy to get if the company went ahead with its IPO, but reports indicated that Vodafone guessed the company wasn't in a position to 'get the float away', which means it wasn't going to raise all the money it wanted.

- ✔ **Apparently being used primarily to raise money rather than to create a tradable market for its stock.** Using the stock market in this way is very common among mining and technology companies, a category of companies that regularly needs to raise finance. Banks or other professional investors in the market are probably indicating a lack of interest in these shares.

Ways to wrangle stock in a float

Twenty years ago, getting shares in a stock market float was a bit like getting into a posh golf club. Knowing the right people always helped. Thankfully, all that snobbery is past — after all, you're the one taking a risk with your hard-earned money when you invest in a float.

Here are the main ways to get shares in an IPO:

- ✔ **Applying as a member of the public:** Most big floats advertise in the financial media. You simply order a prospectus through the mail, or download one on the internet, fill out an application form and send off your money. In the majority of cases, you either succeed in getting all — or a portion — of the shares you apply for.

- ✔ **Applying through your stockbroker:** You can get on the client list for smaller floats by having an account with a stockbroker. Committing to being on a client list isn't as tricky as it sounds; sometimes even a single transaction with a stockbroker can get you on a client list.

- ✔ **Applying through a financial institution:** Sometimes share offers can come through from simply having a cash-management account with a financial institution.

- ✔ **Applying through an investment website or online stockbroker:** Online brokers such as Commonwealth Securities (www.commsec.com.au) regularly offer floats to members.

Chapter 8

Inside Info on the Stock Market

- -

- -

*I*nside the Australian stock market are layers of power that can take many years to understand. At the top is a small circle of powerful players — *market insiders* — who can literally make or break a stock. They can buy or sell stock worth hundreds of millions of dollars with a few quick phone calls. Within this circle are companies like Deutsche Bank, J.P. Morgan, Goldman Sachs JBWere and Citigroup.

What exactly do market insiders look like? Do they wear certain clothes, speak a certain way, give funny handshakes? Well, actually, yes, they do. They still wear tailor-made blue suits, they're predominantly male and they have handshakes that can lift you off the floor.

Beware of anyone who claims to be a market insider. If they're 'inside', then why do they need to talk to someone from 'outside'?

Individual investors who can set the market alight with daring moves (like James Packer or Westfield supremo Frank Lowy) are the genuine market insiders. Only a very small circle of friends and contacts know what exact investment strategies they follow. If too many people find out the investment plans of these master investors, their strategies may not work out. Horseracing is similar — if everybody knows a horse is set to win a race, the odds go down.

But you don't ever have to be this deeply inside the market to invest successfully. You, too, can get inside the market and make it work for you by understanding what makes the market tick. We show you how in this chapter, from following stock ratings to analysing company reports and watching movements in the market itself.

Who Does What in the Market?

Inside the stock market, almost everyone has a role in either buying or selling stocks. At the front line are traders who do the actual buying and selling for various financial institutions. Surrounding the traders are literally dozens of finance professionals who make up the investment markets. Among the most powerful people in the market are investment bankers, corporate finance brokers, and mergers and acquisitions specialists. These executives hatch strategies and plans that involve a huge amount of trading in the market.

With the growth of the superannuation industry and the parallel growth of the managed-funds industry, the executives who manage these funds are the other major power group in any market. These groups of investors are called *institutional investors*.

Sitting somewhere behind all these people employed in the business of shifting money around are the executives who actually run businesses! The folk who run factories, build apartment blocks, grow wheat. The market can be just as much a mystery to these market participants as it is to the private investor.

Reading the Ratings

You may hear some investment analyst on the radio explain that a certain company's share price has risen for the third day in a row on the 'back of re-rating by the market'. What are the rules for rating a company and what exactly does this concept mean?

A rating is a difficult indicator to come to grips with because it's defined differently by different people. At best, the *market rating* of any stock is a reflection of the market's *feeling* about that stock, expressed by the performance of the stock compared with its peers in the market.

When all the key factors that measure a company's share price are going the right way, a stock has a strong market rating.

Making a stock move from inside

What makes a stock price go up or down? Sometimes the forces that move a stock can be inside the company and linked to the company performance. Other times the forces may be outside the company, and the short-term performance of the company itself is barely relevant.

Here are the key factors inside a company that move a stock price. In each case something controlled by the company — profits, dividends or assets — affects a stock price indicator.

- ✔ **Earnings per share (EPS):** The EPS is the portion of the entire profit to which each single share is entitled. The EPS is calculated by dividing the net profit by the number of shares on issue. The EPS is a very reliable ratio and, when you become familiar with a stock, this indicator offers a real insight into how a stock is really faring.

- ✔ **Price-to-earnings ratio (PE ratio):** The PE ratio represents the number of times that a stock's price is trading relative to its earnings (profits), and is calculated by dividing the share price by the earnings per share. In general, a high PE ratio can indicate a share is expensive; a low PE ratio can indicate a share is cheap — though many exceptions to this general guideline exist. For example, a company may have a low PE ratio because it's a basket case, and a basket case is not cheap at any price.

- ✔ **Dividend yield:** This ratio is relatively easy to understand. The dividend yield represents the percentage return that dividends represent relative to the market price of the stock. Just like your cash in the bank pays a set percentage, the dividend your stock pays can be expressed as a percentage, too, and is calculated by dividing a company's dividend per share by the current market price of the shares. Conservative, mature companies can be relied on to always offer a relatively predictable dividend yield.

- ✔ **Net tangible assets (NTA):** Imagine you were able to sell all the assets in a public company and pay off the bills (liabilities). Doing so gives you the 'real' or net value of the company. If you then divide this figure by all shares on issue, you get the net value per share. The NTA of a share is the net value of a company divided by the number of shares. When the share price is below the NTA, a stock is generally seen to be cheap.

Even with a strong history of excellent results, no company is perfect. Just when the market can't say a bad thing about a company, the company is most likely about to fall from grace. Just take a look at the recent history of Babcock & Brown or ABC Learning Centres.

Making a stock move from outside

Outside of a company's day-to-day operations, other forces, which have more to do with the workings of the stock market than the workings of the company itself, can influence a stock. These outside forces include:

- ✔ **Cyclical trends:** When the market is slow and conservative, the majority of investors want safe stocks that grow steadily and pay dividends. When the market is expanding and riding high, the bulk of investors want high-growth stocks, and dividends are a secondary consideration. Very few companies can satisfy both types of investor sentiment.

- ✔ **Liquidity:** A company can have millions of shares in the market but, if all those shares are held by a small number of people, the company shares are said to be 'tightly held'. This type of share, which doesn't trade very often, tends to jump up and down in price quite dramatically.

- ✔ **Overhang:** If a major investor decides to sell a large amount of stock in a company, the decision can put a dampener on the stock price. The reason for this effect is because, until all the major investor's stock is sold, more stock is likely to be available for sale on the market than there are buyers for it.

- ✔ **Market capitalisation:** The total value of the company on the stock market is called *market capitalisation* and is calculated by multiplying every share by the current share price. The 'market cap' tells you nothing about a company's performance, only indicating how big a presence a company has on the stock market. However, a large market capitalisation can defend a stock against takeovers. For example, only a handful of global mining companies would have the ability to orchestrate a takeover of a market titan such as BHP Billiton.

Going into Analysis

Stock prices can move up, down or sideways but, at the end of the day, the operating performance of the company really drives the stock price. In the short term, other issues may affect how the stock trades, but ultimately the share price reflects the results achieved by a company.

By the time you get to read the financial results of a company, very likely the share price has already responded to the 'quality' of those results. The reason for this is because big broking companies have analysts who literally stand by waiting for major results and then instantly do their maths on the back of any changes to profits and revenues. As soon as the analysts are comfortable with their understanding of the updated picture of the company, they give signals to traders whether they should buy or sell its stock.

On your own, you really can't compete with this sort of system. But you can make your own mind up whether a stock is fundamentally worth selling or buying. As an investor, rather than a trader, you're more concerned with the general health of a company than any short-term issues. (At least, you're supposed to be!)

In this section, we discuss what you can read to guide you towards understanding a company's results and ultimately that company's share price, as well as other influences on share prices.

What annual reports actually report

Public companies issue annual results and half-yearly, or interim, results. In some very big companies, results are issued every three months, or quarterly. Generally, the shorter the time period, the less information a company reveals about its business.

The main items to identify in a company's results are:

- ✔ **Revenues, or turnover:** This figure gives you a picture of how much product the company is able to sell. Profits are drawn from the turnover figure, after all expenses are taken care of. The revenue figure is the second most important in the accounts.

- ✔ **Earnings:** Looking at a company's results reveals so many layers of profit that figuring out which one matters can be pretty hard. However, as a general rule, the profit figure that matters most is *earnings before interest and tax (EBIT)*. After you get through all the hype and clutter surrounding a company, the purest guide to the profit a company is making from its operations is EBIT.

- ✔ **Net profit:** The net profit of a company is the most commonly quoted figure and is a very useful guide to the general health of the company. Net profit tells you the final profit that the company is able to declare. Unlike the EBIT, it can be made bigger or smaller by items like tax or interest owing to the bank, which have little to do with the operational performance of the company.

- ✔ **Earnings per share (EPS):** This figure tells you how much those profits are worth to your shares.

- ✔ **Dividend per share:** Here is the figure that matters most of all to you, the shareholder. How much is the company going to pay you for every share you hold?

No company ever went out of business making a profit.

—*Anonymous*

Table 8-1 shows you the full-year results for the 12 months to June 2008 for Foster's Group. You can fairly easily pick out the key items that matter in the profits for the company. After you read the profits, look to see how these profits are transferred to shareholders through EPS and dividend payout per share.

Table 8-1	Annual Results of Foster's Group, 2008		
12 months to 30 June	*2008 $m*	*2007 $m*	*% change*
Revenues			
Beer	2,446.6	2,372.6	3.1
Wine	2,106.5	2,374.3	(11.2)
Corporate	5.4	13.3	(59.4)
Total revenues	4,558.5	4,760.2	(4.2)
Earnings before interest and tax (EBIT)			
Total EBIT	1,140.9	1,116.8	2.1
Net interest expense	(144.7)	(187.1)	22.7
Tax	(279.3)	(260.7)	(7.1)
Net profit after tax	714.6	688.7	3.8
Average shares outstanding (m)	1,938.3	2,013.5	
Earnings per share (cents)	36.8	35.6	3.4
Dividends per share (cents)	26.25	23.75	9.0

From Table 8-1 you can instantly see how the company is performing. The company has had a difficult year in terms of its ability to sell its products — total revenues are down by 4.2 per cent. This fall in revenue translated into a slight increase in earnings, reflecting slightly better profit margins. The EBIT for the 12 months to June 2008 shows $1,140.9 million, a 2.1 per cent increase on the previous corresponding period.

As is clear from the results, wine sales stalled after overtaking beer in 2007. Wine revenues fell 11.2 per cent to $2,106.5 million in 2008, whereas beer sales improved slightly to $2,446.6 million. Beer revenues made up slightly more than half the total revenues of $4,558.5 million. The net profit (the bottom line) for the drinks group in this period shows $714.6 million, a disappointing 3.8 per cent increase on the previous period.

The EPS in 2008 is 36.8 cents a share, up from 35.6 cents a share the previous year. Despite the difficult trading conditions, the dividend per share for the year is 26.25 cents against 23.75 cents in 2007.

Digesting stodgy company statements

Every public company must make a statement to the stock exchange on any development that may materially affect the share price.

If you visit the official website of the ASX (www.asx.com.au), you can see how public companies issue these company statements. Hundreds of statements are made almost every day. Public companies must detail events like takeovers or other forms of restructuring. Providing this type of information creates a fair market where individual and institutional investors have access to the same information.

However, just because a company must make a statement to the ASX doesn't necessarily mean that the statement actually tells you anything.

Very small, or junior, mining companies are notorious for making statements that say nothing. The share price of a mining company may rise or fall by 50 per cent in a single afternoon because something important has happened that can affect the company. In such a situation, the company may get a call from the ASX to issue a statement on the event. However, just as likely, the company may issue a statement that simply says, 'The management has no idea why the share price rose so quickly.' As is often seen in the investment markets, you can actually expect only so much from public information channels.

In mining stocks, share prices can soar ahead on rumour and speculation of great 'finds'. After a hole is drilled, however, poor geological results can send share prices sliding backwards, hence the following caution:

> *Never ruin a good prospect by drilling a hole.*
>
> —*Mining industry proverb*

Speculating on the future

Nobody knows what's going to happen next on the stock market, but a lot of people make a living trying to second-guess tomorrow's news. Market speculation is the fuel that drives stock prices and is probably the most important guide to the immediate trend in a stock price, although it's unreliable.

Here are some rumours that have actually made the front page of our national newspapers in recent times. These rumours (so far) are turning out to be completely untrue.

- Chinese aluminium maker Chinalco sets its sights on BHP
- Deutsche Bank to bid for Babcock & Brown
- Macquarie irrevocably broken
- National Australia Bank to buy St.George Bank (In fact, Westpac seized the prize.)

You need to be aware of the existence of these types of rumours: A stock market rumour invariably has an element of truth in it. Every one of the rumours just mentioned may one day become something more substantial.

Making Waves in the Market

Every day, a million minor events prompt investors to buy or sell shares. Major 'trading' events, however, are the driving force that can almost guarantee a change in direction of a company share price. Moreover, these events can prompt investors to reassess whether they want to remain with a stock in the future.

In some cases, a major trading event directly influences an investor by presenting a choice of options — such as a rights issue. In other cases, the event can simply create a windfall, such as occurs following a demutualisation. We discuss these and other events over the next few pages.

How BHP lost its groove (and finally got it back)

For several generations of Australian investors, BHP — Broken Hill Proprietary Company — was 'the big Australian', the greatest public company Australia has ever produced and one of the few local stocks that ranked with the greatest companies in the world.

Based in Melbourne, BHP was the kingpin of the resources industry. The company did almost everything a resources company can do: It mined coal and copper; it drilled for oil; it manufactured steel. Better still, the company had operations stretching from the Irish Sea to Vietnam. At one stage, to demonstrate just how international the company had become, BHP actually held a board meeting in Vietnam.

As a company, BHP seemed almost faultless. Improved revenues and profits were reported every year. People who joined BHP and played their cards right inside the organisation were almost guaranteed a job for life.

The top brass at BHP had a good life and flew in private jets. In fact, everyone in BHP had a good life. BHP managers attending conferences were able to bring their partners along at company expense. The conditions in BHP mines, although always dangerous, were among the best in the world.

BHP was the ultimate blue-chip investment. In well-heeled circles, giving a newborn child a parcel of BHP shares as a present was common. As the years passed, the allure around BHP was so tremendous that everyone — investors, fund managers, even respected journalists — stopped asking BHP tough questions.

The company had always been something of an insiders' club, but a very successful one. When BHP ignored corporate governance guidelines and allowed one of its own senior managers (Jerry Ellis) to leapfrog the chief executive position and become chairman of the company, nobody in the Australian market cried foul.

By the early 1990s, the performance indicators all started going the wrong way for BHP. The company made huge losses on poor investments offshore, such as the Dai Hung oilfields in Vietnam and the Magma Copper mine in the United States. As the global mining business split into huge conglomerates like Rio Tinto or small-scale specialised mining companies, BHP fell between two stools — it was too small to compete with Rio Tinto and too big and unwieldy to compete with smaller companies.

After a very difficult period when the company reported very poor results in the late 1990s, BHP did the unthinkable. For the first time in its history, control of the company was handed over to someone who wasn't an insider. This new recruit was Paul Anderson, a motorbike-riding American executive who was the very opposite of BHP's dyed-in-the-wool Melbourne Club-style managers.

Within four years, Anderson got BHP back on its feet — but not without enormous cutbacks. In early 2001, BHP merged with the British-headquartered South African mining company Billiton. At the time, there were concerns that 'the big Australian' would be lost inside an international conglomerate, but those fears proved unfounded. In 2001, the company sought a dual listing on the London and Australian stock exchanges. Since then, the company has gone from strength to strength, as it rides the Chinese economic boom and an insatiable demand for Australia's oil and mineral resources. In 2008, under South African-born chief executive, Marius Kloppers, BHP Billiton launched a $122 billion hostile, but ultimately unsuccessful, takeover bid for its arch rival, Rio Tinto.

Floating on the stock market sea

When a company arrives on the stock market, it's called a *new listing*, or a *float*. Most times the company uses the occasion to raise money — officially called an IPO (initial public offering). However, the possibility to list (or float) without raising any money also exists and is often called a *compliance listing*.

New floats, or listings, on the stock market are the spice of life for the investment industry. Suddenly, you have the chance to get a slice of the action in a company that was previously off-limits.

A good example of a successful float (and IPO) is Billabong, the sports and leisure company. Billabong is a household name, especially in houses with teenagers. The Sydney-based company makes clothes known as surfwear — the oversized pants, shapeless jackets and curious headgear that clad the youngsters in every Australian suburb. (Does anyone know what percentage of them ever surf anything apart from TV channels or the internet?)

Billabong was a well-known private company when it announced in 2000 that it was going to be listing on the stock market and selling stock worth $295 million. This move represented Billabong selling most of its assets onto the stock market to a range of institutional and private investors.

With a strong record of profit growth and a well-connected management team, Billabong's issue price was $2.30. Eight years later the stock is trading at $6.83, although it was trading above $14 before the onslaught of the global financial crisis.

Not every float works out quite as well as Billabong. In bad years for shares it's not unusual for investors to lose money on one in every two IPOs.

Raising funds with a rights issue

A *rights issue* is when a public company asks its own shareholders to finance a project. The company pays for the project by issuing more shares, and those shares are divided among shareholders on the same basis as their current holding. So, if you hold 10 per cent of a company, you can be offered 10 per cent of the new shares.

Rights issues are distributed normally on a proportionate basis. A typical rights issue may be on a *one-for-four basis*. This means that for every four shares you hold in the company, you can be offered one more share. Rights issue shares are normally offered at a small discount to the stock price and don't incur any stockbroker's fees because they come directly from the company involved.

A company will try launching a rights issue when it's doing very well and it wants to finance a takeover or a major expansion. And, in contrast, if a company gets itself into trouble and needs money to work its way out of a difficult situation, it will also consider a rights issue.

Companies in the mining and technology sectors, which often have difficulty attracting finance due to the specialised nature of their activities, are very regular users of rights issues for a variety of purposes, such as taking over rivals in the same market.

If an acquisitive company launches a rights issue to support a takeover, it's the same as getting money from the bank, except that the money comes from existing shareholders. The shareholders invest the money in more shares on the basis they will get improved performance from the company. In other words, the company uses its own shareholders — rather than a bank — as the main source of finance.

Placements for the privileged few

A *placement* is where a company asks certain select shareholders, normally institutional shareholders, if they want to buy shares through a special arrangement. The offer of a placement is a bit like a very restricted rights issue.

When the markets are slow or difficult, companies are often very wary of going out in the stock market and asking the general public for money through a rights issue. The fear here is that the rights issue may not be 'fully taken up'. If all those approached don't take up their rights, the result can reflect badly on the company.

Buybacks for a quick boost

The stock market is notorious for changing fashions. At the moment, share buybacks are in fashion. Yet we have little doubt that, in the coming years, major faults will become obvious with buybacks and they're likely to go out of fashion.

A *share buyback* is when a company — believe it or not — buys its own shares and then puts them in the trash. The shares are actually cancelled. The effect of this exercise is to boost the value of the company's remaining shares.

For example, imagine that our infamous company, Awesome Awnings, has 110 million shares in the market trading at $1 each. (What a bargain!) Then Awesome Awnings has a market capitalisation of $110 million — that is, the total value of the company is reckoned to be worth $110 million in the market.

If the company does a $10 million buyback, it buys 10 million $1 shares and cancels them. The market still believes the company has a total value of $110 million, and nothing has changed there! So, each remaining share becomes 10 per cent more valuable, and the share price hopefully rises to $1.10. Share buybacks were associated with banks in the 1990s; they have since become a popular strategy for all major companies.

Share buybacks make sense to people in charge of keeping companies lean and mean. The idea is that no loose money washes around the company. But, at the end of the day, companies spend large amounts of money and time on these buybacks. Many investors believe companies would be better off doing something more useful with their time and money, like buying top assets that give the company a genuine long-term advantage rather than a short-term sharemarket boost.

The demutualisation deal

Boy, these finance guys can come up with some ugly terms! *Demutualisation* is the term applied when a former *mutual company*, which is owned by its members, changes its status to float on the stock market.

Nine times out of ten, demutualisations refer to insurance companies getting listed for the first time. Most big insurance companies, like AMP, NRMA (now IAG) or the former National Mutual (now AXA Asia Pacific), used to have a structure like a club, where every policyholder was an owner of the company.

In the late 1990s, institutional investors put these companies under pressure to modernise and float on the stock market. In almost every major mutual, the demutualisation process went through successfully, and the constitutions of these companies were rewritten. In turn, policyholders were given shares in the companies and the companies listed on the stock market with varying degrees of success. Colonial — the former Colonial Mutual Assurance — is now part of the Commonwealth Bank.

Investors who pick up stock in demutualisations are classic 'accidental investors' — those lucky policyholders who benefit from an event on the stock market that gives them a windfall.

Chapter 9

Getting Access to the Market

In This Chapter

▶ Choosing a stockbroker

▶ Introducing managed funds

▶ Reading the financial media

▶ Knowing how to check investment prices

*A*re stockbrokers necessary? We're afraid so — a legal requirement means that only stockbrokers are licensed to buy and sell shares. Without this system, a free-for-all would predominate instead of the relatively well regulated market investors enjoy.

Try to think of the stock market as a place where parcels of every major company you ever heard about are bought and sold. Think of household names in Australian business, such as BHP, Foster's or Wesfarmers — traders are buying and selling shares in these companies every day. You probably know a lot more about the stock market than you realise. Where did you grow up? If, for example, you grew up in a mining town, you know a lot more about the resources industry and BHP than many other people. If you grew up on a farm, you know quite a lot more than the average punter about agribusiness and Wesfarmers.

Where does your experience come from? From spending some time in the computer industry, perhaps? Lucky you. That industry is always a hot investment sector. The point here is that the markets are not some distant arena. The markets represent a way of buying into the paint factory at the bottom of the road or the software company the whiz-kids at your local university put together.

Investing is not nearly as difficult as it looks.

—*John (Jack) Bogle, legendary US investor and founder of Vanguard Investments*

The real problem is getting access to the market — as soon as you get an understanding of the ways to access the markets, you have the practical information that turns your own experience and expertise into profit.

You can access the markets through shares and stockbrokers, or managed funds and fund managers. A very healthy and attractive spectrum of financial information providers exists to guide you through those choices. Getting information to help you make investment decisions has become much easier in the last decade, especially through the internet. In this chapter, we show you how you can build a strategy in order to access the markets, as well as how to access and interpret market information.

Building a Market Access Strategy

At one time, the market could have been described as a club for a select group of people who knew how the system worked. Thankfully, that club atmosphere has almost totally disappeared.

Today, the market is much more of a level playing field. Your biggest challenge isn't getting information, but digesting and distilling the huge amount of information available.

To minimise the chance of being caught in a market downturn or a disaster in specific stocks — what if your two major stock holdings had been ABC Learning Centres and Babcock & Brown? — you must diversify your investment portfolio.

With a truly diversified portfolio of stocks, managed funds, property and other savings, you can build real wealth and have strong, built-in protection for your portfolio.

Going for broke with full-service brokers

Up until the 1990s, all brokers were *full-service brokers*, but these days the type of services a broker can offer vary greatly. As a general rule, the more you pay, the more advice and help you get.

Among the full-service brokers are the grand old names of the local and international broking sector, such as Ord Minnet, Goldman Sachs JBWere, Macquarie Equities, Bell Potter and UBS.

These brokers promise a full service. If you pay enough, they advise you on what stocks to buy, when to sell and when to take up a rights issue. They may invite you to take up stock in a new listing or IPO (initial public offering).

Depending on how much you have to invest, these brokers are happy to meet you. They'll ask you into the office — at least for an initial introduction — where you can have a coffee with a staff member and get some general advice.

A full-service broker can offer you certain account facilities to make trading easier, and a range of valuable research on the markets is also available. The catch is that for these services a full-service broker charges you more for each trade than an online broker, but brokerage fees have fallen in recent years due to intense competition. A full-service broker will charge you around $50 each time you buy or sell a stock. Alternatively, they charge you around 0.75 per cent of the amount you want to invest in a range of shares. Full-service broking has great advantages — if you have a lot of money to invest or you know very little about shares — but the bottom line means this type of service can be expensive.

Plenty of snobs still offer full-service broking. If you encounter arrogance or patronising behaviour from brokers, pick up your papers and walk out the door. They don't really want your business. Remember, 90 per cent of their revenue comes from just 10 per cent of their clients.

A full-service broker aims to provide you with the following services:

- ✔ **Personal contact:** Providing a single individual who is your link to the brokerage and its services and is someone you can get on the phone to with little difficulty.

- ✔ **Individual portfolio advice:** Offering specific advice about the composition of your share portfolio.

- ✔ **Warnings:** Warning about problem stocks — a good broker would have warned of trouble brewing in recent years in companies with too much debt and not enough cash flow, such as ABC Learning Centres.

- ✔ **IPO invitations:** Inviting you to participate in IPOs that suit your needs. This service doesn't mean you're going to be invited to join in every IPO the firm is involved in financing. Instead, you are notified of IPOs that make sense for you.

- ✔ **Tailored blue-chip investment advice:** Advising you on blue-chip shares with franking credits that suit your specific tax needs.

- ✔ **Ongoing investment advice:** Acting as a sounding board and offering ongoing advice on investment decisions you're about to implement.

Daring to deal with discount brokers

Discount brokers and *online broking* hit the Australian market more or less at the same time around the mid-1990s. The arrival of the internet was the perfect medium for discount brokers, who expect you to make your own choices and give them nothing more than orders to buy and sell investments on your behalf.

Typically, discount brokers want you to deal primarily over the internet or over the phone. You still have to fill out the forms and other legal requirements for buying and selling shares, but nobody's going to give you advice over a coffee. The reward for taking your own advice in the market is a discount on the price of trading in shares.

Discount brokers can buy or sell shares for you for about $30. If you're a frequent trader, you can trade for less than $20.

Among the big names in discount broking are CommSec (from the Commonwealth Bank), E*TRADE, Westpac Broking, Andrew West Stockbroking, Macquarie Bank and National Online Trading.

The problem with discount broking is that you can't get anyone to help you. As it's quite a strict business model, you're simply not welcome to ask for advice; you really have to know what you're doing. So, if you're buying a block of shares in a blue-chip company, then you probably can operate without advice. But, if you're trying to construct a share portfolio with a balance of risk and reward that suits you perfectly, then building the entire portfolio without ever seeking professional advice can be a very risky exercise indeed.

 Because access to market information is no longer a problem for most Australian investors, the challenge now is to build your own information channel. Settle on a package of information providers that suits your needs best. This information-gathering may include a routine of morning newspapers, magazines, investment newsletters, regular visits to certain broker-sponsored websites and a systematic reading of your favourite market commentators (see the section 'Investing in Information' later in this chapter).

Making the best of both broking worlds

Depending on your particular plans and requirements, being able to choose from a wide range of service providers offers certain benefits.

The best way to take advantage of this wide range of service providers is to mix the choices available in full-service and online broking — they're starting to look more like each other anyway. You can use a discount broker for no-brainer moves like buying another 1,000 ANZ shares. After all, if you're comfortable you want these shares, they suit your needs and they're good value at the time, then you don't need advice from anyone to confirm your views. (Remember that brokers always find a reason to recommend why you should buy stocks.)

The outlook on online broking

Online stockbroking really has turned the traditional world of stockbroking on its head — probably because stockbroking is the perfect industry for the internet. At the end of the day, broking is all about information and, if that information is cheap, then a sizeable slice of the package presented to retail investors by traditional full-service stockbrokers is useless. After all, not long ago, if a broker sent you research on the stock market, you were in a privileged group. Now anyone can get top-class research over the internet, and it's often free.

In the late 1990s, when online brokers started to charge about $50 for what was, in some instances, an identical service that cost up to $200 in a traditional broking company, the full-service brokers' value-for-money image diminished.

Online brokers are not going to go away, but trends are changing rapidly. After more than a decade of 'discounting', the fact that nobody can make much of a business selling stocks for much less than $30 a trade became evident. Discount brokers who specialise in online trading are starting to add — and charge for — an increasing range of related services. They're starting to look a lot more like the traditional full-service brokers.

On the other hand, traditional brokers threatened by the new breed of discount brokers are offering their own copycat versions of discount broking. Macquarie Direct from Macquarie Equities is a good example of this trend. As a result, the traditional brokers are starting to act more like discount brokers.

You may start to see in a few years' time that the two sides of the broking industry — full-service and discount — are meeting back in the middle somewhere, not charging as much as they used to and not offering as much as they used to either (except to their very wealthy clients).

Online broking has had an important effect — allowing changes to take place in stockbroking that might otherwise have taken a long time to happen. For example, stockbrokers can no longer pretend they're the gatekeepers to the mysteries of the market — you can get almost any information on the internet — and the greatest challenge now is to classify and understand that information.

Brokers these days can only charge for the real added value they give you as an investor. Until very recently, much of their charging was based on the delusion that they controlled the market. That change is progress!

On the other hand, if you're thinking of buying mining or technology stocks for the first time in your life, or preparing to invest offshore, then you need advice. At the very least, you need the basic *house view* — the view of the stockbroking company's research team on the prospect of a stock. That view is built on key ratios like price-to-earnings (PE) ratios, and the specific outlook for the relevant industry. (For more on stock market indicators like PE ratios, refer to Chapter 8.)

Perhaps the greatest power of full-service brokers these days is their ability to tap into global information networks. An intelligent broker can give you a basic view of a stock's fundamentals, and ought to be able to give you a global view as well. So, if you're thinking of buying shares in Telstra, for example, look for the broker who can quickly summarise the price of Telstra in the local market in terms of its profit outlook, its PE ratio and its dividend policy. Then, to fortify that information, a broker ought to be able to give a global view of the telecommunications industry and to what extent global trends in that industry will be influencing the future of Telstra.

All About Your Average Managed Fund

Managed funds are quite simply pools of money formed by professional fund managers to invest in certain areas. Those areas can be as vague as 'international shares' to something as precise as Australian biotechnology companies.

Once upon a time, the only way to access the markets was through a stockbroker. In recent decades, the managed-funds industry has flourished as investors become more comfortable with letting professional managers manage their money.

The big difference between shares and managed funds — apart from fund manager fees — is that you must make a decision about both the investment and the manager of that investment.

As more money flows into funds, the suite of products offered by the industry becomes more diverse, which in turn brings in more clients. By mid-2008, the value of the managed-funds industry in Australia was a whopping $829 billion, according to research house Morningstar, although this figure was down from its peak of $950 billion in 2007. Australian investors have more than 10,000 different managed funds to choose from.

The advantage of managed funds is that you get to genuinely diversify your investments for as little as $1,000. The disadvantage of managed funds is the layers of financial management between your money and the final investment, which means everybody on every layer has to be paid.

As a result, managed funds' fees are substantial and much higher than any similar fee you're likely to face in holding shares. (See Part III for more information on managed funds.) Worse still, evidence exists that Australians are paying some of the highest management fees in the world.

Paying 1 per cent instead of 2 per cent in fees on your managed funds can make a big difference to your returns, especially if you're expecting to only make something like between 8 per cent and 12 per cent on your money. Over a period of years, the overall effect on returns can be quite dramatic.

One of the big problems in the Australian market is that there are simply loads of fund managers without enough power individually. Australia supports 10,000 funds, more than the number available in the entire US market. While Australian funds are worth in total $829 billion, the US market is worth more than $10 trillion. Australia has too many small funds — small funds get into trouble more easily than big funds because they don't have the one thing you demand from a good fund manager, a genuinely diversified portfolio of investments.

Still, despite their flaws, the majority of managed funds really do offer splendid access to the markets, especially if you have a limited amount of money to invest. For a couple of thousand dollars you can have investments well spread across investment markets. You can invest in different countries; you can put your money on an index that represents a single market by investing in an index fund. Whether you feel the benefits are worth the price of high fees is up to you — we think the benefits are often worth the gamble. (We discuss various aspects of managed funds in Chapter 13.)

Investing in Information

Maybe because Australia has the highest level of share ownership in the world and a long tradition of speculative investing, especially in mining stocks, Australia has a rich and diversified financial media.

This availability of financial information really is good news for investors. All of the major papers have substantial financial sections, and a very strong financial newspaper (the *Australian Financial Review*) publishes daily. You can even watch financial television shows like *Lateline Business* on the ABC.

Here are some of the places you can get good financial information for just a few dollars or even for free:

- ✔ **Newspapers:** The *Australian Financial Review*, the *Australian*, the *Sydney Morning Herald*, the *Age*.
- ✔ **Magazines:** *BRW*, *AFR Smart Investor*, *Money* magazine.

- ✔ **Investor information websites:** Money Manager at www.money manager.com.au, ninemsn's Money at www.money.ninemsn.com.au.

- ✔ **Investor product websites:** These websites back up financial service providers, who offer a range or package of financial products. They often have a wide range of information designed for their own clients who are active investors. The best known is Commonwealth Securities at www.commsec.com.au, the first in the field and by far the biggest as it has continued to buy up smaller rival sites in recent years.

- ✔ **Financial newsletters:** *Huntleys' Your Money Weekly* (www.aspect huntley.com.au), the *Intelligent Investor* (www.intelligent investor.com.au) or the *Rivkin Report* (www.rivkin.com.au).

Interpreting Price Information

Any time you want to find out the price of a share or a managed fund, you're invariably faced with a table. Among the most comprehensive tables in the market are the share tables from the *Australian Financial Review* and the managed-fund tables from the *AFR Smart Investor* magazine (www.afrsmartinvestor.com.au).

Turning the tables on shares

At first glance, share tables look complex, but they're no more complex than reading sports results. The trick is not to try to take too much in at first glance. Try focusing on one share price at a time.

The *Australian Financial Review* presents a wide selection of tabulated data on all publicly listed shares in Australia. Table 9-1 details 10 of the 16 items recorded in the *AFR* for the Commonwealth Bank's share price.

Looking more closely at the items in Table 9-1, their meaning is as follows:

- ✔ **52-wk high and 52-wk low:** These items tell you the highest price ($62.16) and the lowest price ($36.98) that the share achieved over the previous 12 months.

- ✔ **Last price:** This line tells you the last available price of the Commonwealth Bank shares ($45.01).

- ✔ **Div/share:** You can see how much the bank pays in dividend per share — 266 cents (or $2.66) on every share.

Table 9-1	Commonwealth Bank Share Price, October 2008
52-wk high	62.16
52-wk low	36.98
Last price	45.01
Div/share	266.00
Div/tmes cov'd	1.36
Div yield	5.91
Franking	f (fully franked)
NTA	12.38
Earn/share (c)	363.00
PE ratio	12.4

Source: Compiled from AFR data.

- **Div/times cov'd:** An indication of the affordability of a company's dividend policy. Dividend cover is expressed as a ratio and shows how many times over a company's net profit could pay for shareholder dividends. You calculate this by dividing earnings per share by dividend per share; in this case, 363c by 266c, giving a ratio of 1.36.

- **Div yield:** This line tells you how much that 266 cents dividend represents as a return on the money you invested in the shares. In this example, a Commonwealth Bank share is worth $45.01 and the yield is 5.91 per cent. Remember, the yield takes no account of possible capital increases you may have enjoyed in the value of Commonwealth Bank shares.

- **Franking (meaning franking level):** This line tells you that Commonwealth Bank shares are fully franked at 100 per cent, which means you get the maximum *dividend imputation*, or tax credit, on your dividend income.

- **NTA:** This line shows the net tangible assets per share — the amount of assets the bank holds divided by the number of shares the bank has on issue; the figure is $12.38. Asset backing is not regarded as an important ratio in banks because they're largely a service business and don't try to have large assets like property on their books anymore.

- **Earn/share (c):** The EPS is the earnings per share figure, one of the most important guides to the real profitability of any company. At Commonwealth Bank, the EPS is 363 cents (or $3.63).

- **PE ratio:** The price-to-earnings ratio is a key indicator of the value of the share price of the bank. At 12.4, Commonwealth Bank is looking a little more expensive than some of its rivals. ANZ, for example, the same week was showing a PE of 8.8, while National Australia Bank was showing a PE of 8.6 and Westpac was showing a PE of 10.8.

Sifting statistics on managed funds

When you look across the price indicators on a managed fund, as shown in Table 9-2, you see a very different string of indicators compared with share prices, explained earlier in Table 9-1.

Table 9-2	Platinum Asia Fund, September 2008
Morningstar rating	*****
Min investment ($)	25,000
Size ($m)	2,540
1 yr (%)	−11.33
3 yr (%)	13.9
5 yr (%)	20.44
Income return	12.92
Entry (%)	0
Fee (% p.a.)	1.54

Source: Compiled from AFR Smart Investor *magazine data.*

In general, managed-fund statistics are easier to read and understand than share price statistics. These figures give you important information that you need to know about performance, size and even fees. The current entry and exit price of units in a managed fund can be found in the *Australian Financial Review* and on the fund manager's website.

Here are the key features of the *unit trust table* (the table that tells you important investment information) for the Platinum Asia Fund:

- ✔ **Morningstar rating:** The first line shows the Morningstar rating, which is a typical star system assigned by a research house (in this instance, Morningstar). The star system rates the fund according to a number of key criteria, such as management fees and long-term performance. According to Morningstar, the Platinum Asia Fund has a top rating of five stars. A fund can score anywhere between one and five stars.

- ✔ **Min investment ($):** The next line is the minimum investment of $25,000. Some funds have a minimum investment of as little as $1,000, whereas other funds require a minimum of as much as $40,000.

- ✔ **Size ($m):** The size of the fund tells you the total assets of the fund. This indicator is one of the most important signposts for an investor. A very small fund can suffer from a lack of clout; a very big fund can have difficulty moving quickly enough to profit out of certain situations. This example is a $2,540 million fund — that is, a very large fund. In contrast, the Advance Asian Equity fund has $9 million on the books.

- ✔ **1 yr, 3 yr, 5 yr (%):** These figures tell you what the fund makes for its investors, on average every year, over the set periods of time. The figures (expressed as percentages) assume that all dividends are reinvested.

- ✔ **Income return:** This line estimates the return on your investment in the fund in terms of the income it has produced over the last 12 months, in this case, 12.92 per cent.

- ✔ **Entry (%):** This is the up-front fee the fund manager charges you to invest in the fund, expressed as a percentage. The Platinum Asia Fund has no entry fee. Fund entry fees can be up to 4.5 per cent.

- ✔ **Fee (% p.a.):** The annual fee charged by the fund manager to manage your money, expressed as a percentage of your investment. The Platinum Asia Fund charges 1.54 per cent a year. Management fees can range from less than 1 per cent to 2.85 per cent.

Chapter 10

Playing the Stock Market Game

In This Chapter

▶ Settling in to the big picture

▶ Understanding dividends and franking credits

▶ Developing your portfolio

▶ Selling stocks

▶ Avoiding market tricks

*O*ne of the first challenges you face when you trade in the stock market is to reduce your exposure to risk. As you know, avoiding all risk isn't possible, but you can sidestep the worst mistakes in trading stocks by carefully, and sometimes bravely, choosing when to buy and sell.

You're trying to make money in a market where everyone has a separate agenda. Your broker wants your stock to do well but, more than anything else, that same broker wants to make a big salary this year. Similarly, the chief executive at the company in which you invest wants a good result — but sometimes a chief executive's action can hurt the share price and hurt your pocket as well. Important, too, is the fact that often you can be given information by either brokers or company leaders that simply isn't the whole truth about a particular stock or company.

Companies and their supporters in the stock market always put the best possible 'spin' on their performance. Sometimes companies come through rough periods (like BHP Billiton or the banks) and sometimes they never recover (such as Coles Myer, before the business was split up and taken over).

Your strategy has to be to buy and sell your investments at the time that you believe is the very best possible moment for your share portfolio — nothing else matters.

Regardless of how thoroughly you analyse individual stocks, for every handful of stocks you choose, you always stand to get caught with one loser, because nobody can ever know what the market is going to do next. But, in this chapter, we give you some tips on how to select your stocks, how to time your investments to make the most of dividend payments and when to sell. We also look at some of the market tricks to watch out for.

Picking Your Investments: The Big Picture

As soon as you begin to understand the basic factors that make up a share price, you may find that quite a number of companies satisfy your criteria for investment. How do you go that extra step and actually choose one stock over another?

Four key factors can help you formulate your final decision. They have more to do with the 'big picture' than any information the number crunchers in a broking house are likely to throw at you. These factors are:

- ✔ **Fundamentals:** Are you fully comfortable with the fundamental situation at this company? For example, your research shows great numbers, but maybe this company is a tobacco giant, and you don't like smoking. Maybe the profits look great, but you just can't see how this particular industry can keep churning out profits. Your reaction may be no more than a gut feeling.

- ✔ **Cyclicals:** In a recession, investors rush to invest in *cyclicals*, or *defensive stocks*. A *recession* is officially defined as two consecutive quarters (three-month periods) when the economy doesn't grow. During recessions, investors aim for stocks that are guaranteed to do a certain level of business no matter how bad overall economic conditions become. These types of companies sell basic items like bread and butter, healthcare and electricity. In contrast, during a boom, people are more likely to invest in speculative companies like oil and gas explorers or tourism projects.

✔ **Takeovers:** If a stock shows signs of having a realistic chance as a takeover target, then the share price, too, has a good chance of staying strong, even with lukewarm operating results. Moreover, if a takeover offer finally does hit the table, the stock jumps in price. Certain sectors can become ripe for takeover, like mining companies in the early 2000s or non-bank lenders during the global credit squeeze of 2007–08. A *takeover premium* is the extra strength in a company share price attributed to the possibility of the company being taken over by another.

✔ **Management:** Investing in a stock if you don't believe in the management makes little sense. Also, if a new big-wig replaces the chief executive and that CEO brings in a new team, then remember that you're investing in a very different company. Make sure you're comfortable with the management, which is ultimately the most important factor driving the share price of any company.

Getting It Right: Timing Dividends

As a smart investor with your eye on medium- to long-term share price growth (often with a top-up from a nice big juicy dividend), timing isn't the most important consideration in your overall investment strategy. However, timing still matters. What does carry weight with the smart investor is the company's dividend policy — that certainly bears investigation!

Timely decisions

Among the factors that prompt you to make that call to your broker (or press that button on your computer) are the following:

✔ **Trading history:** How has the share performed in the past year? Is the share priced reasonably against its peers in the local market? Positive signs include a price increase over a set period showing less than the overall increase among an average of the company's peers in the market, such as the financials index or the metals and mining index. For example, you can measure the share price performance of a mining company against the metals and mining index, which just measures this industry.

✔ **Profit outlook:** What is the realistic outlook for profits in this company? For an answer to this question you must look to the management statements on future profitability that will be offered when results or other important announcements are made by the company.

Projections of future profits, however, are no more than hazy indicators, even from the most reputable companies. When times are good, profits can be much higher than expected, and, when times are bad, profits can nosedive spectacularly.

Dividend policies and plans

As well as assessing the company's profitability, you need to check its dividend performance:

- ✔ **Dividend policy:** Independent of its share price, can this company give you an income on your investment? What is the dividend history of this company? Has this company ever missed a dividend payout in the last five years? What is the dividend yield at this company? (Table 10-1 shows a list of companies with high dividend payouts.)

- ✔ **Franking policy:** Does this company pay fully franked, partially franked or unfranked dividends? How likely is the company to retain its franking policy? The answers to these questions can give you a guide to the tax advantages of investing in this company (see the next section, 'Dividend imputation').

- ✔ **Dividend-reinvestment plan (DRP):** Does the company offer a dividend-reinvestment plan? This scheme allows you to reinvest your dividends back into the company at no extra cost and with no additional paperwork. Sometimes companies give you an opportunity to reinvest your dividends and buy shares at a discount to the current share price.

Dividend-reinvestment plans are a great bonus if you've already decided to invest in a stock. Nobody wants a dividend cheque for just $50, because often times you just fritter the money away. DRPs, too, make you save your money — always a good habit.

Dividend imputation

The idea behind dividend imputation is good: Nobody ought to pay tax twice. So, the policymakers in Canberra came up with a scheme in 1987 in order that investors don't have to pay tax on dividends; after all, those dividends are no more than slices of profits that have already incurred tax at the time the company pays its own tax bill. It's not fair to ask you to pay tax a second time when you get billed for income tax.

So the powers-that-be decided how to implement the scheme. The government introduced the notion of *fully franked dividends*. (Dividends can be partly franked, but for sanity's sake we keep the explanation here simple.) When a company pays you a dividend, if it has already paid full taxes on the profits used to create that dividend, then the dividend is fully franked.

Table 10-1	Top 15 Dividend Yields, 2008		
Company	*Closing Price (31 Aug. 2008)*	*Franking (%)*	*Dividend Yield (%)*
Adelaide Brighton	3.62	100	4.1
Alesco Corp	6.91	100	9.7
AMP	6.96	85	6.6
ANZ Banking Group	16.61	100	8.2
ASX	35.36	100	5.4
Caltex Australia	12.55	100	6.4
ConnectEast	0.82	0	12.8
David Jones	4.35	100	5.0
DUET	2.99	0	9.0
Macquarie Group	44.04	100	7.8
National Australia Bank	24.50	100	7.4
Pacific Brands	2.23	100	7.6
Platinum Asset Management	3.59	100	6.7
QBE Insurance	23.95	50	5.1
Stockland	5.27	0	8.8

Source: Compiled from AFR Smart Investor data.

How you get an advantage from this system is largely to do with the possibility of offsetting what's called the *dividend-imputation tax credit* against your tax bill, making it lower.

Companies pay around 30 per cent in tax on profits. So, if you get $100 in dividends, fully franked, then the dividend-imputation tax credit (or the amount you can offset your tax bill by) will be around $42. This credit will be very useful when you come to pay tax on your earnings, as the following example shows.

The tax system works like this: If you get a $100 fully franked dividend, that means the company issuing the dividend has already paid tax on the money in your dividend. Company tax is 30 per cent, so really you only got 70 per cent of what you should have. The total (100 per cent) figure before tax would have been $142.86 (this is called *grossing up*), bringing the figure back to its pre-tax total.

According to the tax system, your taxable income relating to this dividend is declared at $142.86. However, the government says, to avoid double tax (that is, taxing this slice of company profit and taxing your income as well), you can have a dividend-imputation tax credit equal to that grossed-up value of $42.86. When you work it out, the tax due this way (at about $16.43 for people on the 41.5 per cent marginal tax rate) is a lot lower than the tax that would have been due if you just paid 41.5 per cent on $100. In fact, it's less than half as much ($16.43 against $41.50) so, believe it or not, it's all worth the trouble, especially if you're in a high tax bracket.

Investing in shares offering dividend-imputation tax credits can be a smart strategy, but make sure you get tax advice on how to treat your dividend-imputation opportunities.

Alternatively, you can buy into a managed fund that specialises in shares that have 100 per cent franking. These funds handle the tax issues for you and simply send you a regular statement of your income and the tax treatment that applies to that income. You can then hand these statements to an accountant at the end of the financial year, when it's time to do your tax returns.

Building Your Stock Portfolio

Ideally, a stock portfolio gives you a balance of growth, income and speculative opportunity. If a portfolio is too small, achieving this balance is impossible, and, if it's too big, then the logistics of managing the portfolio become tricky.

For beginning investors, the optimum number of stocks is somewhere around ten — a reasonable number of stocks to keep tabs on.

During the building phase of your portfolio, you ultimately have to follow your instincts. In the end, you probably create your own personal blend of different styles in the market. For the record, though, here are the main approaches that investors traditionally take to building a stock portfolio. See which style suits you best:

- ✔ **Aggressive:** The aggressive investor is willing to take speculative positions in a stock. This investor is looking for a big capital gain and is willing to take a big risk. Looking for turnaround situations or situations where a stock may greatly increase in price rapidly, this investor likes mining and technology stocks.

- ✔ **Passive:** The passive investor sits back, confident in the belief that the stock is such good value that the mere passage of time pays sufficient returns. This investor diligently looks for strong, well-managed companies that are financially very sound. These stocks can include companies from sectors such as banking and manufacturing.

- ✔ **Top-down:** The top-down investor looks at the economy first, then looks at the stock market. These investors make decisions based on the big picture. They are well aware that Australia is going to have one in four people over retirement age in 2050. On this basis, the top-down investor may choose to invest in the healthcare industry.

- ✔ **Bottom-up:** This very sober investor doesn't pay too much attention to fashion or futurologists. Instead, the bottom-up investor looks at the financial fundamentals of a business and makes decisions on that basis. This approach may completely ignore the healthcare sector and concentrate on poker machines — if the gaming companies match the investor's criteria, they don't worry about big-picture, or macro, trends.

- ✔ **Ethical:** The ethical investor represents a growing trend of investors first eliminating investments they oppose in principle. These investors may avoid companies that make cigarettes or sell uranium to nuclear power companies, regardless of the financial attraction of these stocks. Some ethical funds actively seek out sustainable and ethically managed businesses. Ethical investing results show a very strong track record in recent years, thanks to a number of outstanding managed funds.

In building your portfolio, don't get confused between popular companies and great stocks. Foster's is a company with products enjoyed by most adult Australians, but the track record of this company reveals a stock in some difficulty. Conversely, few banks get more criticism than the Commonwealth Bank about fees and service, but the stock continues to be strong.

'Sell, Sell, Sell!' When to Sell a Stock

You don't buy a share forever. Stock has a life span, a period of time when keeping it makes sense, and then, more than likely, a period of time when having it as part of your portfolio no longer suits your needs. Nine times out of ten, after you buy a stock, you're going to have to consider selling it in the future.

If you trade too often, you're going to have to make the money back that you lose on tax and commissions before you can count it as profit.

The secret is to make good buying decisions so that situations that force you to sell don't come around too often. Here are some guidelines for selling stocks:

✔ **Don't sell just because everyone else seems to be doing so.** Selling at the bottom of the cycle leaves you with the worst possible feeling. If you believe in a company, then hang on through weak periods in the economic cycle when all companies are doing it tough.

✔ **Don't sell just before a company is due to pay a dividend.** Check with the company when it expects to pay its next dividend. Waiting nearly always makes sense, especially if you're in a dividend-reinvestment plan (refer to the section 'Dividend policies and plans' earlier in this chapter).

✔ **Sell when you've found an alternative use for your money and you're convinced the time is right for you to get out of a stock.** The timing doesn't have to be perfect.

After you sell stock, don't bother looking at the share price to see what may have happened if you had stayed 'in'. Forget it, you're onto new pastures!

Down and Dirty Stock Market Tricks

'The stock market is no place for widows and orphans' — an old saying, perhaps, but behind that piece of folksy wisdom sits a warning that, when you're in the stock market, you're swimming with sharks.

Detailing the sort of skulduggery that takes place in the stock market every day, ranging from basic misdemeanours to outright scandals, could take up a whole book! The stories all have one thing in common, though — they involve attempts to influence the market in favour of one group of people at one time.

Here are some of the most common forms of trickery:

- **Takeover talk:** Some company executives would sell their grannies to get their way in a takeover situation. The prospective acquirers exaggerate the faults of the takeover company. The takeover target underestimates the value of its acquirer and overestimates its own value. The collapse of an $11 billion private-equity takeover of Qantas in May 2007 began as an agreed takeover, but ended in a heavy cost to the reputations of all the senior executives involved.

- **Ruling off the books:** Fund managers buy or sell stocks when sometimes doing so doesn't make sense, other than to achieve certain ratios. A fund manager may have told investors that 25 per cent of all stocks will be held in the United States. Two days before the books close for the end of the year, the manager may have 27 per cent of stocks in the US market. A selling program may be introduced to bring the ratio back to 25 per cent — even if the stocks are sold at a loss. In doing so, fund managers can completely bamboozle small shareholders, who can't possibly expect to second-guess their actions.

- **Spin:** Literally thousands of people are employed in financial markets to do nothing more than 'make the company look good'. For example, lurking in large corporations (like Telstra) are dozens of spin doctors, when press officers, community relations officers and various investor relations personnel are taken into account. Somewhere behind this torrent of spin lies the real story of the company's performance.

 If you see something you think is irregular or illegal in the stock market, contact the stock market regulator, the Australian Securities and Investments Commission (ASIC).

Don't get caught by window-dressing

On Friday 29 June 2001, a day that should have marked the end of another sleepy week on a market still recovering from the dot-com boom a year earlier, the All Ordinaries Index rocketed by 2 per cent. A lot of good news is needed to make the market jump 2 per cent in a single day, and the good news was decidedly lacking that day — in fact, more bad news was making an appearance as more companies announced downgrades in profit forecasts.

Stranger still, the bulk of the $4.45 billion worth of shares that traded on the market that day traded in the last quarter of an hour of trading on Friday afternoon.

Nobody could prove anything on the day, but a flood of fund managers were needing to window-dress their books before closing them off for the financial year to 30 June 2001. As a result, the fund managers put through huge orders to touch up their portfolios in ways that made them look better to anyone reading their full-year statements.

The proof that the 2 per cent lift on the ASX was built on nothing other than window-dressing came when the ASX reopened for business on Monday morning, 2 July — the All Ordinaries Index finished the day down 1.5 per cent, the biggest one-day fall for the previous 16 weeks.

The Australian Securities and Investments Commission announced that very Monday morning an investigation into the matter. But everybody in the market knew the reason — fund managers artificially tweak their books on the last session for the financial year.

The story matters because it shows how isolated a private investor can be from the games professional investors continually play in the market.

You, the private investor, may easily have decided to sell shares on Thursday 28 June, not knowing that fund managers were about to boost the market by 2 per cent the next day with their style of window-dressing.

In September 2001, ASIC introduced new regulations to stamp out window-dressing. But there will always be a gap between fund managers and private investors — don't expect to bridge that gap too easily.

Chapter 11

Putting the Web to Work: Online Trading

*T*rading online is the biggest thing to hit financial markets in your lifetime. If you think online investing is a flash in the pan . . . think again! Experience from the last decade indicates that financial services are perfect to deliver online because financial services have a high value and no physical presence. Long after the excitement about online books or online music passes, online financial services are likely to continue steaming ahead.

Major-league financial institutions were very quick to realise the long-term benefits of presenting investment options online. (After all, if you're willing to do the computer work previously done by bank and stockbroker clerks, why wouldn't they be happy!)

In 2007, ANZ Banking Group spent $432 million buying Australia's second-largest online broker, E*TRADE. Although this sounds like a lot of money, ANZ has bought itself a major slice of the online broking industry, which is dominated today by the country's four biggest banks, the Commonwealth Bank, ANZ, Westpac and NAB.

In the late 1990s, stockbrokers led the financial services industry into the online world with the emergence of the Commonwealth Bank as a major force. By 2008, the bank's CommSec online broking service (www.commsec.com.au) had about 1.4 million customers.

For you, the investor, some great advantages exist in online investing. The greatest advantage is the availability of information. Information is the fuel that drives investment decisions. Even just a decade ago, the private investor was able to collect extremely limited financial information in the market. Now, with a simple internet connection, you can get the same information that is available to professional investors and much of it's free-of-charge. As soon as you know where to find key information, you can become a better investor. First, however, you must become familiar with the online world.

Trading in Cyberspace

Investing via cyberspace is fundamentally the same as investing any other way. You're simply dealing over the internet instead of person-to-person or on the phone. But the information you need to know is presented in an enormously different way on the web. Because access to information is no longer an issue for investors, the challenge is now taking control of this information and using it to make money. (Many market analysts believe that information and good research on the markets are now as easily available to retail investors as they are to professional investors.)

The next stage is the age of value; how we use information to create value.

—Edward De Bono, lateral-thinking guru

The secret to online trading is learning to enjoy the speed of web-based investing without becoming lazy. Remember when you began using your first credit card and how easy buying a meal was, just by signing with your card? Compared with hauling the notes out of your wallet, using credit cards is a piece of cake. In fact, the process doesn't feel like spending at all!

Online trading is similar. You have to be very careful not to be seduced by the technology. Buying and selling is very easy because you just click a button. However, the important question to ask yourself is: Does it always make sense to trade?

Bear in mind the following key points as you weigh up each online trade:

- **More than anything else, stockbrokers want you to trade often.** They make a living from commission each time you buy and sell an investment.

- **You, the investor, have to pay fees every time you trade.** When you invest online, you may pay less commission than through a broker, but the great temptation is to trade more often.

- **Every time you buy or sell, you have to cover your fees before you assume any profit.** If you have relatively modest investment funds, those fees can make the difference between a profit and a loss.

Making the most of online broking

Getting confident with the online broking process is important if you really want to make some savings on your investment. The costs of dealing with an online broker can be only one-fifth of those payable if you were dealing with a full-service broker — a huge saving.

The gap between online broking and full-service broking is a bit like the difference between budget airlines and full-service airlines. The budget airline asks you: 'Why pay twice as much for little extras like food?' Of course, the whole service picture isn't really as simple as this statement implies. Budget airlines are fine as long as nothing goes wrong. If you get stranded at a foreign airport with a budget airline, you very soon realise how lean and mean these companies have to be in order to offer those cheap prices.

Similarly, the process of online broking works just fine, as long as you know exactly what you're doing. For example, you may unwittingly opt to sell your stocks on the worst day of the year, but an online broker isn't going to 'talk' to you about your investment activity and alert you to the fact that the decision is a bad one.

The other essential difference between online and full-service broking is that online broking is amazingly fast. When you deal with full-service brokers, you have to find your broker and talk to him. He goes to the market to do your trade and comes back to you after a few hours to tell you the transaction is complete.

With online broking, the deal can be done in a cyber-second. On the internet, you fill out a form, click a button and, hey presto, the transaction is complete — for better or worse. All online brokers still provide you with a contract note every time you trade. Some brokers allow you to receive this note on paper, but the majority of online brokers prefer to send you the contract note electronically by email.

Online broking has no safety net or recall button — after you click the button, the deal is done. However, some online brokers now recognise that new investors value advice and offer a phone helpline to talk you through your online transaction.

Ogling an online site

Financial information or stockbroking websites, such as www.commsec.com.au and www.etrade.com.au, offer a whole new way of looking at investment markets.

Yet, in one sense, the internet is quite restrictive — only so much information can fit on a single screen. In fact, a screen-load (the amount on the screen in front of you at any one time) can only pack in around 500 words compared with 1,000 words on a magazine page.

This layout means that when you go to the homepage of a website, you have to look around the page to get a sense of how the links work. A good and functional site has basic information across the top of the page.

In most cases, the information across the top of the page is about the company, its services and contact information. Elsewhere on the page you most likely see practical information on products, fees and the important information that you're looking for to complete a transaction in the stock market. The ANZ Banking Group has gone back to basics and redesigned the E*TRADE website with new investors in mind (see Figure 11-1).

Almost every website provides a phone number discretely displayed. You can find this number under a tag called *contact us*. You can get very useful information about any company for the price of a local call.

If talking to the people who run the website makes sense to you, don't hesitate to do so the first time you use the facility. Alternatively, most online brokers offer virtual tours of their sites. After you go through the process, you probably don't need to do it again. Most financial institutions don't encourage small investors to call their investor relations staff, but if the investors make the call, those institutions aren't so stupid as to lose them by being unhelpful.

Trading online: The pros

In the old days, investors sent their sell or buy orders in to stockbrokers through the post. Online trading has a string of advantages:

- ✔ **Price:** Nothing beats online broking for price savings. Online broking can be one-fifth of the price of full-service broking. The average trade is around $20 to $30 against up to $150 for full-service broking.
- ✔ **Straight-through processing (STP):** Online brokers can offer instant transactions between you and the market, without the intervention of a middleman. This STP facility can make a big difference if a stock price is rising or dropping quickly.

✔ **Fresh information:** Information is power on the stock market, and up-to-date information is the most important requirement for you. On the web you can make decisions armed with the very latest publicly available information and real-time share prices.

✔ **Flexibility:** You can carry out an online trade when it suits you, rather than when it suits a busy stockbroker. You control the timing of transactions.

✔ **Organisation:** Not long ago, a major challenge for a private investor was keeping track of previous transactions. With web trading you have an *audit trail*, or a record of everything you've done online. This record is a great way of helping you build a better picture of your investment strategy.

Figure 11-1:
Finding your way around a website is made easy by a good and functional layout.

Source: E*TRADE www.etrade.com.au.

Trading online: The cons

The dangers of online trading are close to the dangers of shopping with a credit card — sometimes the money you're spending just doesn't seem real. As an online trader, you're acting very much on your own in an isolated manner. Here are a few dangers that face any investor choosing to deal with an online broker:

- ✔ **No advice:** You're on your own and any mistake you make can be blamed on no-one but yourself.

- ✔ **Too easy:** The ease of online trading seduces you to do less work. For example, you're less likely to read all the documentation for an IPO on a computer screen, especially if the IPO is more than 100 pages long.

- ✔ **No documents:** Forget about share certificates for every block of shares you buy. Online trading is almost paperless. You have to be able to trust computer trading, because you don't have substantial documents proving your ownership of each share. However, even with online trading, you still get a *contract note* every time you buy or sell, recording the various trades you've carried out and the specific details of your account.

- ✔ **Funds at the ready:** Because you're trading through an online account, your broker insists on you putting sufficient funds in that account before you trade. This money-management style can be an inefficient way for you to handle your cash.

- ✔ **Trigger-happy:** You're tempted to trade more often on the internet because completing a transaction is so easy. However, impulsive trading can ruin a well-planned strategy. Every time you trade, you must cover your fees before you can assume any profit from your alternative investment.

Beware of those incredibly low fees advertised for online broking. The lowest fees can be highly conditional and often depend on a certain volume of trade. Don't get caught up in that sort of relationship.

Table 11-1 shows some of the most popular services in online broking in Australia.

Table 11-1	Australia's Most Popular Online Brokers (2008)	
Name	**Web Address**	**Publisher**
Bell Direct	www.belldirect.com.au/trading	Bell Potter Securities
CommSec	www.commsec.com.au	Commonwealth Bank
E*TRADE	www.etrade.com.au	ANZ Banking Group
Goldman Sachs JBWere	www.gsjbw.com	Goldman Sachs JBWere
Macquarie DirecTrade	www.macquarie.com.au/trade	Macquarie Bank
NAB Online Trading	www.national.com.au/trading	National Australia Bank
Westpac Broking	www.westpac.com.au/broking	Westpac Banking Group

A Short History of Online Trading

The arrival of online broking coincided with one of the most bullish phases of the longest bull market remembered in Australia's lifetime — an unfortunate coincidence. Between 1997 and 2001, at the peak of the dot-com boom, the online-broking sector in Australia went from nowhere to almost a million *registered users* — that is, people with online accounts. Figures are hard to come by but, by the end of the bull market in 2008, Commonwealth Securities alone had 1.4 million customers and close to half the total market.

Of course, any fool can make money in a bull market, and any fool can make that money just as easily without advice, under the same conditions.

The market, like the Lord, helps those who help themselves. But, unlike the Lord, the market does not forgive those who know not what they do.

—Warren Buffet, the world's greatest living investor

The tail end of the 1990s heralded a new generation of investors entering the market, who didn't seek professional advice and who did very well, thank you ... until, that is, around January 2008, when the market entered its worst trading period in living memory. Along the way, young professionals, mums and dads, grandmas and granddads took to online trading like ducks to water.

Not surprisingly, the big four banks were quick to realise the money-making potential of online broking and the opportunity it offered to keep existing customers from migrating to competing banks.

The fierce price competition of the early years lessened as more and more people began to buy and sell shares online. The emphasis in recent years has been on expanding the services on offer. These days, you can trade local and international shares, options and warrants, managed funds and contracts for difference (CFDs). You can set up a margin loan, buy shares in new floats, manage your self-managed super fund and trade via your mobile phone. Most online brokers offer some research and trading tools free-of-charge, or more extensive services for a monthly charge.

The good news is that the market downturn and the emergence of aggressive new players such as Bell Direct are likely to bring prices down again. Bell Direct offers simple trades for as little as $15.

Exploring the Best Websites

Since the internet hit the Australian finance market around 1997, an explosion of financial websites means you can navigate freely for information. The sites range in quality dramatically. In the early days, the Australian Securities and Investments Commission (ASIC) forcibly removed one website because it was so undependable.

Websites are relatively cheap to build (the cost is in the maintenance); consequently, backstreet brokers who can barely afford to advertise in their local paper can launch a good-looking website. As they say, 'In cyberspace nobody knows who you really are.' Online investors who find these websites through search engines can easily be seduced into thinking the website promoters are in a much bigger league than is really the case.

Apart from facilitating direct trading on the internet, websites can be an excellent place to collect information about the market. Many of the best websites are run by large banks and financial institutions and are updated daily. Unfortunately, the best information is mostly for members only — you have to be a subscriber with these companies before you get access.

More commonly, some websites offer a certain amount of information for free and then more detailed information at a price.

You don't have to spend a cent in order to download very useful information on the investment markets. Among the best free general investment websites are:

- ✔ **ASX** (www.asx.com.au): The Australian Securities Exchange site offers a wide range of information on listed companies and securities.
- ✔ **ATO** (www.ato.gov.au): The Australian Taxation Office website is generally regarded by the internet sector as one of the most advanced public service websites in the world.
- ✔ **ASA** (www.asa.asn.au): The Australian Shareholders' Association is a representative group for small shareholders. The website contains useful commentary on investor issues.
- ✔ **ASIC** (www.asic.gov.au): The Australian Securities and Investments Commission is a good site for reviewing regulation and investment issues, and for seeking information on the track records of financial advisers and stockbrokers.

Among the best websites presented by investment companies (including subscription-only sites) are:

- ✔ **AMP** (www.amp.com.au): The website of one of Australia's biggest financial services companies, AMP, offers information for investors, managed funds and superannuation services, as well as investment tools and calculators.
- ✔ **Commonwealth Bank** (www.commbank.com.au): The website of the Commonwealth Bank has a range of information and calculators that can be very useful for any investor, including clients of online broker CommSec and fund manager Colonial First State.
- ✔ **InfoChoice** (www.infochoice.com.au): A website devoted to comparing financial products and services, including online brokers and bank products. An extremely useful site for anyone beginning their search for a loan, a broker or an insurance product.
- ✔ **Macquarie Bank** (www.macquarie.com.au): This site offers an insight into how a major power in the market — in this case, the investment bankers at Macquarie — views the market. The site also offers a staggering array of investment products and services for the bank's mostly wealthy clients.
- ✔ **Westpac** (www.westpac.com.au): Similar to the Commonwealth Bank's site, Westpac offers online broking, investment tools and calculators, managed funds and other investment products.

Shooting the Breeze with Your Online Chums

If you want to 'talk' online or swap emails with other investors, online investor sites offer facilities like message boards or chat rooms that will interest you. A *message board* is a unit of a website where people can ask each other questions and answer them, or create ongoing discussions — a bit like a community noticeboard for investors and market traders. A *chat room*, on the other hand, is basically a real-time forum where users can view each other's responses as they're posted. Despite their immediacy, chat rooms generally aren't as helpful as forums.

Some of the most popular and useful message boards that deal with Australian stocks are ShareScene (www.sharescene.com), Aussie Stock Forums (www.aussiestockforums.com) and HotCopper (www.hotcopper.com.au). Even if you don't wish to actively participate in one of these online communities, they provide an invaluable insight into the hot sharemarket topics of the day.

At best, chat rooms give isolated individual investors a chance to see what other people are doing on the market. Chat rooms are loaded with emails from investors who boast of the great profits they make in certain trading situations. Strangely, people rarely seem to write in about their mistakes or their failures!

At worst, investor chat rooms are wealth-destruction sites where a bunch of nameless rogues promote their favourite stocks to investors who are sitting ducks if they don't know better.

We have very little time for chat rooms. However, they have their uses, especially if you know nobody else in the investment game and you want to see the investment picture in certain circles. But you're a lot better off spending half an hour reading an annual report or an IPO prospectus.

If you want to connect with other investors online, a host of resources now exist, including investor newsgroups, blogs (short for web logs) and podcasts. Social-networking websites such as Facebook (www.facebook.com) allow people with similar interests to connect; this same technology has produced the phenomenon known as social investing, where you can monitor the successes and failures of other investors as they happen. For a thorough look at these types of online resources, pick up a copy of *Online Share Investing For Dummies*, Australian Edition, written by James Frost and Matt Krantz (Wiley Publishing Australia).

The shortsighted online innocent

Back in April 2001, James walked into an optician's consulting room to have his eyes examined. His optician, a talkative intelligent man in his mid-40s clearly had plenty of spare time (and spare money). As James sat in semi-darkness pretending he could read the fuzzy letters on the testing board (which suddenly seemed very far away), this enthusiastic online investor outlined an investment strategy that was nothing short of dangerous.

His investing history began a year earlier through an online broker. His first investment had been the telecom services company, Davnet, and he doubled his money in a matter of months. Emboldened, he multiplied his investments across the technology sector and more recently he had begun to invest directly in the US stock market.

He didn't seek advice from a professional stockbroker and he didn't read a prospectus, the document that accompanies a company's initial public offering (IPO). Instead he relied on what he called 'a gut feeling'.

This is the way this guy looked at things: If more people look like taking up the use of mobile phones in the future, he invested in phone companies. If everyone in Australia is getting older, he thought his idea to invest in medical technology companies was a good one.

Worse still, he told James that he'd recently bought a market-trading software program, and he makes many of his moves on the basis of the trading patterns, or 'charts', arriving on his screen. Watching trading patterns, or charting, is an area that used to be the sole preserve of highly qualified stockbrokers before computers turned the stock market upside down. Charting is something like the stock market equivalent of aromatherapy — support abounds from those who gain from it. For others, the method isn't taken very seriously.

After telling me that he was back from a skiing holiday in Japan, he grandly informed me he was very keen on buying stock in Telstra Corporation: 'I've been looking at the charts and it looks perfect,' he said.

'Hmm …' James mumbled from behind his eye-patch. 'I'm a bit worried about telcos at the moment. They're very expensive — Telstra has problems at board level, the government doesn't know what to do with its shareholding, and the company is looking at buying into a big deal in Hong Kong with a tycoon who runs circles around everyone who ever deals with him.'

'Is that so? I don't know about any of that, but I know a perfect chart when I see one,' said the high-flying optician.

As history shows, after April 2001, Telstra went downhill all the way. By September 2001, the stock was selling at $4.89. James' optician had to pay a hefty bill of $7 for each Telstra share he held — he was sitting on a loss of around $2 a share.

James hopes for his sake he didn't go 'too big' for Telstra's overpriced shares. (The numbers for Telstra never did add up.) But for innocent online investors like the shortsighted investing optician, the lesson is clear. If you aren't fully informed about a stock — internet or no internet — you're very lucky not to lose money.

Part III
Managed Funds, Bonds and Cash

Glenn Lumsden

'I'm having second thoughts about our choice of fund manager ... I believe that's him clearing Table 7.'

In this part ...

Over the next four chapters, we look at managed funds. If you haven't considered this part of the market before, now is the time to start. At its best, a managed fund allows you to let the experts 'manage' your investments. We also look at the important world of bonds and cash.

Chapter 12

How Do You Do? Getting to Know Fund Managers

A friend of James recently inherited the best part of $20,000. This windfall means she has a large amount of money to invest — for the first time. She said to James: 'I've no idea what to do ... and interest rates are not so great ... you can't just park the money in the bank.'

James told her that the time was clearly right to think about managed funds. Anyone can make money in a strong stock market, but the challenges of making money in tougher markets are often best left to professional fund managers.

'I see what you mean,' she said, 'but I'm not sure about managed funds ... wouldn't that be the easy way out?'

Exactly! And why shouldn't investing be easy? A big problem for managed funds is that many people believe they should manage their investments themselves. In some quarters, handing over to a fund manager is seen almost as 'giving up'.

But James' friend is nearly 50 and she doesn't manage any investments of any kind. More importantly, she's completely uninterested in the markets or investment and James doesn't think she's going to change. (This person is, after all, the same woman who recently told James she had 'bits of superannuation all over the place'!)

Managed funds are an ideal complement to your existing investments or, in some cases, ideal as the primary investment if you don't have the time or interest to get involved in the markets.

Over the last two decades, managed funds have become increasingly popular with Australian investors. Every investor can benefit from knowing the basic elements of the Australian managed-funds industry. In this chapter, we cover the main aspects of the managed-funds sector, including how to select a fund manager and how to keep an eye on the fees a managed fund charges.

Interesting Stuff About the Fund-Management Business

Financial institutions kick off managed funds (or unit trusts) when someone gets the bright idea that putting a block of money into one particular investment makes sense. This block of money may go into one type of share, such as Australian shares that pay 100 per cent franking credits (refer to Chapter 10). The money may go into shares from one geographical region, such as China, or they may invest in a specific area of industrial activity like mining, telecommunications or property.

In Australia, the terms *managed fund* and *unit trust* generally mean the same thing. You should always check if a fund is new or if it has been running for a number of years. As new funds have no track record, you'll be depending totally on the promises of the fund manager. The term *fund manager* can mean either the fund-management company or the actual individual who manages a fund for the fund-management company.

When opening a new fund, a financial institution normally puts in a certain amount of its own money to get the ball rolling. For example, it may put in $10 million for a start, with a target of raising $50 million. The fund is advertised or, more commonly, the financial institution informs the financial adviser industry that the fund is up and running. (Australia has more than 12,000 financial advisers — they can make or break a new fund.)

Assuming the fund manager attracts the desired $50 million from investors to the new fund, he now has a total of $60 million (adding in the $10 million 'put in' by his employer). The fund manager can then issue 60 million $1 units in the fund. If you apply for units in the fund, you will get one unit for each dollar you invest.

For the first few months, the new fund probably won't make you any money, as the team behind the fund has to get their offices set up and consider their first investments. More importantly, these managers have to be paid every week for their efforts. So the fund doesn't make any money until its initial investments start to pay some dividends. However, after the first year, the fund may give you a total return on investments of 10 per cent, or $6 million on the original $60 million raised.

Now, to distribute this money, the fund manager splits the profit equally between every unit-holder. But, rather than giving the money in cash to you and the other investors, he distributes the money in units.

Assuming you put $6,000 in the fund when it advertised its launch a year ago, you therefore kick off with 6,000 units. Assume also that you tell the fund manager you want to reinvest any profits distributed by the fund. With a 10 per cent total return, you're entitled to $600 worth of units. Assume the unit price is still $1 a unit (though in reality the unit price improves if the fund is doing so well); that's 600 units. The fund manager sends you a statement informing you that you now have 6,600 units worth $1 each in the fund.

As soon as the fund is motoring along in top gear, it probably pays all its investors distributions twice a year. In the early stages, the fund has certain advantages: Being relatively small — say, less than $100 million — the fund can move quickly and almost unnoticed in the stock market.

As time passes and the fund gets bigger, it may not have the same success of the early years, unless the original management team can retain their early enthusiasm. More importantly, if the fund gets very large — in excess of $500 million — it becomes less flexible and, like an aircraft carrier compared with a destroyer, the managed fund has lots of power but lacks speed and flexibility.

New funds will always be a speculative investment. If a blue-chip fund has a ten-year track record of making 7 per cent a year, the chances are strong that it will make 7 per cent a year over the next few years as well. With a new fund, you're in uncharted waters, but there's always the promise those waters will yield big rewards. Often, new funds will be trying new investing techniques or even new managers who are trying to prove themselves. If your investment style matches the objective of a new fund, investing in the fund may be the opportunity you're looking for.

Unlike shares, managed funds tend to perform in more reliable patterns — they go up slowly and down slowly.

The Australian fund-management industry is still very much dominated by well-established financial institutions. In general, standards are high. Unlike broking and financial planning, the industry doesn't have a history of scandals. In the United States, however, following the scandal over the collapse of Bernie Madoff's $50 billion Ponzi (or pyramid) scheme, focus has turned to the due diligence performed by fund managers before they invest. Some people who didn't invest directly with Madoff are finding out that their fund managers did, and that they've lost that portion of their fund, and that's causing a lot of people to ask big questions. Time will tell whether this scrutiny will extend to the Australian industry.

Finding Your Comfort Zone

You probably believe that medicine is best left to doctors and that plumbing is best left to plumbers. How about applying the same thinking when managing your investments? The chances are that you don't have the time or the skills to compete with professional money managers in many situations.

We're not saying to hand over your investments lock, stock and barrel to fund managers or even that they always do well (in fact, they have a mixed record). But every beginner investor can benefit from a mixed portfolio in which shares are only one element of a total package of investments in the market, which also includes managed funds, bonds and cash.

You may like to control your investments yourself and keep buying shares until you feel that you have a diversified portfolio. But building a truly diversified portfolio without using managed funds is an impossible task for most people. Even if you have 30 different stocks on the ASX (Australian Securities Exchange), you would still probably have little exposure to the rest of the world. Keep in mind that the Australian economy represents less than 2 per cent of the world's economy. If you visit a foreign city and you only see 2 per cent of the great sights, do you feel like you're giving that city a fair go?

Think of using professional fund managers as giving you a fair go. For the sake of a well-rounded portfolio, shrug off the notion that you can 'do it entirely yourself'. The chances are that, through your superannuation fund, you're already depending (perhaps even for some years) on the ability of professional managers. Don't ignore professional managers when you invest in the markets.

Not what they do but the way that they do it

Who's the best fund manager for you? The answer to this perennial question is: The best manager is the one whose style suits the market best each year.

We know this answer is like one of those irritating answers you always get from the finance industry. But allow us to explain a little further. Professional fund management attracts all types of people. There are cold people and warm people; managers who want to go into the office every day and take a risk, as well as managers who never want to take a risk from one end of the year to the other. You need to get the manager who suits your style. In the end, fund management comes down to two essential styles:

- ✔ **Aggressive:** Aggressive managers take risks and 'push' your money into situations that are likely to make high returns in exchange for high risk. These managers make heaps of money in strong markets and often do very badly — losing money — when markets go sour. If you can weather the ups and downs of these funds, then by all means go with aggressive fund managers.

- ✔ **Value-based:** Value-based styles of fund management occur where managers completely avoid taking risks with your money. They look for investments that are undervalued by the market and believe that true value always shines through in any investment. These managers are less likely to make a loss and they can nearly always make money. The problem is that, when the markets are strong, they make relatively small amounts of money. If you want security, and you can bear losing the chance to make big returns when the bull markets are roaring, then go with value-based managers.

In the good times, the value-based managers look like laggards; in the bad times, aggressive managers look like losers. Because investment markets always run in cycles, everyone gets the chance to look both very good and very unimpressive at regular intervals.

The problem for you, however, is that neither aggressive nor value-based managers ever get the better of each other. Of course, many managers opt for a balanced approach, mixing aggressive and value-based strategies. Although this approach sounds like a smart strategy, it isn't the magic formula — at worst, this style dilutes both the good times and the bad times, and what you can be left with are pretty ordinary returns.

In choosing a fund manager, keep these basic principles of aggressive and value-based investing styles in mind. A huge variety of fund-management styles exist in the market and at least a handful of funds will suit your needs. When picking an individual fund, read the details in the fund prospectus on the fund's objectives closely — the trick is to closely match the objectives of your fund with your ambitions as an investor.

Investing successfully in managed funds is ultimately determined as much by the people behind your fund as by what you choose to invest in. Making money in any market is hard for a hopeless fund manager; a superb fund manager makes positive returns even in the most difficult circumstances.

Of managers and manglers

If you want a picture of the best possible fund manager in Australia, there he is sitting in his plain office. He's there from early morning reading financial data, talking to company managers and, most importantly, making skilful decisions on the future of your money. A brilliant number-cruncher, he can digest an earnings statement in five minutes and can just as easily visit a leather factory and understand the mechanics of an industrial company. This manager is a lone ranger and a long-term investor. He puts his best ideas and contacts towards the success of his fund. He doesn't follow the pack when making investment decisions; he follows his own instincts.

If you want a picture of the worst possible fund manager in Australia, there he is sitting across the corridor. He's just back from a very expensive lunch with three old mates after making a decision to follow the latest trend in the market — together. He's not at all aware of what's really happening in his area of responsibility. But he fully understands that you can survive in a major financial institution by following the herd and upsetting as few people as possible. This worst-of-breed fund manager is focused only on the figures he produces over the next three months — for him, six months is long term.

The million-dollar question is whether these two fund managers are working for the same company. Maybe one guy runs Australian equities; maybe the other runs foreign equities. This is the dilemma of having other people manage your money. You want only the best people but how do you get them?

If you buy the same securities as other people, you will have the same results as other people. It is impossible to produce a superior performance unless you do something different from the majority.

—John Templeton, legendary UK fund manager

Knowing the professional ability of every individual fund manager is not possible, but help is at hand with a range of rating services that keep tags on the major funds through rating systems such as Standard & Poor's and Morningstar (see Chapter 13 for more information on the rating systems).

What's in it for me?

You can't do everything yourself. The resources and contacts held by fund managers are going to be very hard to beat. Before you decide to pit yourself against a professional fund manager, consider some of the advantages of managed funds:

- **Regular distributions:** Shares pay dividends, funds pay distributions. The difference is that funds — especially fixed-interest and balanced funds — nearly always pay distributions on schedule, due to the fact that funds keep reserves for the bad times.

- **Diversification:** For as little as $1,000 you can get started with $1,000 worth of units in a managed fund. However, if you go into the sharemarket directly, armed with $1,000, you won't be able to afford much diversity. In fact, with a minimum limit of about $500 on share purchases, you'll be lucky to hold two shares.

- **Clout:** Having money in a managed fund allows you to take advantage of the power amassed in the market by some of the giants of financial services, such as AMP or Commonwealth Bank.

- **Comfort:** Keeping money in managed funds means the funds are doing a lot of the work for you. At the end of each year, they dispatch all your tax affairs to you in a single letter that you can hand over to the tax office.

- **Information:** Fund managers are 'inside' the market. They hear the news first and can take advantage of their connections by trading on this information.

- **Choice:** Investing in managed funds allows you to invest in almost any sector of commercial activity or any geographical region of the world.

- **Specialisation:** Fund managers can become thoroughly expert in one area, such as mining or technology.

I can do without ...

Almost every problem you encounter with managed funds relates to the fact that other people are managing your money and they want to be paid, regardless of the outcome, for their services. Here are some of the pitfalls of putting your money in managed funds:

- ✔ **The herd instinct:** Fund managers are notorious for moving as a pack. Following the crowd, even though you're making ordinary returns, is always safer when you work for a big investment fund.

- ✔ **Mixed results:** Every area of fund-management activity has a sector index. For example, Australian property funds have a sector index that represents the average performance of all funds in that sector. Amazing though it may seem, considering all the expertise that fund managers have in their favour, many funds don't even match their sector index in their area of activity.

- ✔ **High fees:** Working in financial services leads people to believe they deserve big salaries. Australian managed funds have high fees by international standards.

- ✔ **Absence of power:** A fund has clout but you, the investor, have virtually no power within the fund. As soon as they have your money, fund managers can do more or less what they like with it. The 'constitution' of most funds is vague and allows managers wide powers over your money.

- ✔ **Waste:** Paying someone else to invest money in someone else's business activities means several layers exist between you and the profits. Everybody at every layer wants a slice of the profits.

- ✔ **Insufficient liquidity:** Selling a fund can take days, even up to a month. More importantly, if too many people try to sell at the same time, the fund manager has to sell assets of the fund at bargain prices to raise cash. Most managed funds aren't as liquid as shares.

As a group, lemmings may have a rotten image, but no individual lemming has ever received bad press.

—*Warren Buffett, US investment legend, on fund managers*

One of the worst aspects of managed funds is that you're charged management fees whether the investment is successful or not. Paying fees to someone who has lost you a lot of money always hurts.

Looking at the pros and cons of managed-fund investing, it's plain to see the best fund managers will be able to outweigh the problems relating to the sector. You're probably quite prepared to pay high fees and suffer the restrictions of managed-fund investing if the returns are consistently better than you can manage by directly investing in the market.

Doing your homework

Finding a fund manager means taking your pick from the wide selection of fund-management groups in the market. You can find a fund manager yourself through examining advertisements, reading the financial press, cruising the internet sites of fund managers or talking to friends who already have money with fund managers.

Getting to know the fund-management market requires a bit of reading and selection. A good idea would be to look at the monthly personal investment magazines *AFR Smart Investor* and *Money*, and the quarterly supplement on managed funds issued by the *Australian Financial Review*.

Once you pick a fund manager, the next decision is to pick the fund — or range of funds — that suits you best. Collect an armload of prospectuses from your chosen fund managers and find the funds you want through a process of elimination.

Reading fund-management documents is much easier than it used to be; financial information is much more attractively packaged these days compared with ten years ago. But, remember, all that matters is performance. Past performance may not be a firm indicator of future performance but it's still the best measure of consistency.

How much of your portfolio should be in managed funds? As much as you like. If you love the idea of having your money managed by professionals and you're happy to pay their fees, you could have 100 per cent of your holdings in managed funds. After all, you can find a managed fund to invest in almost anything from cash to property to foreign shares. Legendary US investor and pioneer of index funds, John (Jack) Bogle, has 100 per cent of his money in funds.

However, diversifying your investments is always wise. For example, if you had 100 per cent managed funds, you'd lose the opportunity of directly owning an investment property. Always diversify your assets.

Useful tips for selecting a fund manager

A vicious circle develops: The best fund-management companies attract the best fund managers, and bad fund-management companies can't attract the best people so they don't get any better. In the middle of all this cause and effect, you have to choose the best fund for your purposes. And the slick advertising rolled out from fund managers makes the task even harder for you, the investor.

Here are a few tips for selecting a fund manager:

- ✔ **Don't be fooled by brand names.** Names of wonderful old banks and financial institutions are no guarantee of quality.

- ✔ **Advertising means almost nothing.** The worst fund manager may spend the most on advertising. In fact, this pattern is often the case, but all that really matters is performance.

- ✔ **Don't trust short-term performance.** Being the best fund manager in a certain situation over a short period doesn't mean a fund is any good. The fund's performance may be the result of luck. You need to look for consistent performance over at least three years.

- ✔ **Watch for fees that are higher than average.** Remember, fund managers generally do similar work and should be charging similar fees (see 'Fees: Are you being served?' later in this chapter). The standard rates are 3 per cent for aggressive or active, 2 per cent for balanced, less than 2 per cent for cash funds and around 1 per cent for index funds.

- ✔ **Take note of personnel changes.** If a number of top managers leave a fund-management company, it's very bad news. Funds can survive such exits but surviving successfully is a major challenge.

- ✔ **Don't be misled by smart-sounding concepts.** Just because many companies in one area — such as alternative energy — are doing well doesn't mean a fund manager can open a fund and perform well automatically. In fund management, anyone can have a bright idea, but few have the expertise to turn those ideas into profits for their investors.

Now, having reviewed some of the factors that may influence your decision when selecting a fund manager, we turn to four specifics that we recommend you investigate further. Here they are:

- ✔ **Performance:** How good is the performance? How does it rate against other managers and against other benchmarks such as stock market indices?

- ✔ **Consistency:** How often has the manager turned in good performances? Is there a strong track record?

- ✔ **Fees:** Are the fees charged by this manager reasonable and comfortably within industry standards?
- ✔ **Risk factors:** How much risk does the manager take to achieve your return? Is the volatility score normal for this fund type? (Refer to Chapter 2 for more on managing risk.)

How Managed Is My Fund?

The descriptive hype all sounds so good when you hear it on those television ads: The smartest people in the market can manage your money for you — all you have to do is sit back and take the profits.

If only the system worked so easily. In fact, you have to pick the right fund and make sure the manager is the best for your purposes.

The two most important questions for you to answer in relation to any managed fund are:

- ✔ What sort of returns is the fund actually achieving?
- ✔ What level of fees and charges is the fund imposing?

Keeping track of managed funds is something we look at more closely in Chapter 13. But, before you even start thinking about the returns a fund claims it's achieving, you have to understand what price these guys are charging for the privilege of managing your money.

Fees: Are you being served?

Figuring out the level of fees you're being charged by a managed fund is important, not just to see whether the fund manager is overpaid (don't worry about that ... they're all overpaid!), but to reduce the effect of high fees on your overall return.

For a typical managed fund that's not listed on the stock market (or unlisted, something we discuss further in Chapter 13), you can expect management fees to include:

- ✔ **Up-front fees:** You pay these fees upon joining the fund. The average up-front fee, often called an *entry fee*, is about 3 per cent of the total amount you invest. If the fund doesn't impose an up-front fee, it's called a *no-load* fund.

- ✔ **Annual management fees:** These general administration fees are normally about 1 per cent of the *net asset value* (the price of the fund). More aggressive fund managers often charge performance fees — yes, they take a slice of your profits, but rarely share your losses — on top of the usual management fees.

- ✔ **Trail fees:** Financial planners often receive a trailing commission from the fund manager of 0.25–0.8 per cent a year. Trail fees are, in effect, an ongoing fee for introducing a client.

- ✔ **Exit fees:** Some funds charge a special fee if you withdraw your money inside a set time period. A typical exit fee for a fund that expected you to keep your funds invested for three years is 1 per cent of the amount you withdraw (if you withdraw before the three-year time period ends).

- ✔ **Other fees:** Funds can also add certain fees outside basic administration charges. An example of a typical 'extra' fee is a charge relating to the fund's own costs incurred from legal obligations, like employing a custodian for the fund. (A *custodian* records and stores transaction information.)

At the very least, fees charged by any fund manager should remain within the standards of the industry. The fees should also reflect the level of risk in your fund. The higher the level of risk in your fund, the more fees you can expect to pay.

You can judge whether your fund manager is being reasonable in relation to fees by checking the *management-expense ratio (MER)*. Here's how:

- ✔ The MER is calculated by adding the total of the management expenses and fees of a fund and dividing that figure by the total value of the assets under management. Take the example of a fund with $100 million of investment assets and operating expenses of $1.6 million. Divide $1.6 million by $100 million and you end up with an MER of 1.6. The MER is an indicator of the efficiency of a fund manager.

- ✔ The average MER in the Australian market is around 2 per cent. The lower the MER, the better. Fund managers nearly always advertise their MER rates in their promotional material.

Spreads: Do you know the difference?

Apart from management fees, you also have to contend with the 'spread' in unit prices. Spreads are very easy to understand because two prices exist and whatever way it works, you always get the worst one! When you buy into a unit trust you pay the high price (entry price); when you sell units in a trust you get the low price (exit price).

Strictly speaking, a *spread* is the difference in a price quotation between the bidding price and the asking price. In managed funds, a spread is the gap between the *entry* price a fund manager charges you for units and the *exit* price the fund manager pays for units. So, even though your fund is reporting an entry price of $1 per unit for new investments, the fund manager may only pay you an exit price of 99.4 cents a unit if you sell your units, representing a buy–sell spread of 0.6 per cent.

The buy–sell spread in most unit trusts is normally around 0.5 per cent. Fund managers have a spread because a range of costs are incurred in running any fund. If you cash out a large volume of units, the manager may have to sell stock in the market to collect enough money to pay you out. In turn, the manager has expenses in carrying out these transactions.

More importantly, the spread ensures that investors don't sell out of funds without thinking seriously about the cost involved in taking that decision!

Figuring out the fees, charges and spreads that fund managers are imposing on investors has been one of the big debates in the managed-funds industry. Inside the industry they call it 'transparency', the ability to clearly see all costs faced by the consumer.

Things have improved with the publication of MERs and other ratios in recent years, but, as long as keeping the charges a mystery suits the funds' interests, it's unlikely you'll ever see full 'transparency' from them. The best you can hope for is that your fund is in line or better than industry standards.

Chapter 13

Up Close and Personal with Managed Funds

*A*ssuming you're willing to pay the fees charged by fund managers, the challenge really is choosing a fund or portfolio of funds that suits you.

Choosing a managed fund isn't as hard as choosing shares. Even though you have more managed funds to choose from than stocks — about 10,000 funds (including those for general savings, superannuation and allocated pensions) versus 2,200 stocks — the challenge is actually easier because many funds have similar objectives. Every stock on the stock market is completely individual (ten retailers can operate ten dramatically different businesses). In contrast, managed funds can be almost identical in nature. Every major fund manager has an Australian mining fund or an overseas growth fund, for example. We talk about funds and fund managers in general terms in Chapter 12. In this chapter, we discuss things like fund structure and investments, and the major players, as well as the overall shape of the managed-funds market in Australia.

The big dilemma in choosing a fund is whether you're aiming for income or growth. This is what it means:

- ✔ If you want *income*, then you select cash, property and conservatively managed funds that aim for blue-chip shares and the prospect of regular and predictable income through distributions.
- ✔ If you want *growth* from your funds, then your main aim is to see the unit price head skywards — the distributions aren't as important to you as a consistently increasing unit price.

Accordingly, fund managers are either *value-based* — also known as *conservative* — where the emphasis is on creating income, or they're *aggressive*, where you're offered funds that improve in price fast. Of course, between these two extremes, hundreds of fine distinctions exist where fund managers claim to achieve a 'balance' between income and growth funds. The fact that some of the biggest funds in Australia are *balanced funds* is really no surprise.

Funds employ very smart, sophisticated public relations people to write their websites, brochures and newsletters. Read the numbers, look at the past performance, not the future promises, and make up your own mind about the funds you want. As you read, remember that, in Australia, the terms *managed fund* and *unit trust* generally mean the same thing.

Listed Versus Unlisted Funds

Before a fund-management company releases a fund onto the market, the fund promoters have to choose how to structure it.

The first decision is whether the fund is to be managed as an *unlisted fund*, or trust, where the managers run the fund from inside their own institution, or to list the fund on the stock market. With an unlisted fund, the fund manager is in charge of the market for the units in the fund. Basically, the fund manager 'runs a book' on the units trading in the fund. In contrast, the manager may decide to list the fund on the stock market. This means the stock market itself is the manager of trading in the units.

Putting your trust in unlisted funds

The points to note about unlisted funds (or trusts) are as follows:

- ✔ Unlisted funds are totally managed within the four walls of the finance house that creates and promotes the funds.
- ✔ The fund manager is responsible for the trading in the units of the funds.
- ✔ Unlisted funds are the most popular form of managed funds.
- ✔ The entry fees charged by unlisted funds tend to range between 3 per cent and 5 per cent of the amount invested. Ongoing fees range from 1.4 per cent a year for a fixed-interest fund to 2 per cent for a share fund specialising in high-risk smaller companies. Ongoing fees for wholesale funds you can access via an investment platform such as a wrap account or a master trust are slightly lower (see Chapter 21 for more on fund management in the superannuation arena).

Trying your luck with listed funds

The Australian Securities Exchange (ASX) has a rapidly expanding menu of listed managed investments. Listed investment companies (LICs) and exchange-traded funds (ETFs) provide a very low cost alternative to unlisted managed funds. Other listed funds include Australian real estate investment trusts (A-REITs), infrastructure funds and absolute-return funds (or hedge funds). The points to note about listed funds (or trusts) are as follows:

- ✔ They're available on the stock market.
- ✔ Trading in listed funds is no longer the responsibility of the fund manager. Instead the funds are trading on the stock market like any other public company — except the business of this company is operating a managed fund.

A listed managed fund (or unit trust) doesn't have entry fees; instead, you pay broking fees and ongoing management fees. Ongoing fees for ETFs range from 0.09 per cent to 0.75 per cent of the net asset value of the trust. If you're buying or selling these funds, the main expense is stockbroking fees. Ongoing fees for A-REITs are around 1.7 per cent, whereas fees for infrastructure funds and absolute-return funds are closer to 2 per cent.

Should I have the open-ended or closed-end fund?

After you make your choice between a listed and an unlisted fund, the next decision is whether it's to be an open-ended fund or a closed-end fund.

✔ An *open-ended* fund means that the fund is always capable of expanding the number of units on issue. As the fund grows, the fund manager continually issues more units. An open-ended fund is the most common structure for managed funds.

✔ In a *closed-end* fund, the fund manager issues a set number of units and then 'closes' the fund. No more units are ever issued and the fund has a limited lifespan, typically of five years.

Choosing from the Fund Menu

When you research what a managed fund invests in, you're confronted by many choices, though in fairly predictable categories, such as foreign shares or commercial property. During the last few decades, fund managers have tended to concentrate their fund-management products in one of the following categories:

✔ **Multi-sector or balanced:** The classic smorgasbord approach, where a fund manager promises to invest in just about everything under the sun, including shares, bonds, other funds, currencies, derivatives, property, fixed interest and cash.

✔ **Diversified shares:** The fund restricts itself to investing in public companies through investment in stock markets.

✔ **Industrial shares:** The manager only invests in the stock market's biggest single sector — industrial shares.

✔ **Small caps (shares in smaller companies):** In Australia, small companies have a market capitalisation of less than $100 million. In major overseas markets like the United States, a small cap has a market capitalisation of less than $2 billion.

✔ **Resources:** One of the favourites of Australian fund managers due to our huge mining sector and the level of expertise local fund managers possess in the resources industry.

✔ **Listed property:** The fund invests primarily (85 per cent or more) in listed property trusts or stocks on the ASX.

✔ **Diversified property:** The fund invests in any type of property investment.

Property trusts specialise in investment property and are favoured by people who want to invest in property but don't want the hassle of negotiating with real estate agents and lawyers. We give a full discussion of both listed and unlisted property trusts in Chapter 19.

Outside these commonly available options within managed funds, you can also use fund managers to reduce or increase your exposure to risk in very specific ways. In terms of reducing your risk within markets, the main option is *index funds*, where managers 'track' (or copy and reproduce the performance of) an index. If you're seeking high returns and you're ready to take higher risk, then you have the option of *commodity funds*, which invest in futures contracts for everything from iron ore to agricultural products such as wheat and wool, or *hedge funds* (see the section 'High-rolling with hedge funds' later in this chapter).

Playing it safe with index funds

Working on the notion that key stock market indices beat the average returns of many fund managers over an extended period, index funds simply create a fund to precisely reflect any index, such as the *All Ordinaries Accumulation Index*, which measures price increases as well as dividends, treating all dividends as if they're reinvested. The fund manager creates a computer program that exactly matches the composition of the index and then follows every move in the index.

If a company leaves the index, the manager sells its shares in that company. If a new company graduates into the index, the manager buys shares in that company — but only enough to exactly match the share of the index controlled by the company. As the index moves up or down, the returns of the fund follow very closely within fractions of 1 per cent.

Expecting a fund to beat the market average all the time is asking the impossible. Fund managers say they expect to out-perform the average, but they can't all achieve that aim. After all, the average is what the combined returns of the bulk of fund managers represent! Index funds seek to take advantage of this situation.

A traditional index like the All Ordinaries Accumulation Index generally posts a reliable return — for example, although it was down 15.5 per cent in the year to June 2008, in the middle of the global market meltdown, the ten-year average annual return to that date was 11.52 per cent. An All Ordinaries Accumulation Index fund can match that return accurately over the same period.

Knowing that a fund manager can devise a computer program that gives you a return as good as the index is useful, but shouldn't any half-decent manager be able to do that anyway? And don't forget the return of an index like the All Ords includes all the below-average companies among the 500 stocks carried in the index.

Index funds only match an index that is an 'average' of good and bad returns. When you choose to buy an index fund you're choosing to include bad returns from companies you wouldn't invest in otherwise.

At their worst, index funds offer mediocrity. More importantly, when an index actually goes down, you find yourself paying someone to run a computer program that bolts your investment to a falling index.

A US company called Vanguard Investments pioneered index funds in Australia, but today most major financial institutions offer an index fund. The fees of index funds are lower than ordinary funds — as they should be, for running a computer program!

The best way for you to consider incorporating index funds into your portfolio is as a stabiliser, in the same way that an investment in bonds or fixed-interest securities can help underpin your overall returns. Index funds are available in any investment category from shares to cash, and the more reliant you become on index funds, the closer your overall return will be to the overall performance of the market. Ultimately, this approach means you'll do as well or as badly as the average investor will in an average year. The choice is yours.

High-rolling with hedge funds

You've probably read about hedge funds — those mysterious funds that use complex financial techniques to 'attack' (or try to profit from) the mis-pricing of financial assets. *Hedge funds* are managed funds that trade, speculate and invest in derivatives, like options and futures, or commodities, currencies, shares or any other investment assets.

Hedge funds, or *absolute-return funds*, as they are also known, aim to make high returns in exchange for high risks. The people behind hedge funds are usually international fund managers who trade in any market where they think a profit is possible. Hedge funds can profit from both rising and falling markets, using strategies such as *short selling*, where a fund manager sells securities it doesn't own in the expectation of buying the securities back after the price falls.

Investing in a hedge fund offers access to the 'sharper' end of investment markets. Hedge funds trade when a special situation appears in the market, such as when a currency is clearly trading too high or too low. They may also invest in a company that looks likely to have a major rebound in price as soon as a certain objective is achieved.

During the global credit crisis of 2007–08, hedge funds exacerbated the steep decline in sharemarkets by short-selling the shares of vulnerable companies with high levels of debt. Governments in many developed countries, including Australia, stepped in to stabilise markets by placing a temporary halt on short selling. In the early days you had to have a lot of money — at least $50,000 — to get involved in hedge funds, but that entry level has dropped dramatically and hedge funds are now available for a minimum entry of $5,000. Listed hedge funds have no minimum investment amount. Fees are often high, with ongoing management fees of 1–2 per cent and performance fees of up to 20 per cent.

Investing in hedge funds is risky but the returns can be very strong. In a good year, returns can be well in excess of 20 per cent. In a bad year, such as the 12 months to June 2008, most hedge funds reported a negative return, despite their aim to profit from all market conditions. Hedge funds are also quite *illiquid* — hard to get your money out of quickly. Prices for hedge funds are often only on display from the hedge fund managers once a month, and selling units can take more than two months.

Hedge funds are becoming much more popular with superannuation funds, which are now putting more money into this type of investment. But, as more money chases high returns in this very specialised market, the danger of a disaster is ever present. Big dramas have already rocked the hedge fund market — including the spectacular failure of celebrated US hedge fund Long Term Capital Management in 1998 and the collapse of several absolute-return funds in Australia during the credit crunch of 2008. If you invest in these funds, you're taking maximum risk.

Going Global with Funds

Hunting for the highest possible returns, some fund managers believe in the maxim, 'There's always money being made somewhere.' With new technology and global stock markets, comes the possibility of buying shares almost anywhere.

Despite the huge power of the US stock market — about 27 times bigger than the Australian market — all stock markets don't move the same way on the same cycle.

Some fund managers also like betting that a certain region at a certain time is going to provide investments with exceptional returns. Sometimes they're correct; sometimes they're wrong. Here are some examples of good and bad calls:

- **Good call (Asia in the late 1980s):** The South-East Asian economies absolutely roared ahead between 1985 and 1990.

- **Good call (Western Europe 1997–2000):** Many fund managers believed the US technology-led boom in the mid-1990s would be repeated a few years later in Europe. They were right.

- **Good call (emerging markets in 2006–08):** Fast-growing economies in Asia and South America opened up to a wider range of investors. In 2007, China became the world's second-largest economy and India the fourth-largest. Fund managers cashed in on the boom with funds that invested in a range of developing economies, single-market China funds and funds targeting the BRIC economies of Brazil, Russia, India and China.

- **Bad call (Eastern Europe in the early 1990s):** The former Soviet bloc countries held the promise of strong returns if they could get up to speed with Western Europe. This never really happened.

- **Bad call (Japan 1999–2001):** Fund managers believed a succession of new Japanese governments that said they were going to kick-start the world's second-biggest market back to life. They were wrong.

A fund that invests in a geographical region because the fund manager believes the region itself is the key to exceptional returns is a very good example of an aggressive style. Investing for this reason is also a very good example of *top-down* investing. Basically the fund manager is taking a helicopter view and working on the basis that, if the economy is roaring ahead, then investments in the stock market are going to move in tandem.

Among the main regional or international choices you can come across in the managed-funds markets are the following classifications:

- **International:** These funds typically invest in the world's best-known companies, wherever they're based.

- **Emerging markets:** Fund managers in this area are risk-takers. They look for up-and-coming companies in developing markets overseas, like Asia, South America or Eastern Europe. The funds can be very volatile and very profitable.

- **Europe:** The European markets offer a very broad range of investing options — second only to the United States. They also run on a different cycle to the United States, so they can be popular with investors looking to diversify their portfolios.

- ✔ **Japan:** The world's second-biggest stock market made fortunes for investors in the 1980s. Since then, fund managers continue to bank on a rebound in this market but conditions have been very disappointing since the early 1990s.

- ✔ **United States:** Even though the United States is the world's biggest stock market, relatively few funds specialise in investing there. This is probably because most 'international' funds already have more than 50 per cent of their investments in the United States.

- ✔ **South-East Asia:** The boom sector for decades, the Asian markets are very diversified and, more importantly, are very hard to access as an individual investor. As a result, managed funds are probably always likely to be popular for this market.

The Big Guns in Fund Management

Controlling most of the action in the Australian investment markets are fund managers. They're the people behind the bulk of shares traded on the stock market. They're the people behind the trading in options and futures. Increasingly, fund managers own the building you work in and sometimes the building you live in!

There are about 10,000 managed funds to choose from, but don't be fooled into thinking you have a truly diverse range of choices. Looking closer, you'll see the choice of funds is large but the number of fund-management companies available to you is relatively small. In addition, many funds are issued in slightly different forms for different types of investors and investment vehicles, such as retail investors, wholesale investors, retirees and superannuation funds. And, more importantly, many funds launched in this market are too small to operate efficiently.

Among the most popular (though not necessarily the best) names in the fund-management industry at present (in alphabetical order) are:

- ✔ AMP (formerly the Australian Mutual Provident Society)
- ✔ AXA Asia Pacific (formerly National Mutual Life, now owned by AXA of France)
- ✔ BT (formerly Bankers Trust, now owned by Westpac)
- ✔ Colonial First State (formerly Colonial Mutual Life, now a subsidiary of Commonwealth Bank)
- ✔ ING/ANZ (a joint venture of ING of Holland and ANZ Bank)

 ✔ Macquarie (Australia's only ASX-listed investment bank)

 ✔ MLC (a subsidiary of National Australia Bank)

 ✔ Perpetual (an Australian-owned, ASX-listed finance house)

Other fund managers can make a big impact as specialists in certain areas of fund management. Among the biggest (though, again, not necessarily the best) names are:

 ✔ APN (property)

 ✔ Australian Ethical (ethical funds)

 ✔ BlackRock (multi-sector funds)

 ✔ Goldman Sachs JBWere (emerging companies)

 ✔ Hunter Hall (ethical funds)

 ✔ IOOF (balanced funds)

 ✔ J.P. Morgan/Ord Minnett (structured products, emerging markets)

 ✔ Macquarie (cash-management and infrastructure funds, structured products)

 ✔ Platinum (international shares)

 ✔ Vanguard (index funds)

You see in these two lists the household names of Australian finance, although, in the last decade or so, many of these grand names have become owned by overseas institutions.

Because of the way the system works, you hear the big names more often than the smaller players, even if some of those players are excellent in their field. For example, in the three years to June 2008, the SG20 Australian shares fund managed by SG Hiscock & Co returned an average of 15.39 per cent a year, compared with the overall market return of 3.93 per cent. But the SG Hiscock fund, a fraction of the size of its rivals, doesn't advertise heavily. Although you see the leading names in fund management everywhere in the media, that exposure is no guarantee of performance.

Table 13-1 shows the assets of the biggest fund-management companies in Australia as at 31 December 2008.

Table 13-1	Market Leaders in Funds Management	
Company	**Assets under Management ($ billion)**	**Market Share (%)**
1. Commonwealth/Colonial	94.27	11.1
2. Macquarie Bank	68.38	8.1
3. AMP	59.38	7.0
4. ING/ANZ	47.58	5.6
5. State Street Global Advisors	43.17	5.1
6. Vanguard Investments	43.14	5.1
7. AXA	40.37	4.8
8. BT/Westpac	34.56	4.1
9. Barclays Global Investors	28.30	3.3
10. Perpetual	23.44	2.8
Top Ten Total	482.58	56.8
Industry Total	849.67	100.0

Note: Calculations may be affected slightly due to rounding.
Source: © Morningstar Australia, December 2008.

No firm link exists between the top funds in terms of size of total assets and the top funds in terms of investment performance.

If you look at the figures for all funds over a ten-year period, the average annual return is 18 per cent, and a pattern emerges — the big funds and the smaller boutique funds are equally as likely to be near the top, and the bottom, of the pile.

Strangely enough, when you talk to representatives of any of these big funds, they claim to beat the market average. But the figures tell a different story.

To get better-than-average returns from your fund-management investments you either have to concentrate on the riskier investments offered inside the big funds or hunt outside the top ten managers for boutique managers who are doing things differently.

Getting to know boutique fund managers takes time. The managers in these outfits tend to have been exceptionally successful in the bigger companies like Perpetual or BT and then struck out to build their own empires. By closely studying the form in the funds-management industry, you can come to know these smaller companies, who rarely advertise.

Be Ready to Jump Ship

Performing to investor expectations is the main target of any fund manager. Springing up over the last few years are a string of agencies to help investors, and the fund managers themselves, observe how they're performing.

As an individual investor, keeping track of the relative performance of your fund by matching it against others at any time is an important part of the keeping-watch process. Although no benchmark system for doing this exercise exists, we give you some useful pointers to guide the way.

Among the easiest systems to understand are the star-rating systems that you can find wherever managed-fund prices get published. The star system weighs up a range of performance indicators for most of the bigger managed funds.

The Standard & Poor's (www.standardandpoors.com) star-rating system or the Morningstar system carried in the *Australian Financial Review* (weekend edition) and *AFR Smart Investor* magazine are two of the most popular systems. Both these systems rate managed funds from five stars (the highest rating) down to one star (poor quality). Like many other in-house benchmarks in financial services, the star system can tell you important information about a fund.

Unlike shares, the managed-fund sector is seen as boring by the financial media. As a result, very important developments like personnel changes at funds can go unreported.

If a fund isn't rated, it doesn't mean the fund is in trouble: Remember that not every fund is monitored by the rating agencies.

A fund with a healthy star rating warrants attention — continually. Although a fund may be awarded five stars the day you buy it, two years later it might only rate one star. You can't say you weren't warned.

The best way to analyse a fund's performance is to check its past performance in the managed-fund tables published in all the daily papers and in specialist investment magazines. (To figure out how to read managed-fund tables refer to Chapter 9.) A very useful publication for tracking managed funds is the quarterly performance review published by the *Australian Financial Review*.

If you keep a close eye on the performance of your funds through publications like this and rating systems, you'll be able to see whether a fund is losing its way. Star ratings for funds change all the time, so you need to keep a close eye on the ratings tables. Most fund prices are now available at least twice a week in the press and every day on the internet.

When everything goes wrong: The BT story

Keeping a close eye on the performance of your fund and on the overall health of your fund manager is essential. In any market, financial institutions tend to have periods when they're stronger or weaker. An insurance company can be 100 years old but, during that century, it may endure one or two dreadful periods when it nearly loses its reputation.

Bankers Trust Australia (BT) became one of the top financial institutions in Australia during the mid-1980s. The company could do no wrong, and it hit the jackpot in 1987, when it got many of its investors out of the stock market before the October 1987 stock market crash.

Over the next decade, the top team at BT became some of the most influential executives in Australian financial services and the financial adviser community in Australia backed BT to the hilt.

By the mid-1990s, BT was a household name in Australia and its only serious rivals as fund managers were long-time arch-rival AMP and the up-and-coming Colonial Group (which is now part of the Commonwealth Bank).

However, around this time, things began to go very wrong at BT. A number of key figures left the company (including Kerr Neilson, who formed the Platinum fund-management group) and BT's overall performance lost some of its gloss. By the late 1990s, BT's fund performance was mixed. It had good results in many areas but a few embarrassments, such as poorly performing funds specialising in property and Asian sharemarkets.

In 1998, the company was put up for sale by its US owners and it was sold to US company the Principal Group of Des Moines, Iowa. Unfortunately, the lengthy sale process brought out some of the worst aspects of BT. Against a background of mixed returns, the local investment community was treated to details about huge salaries at BT and a management that seemed to have lost touch with realities in the market.

By 2000, the rot had seriously set in at BT. The group started to show very poor returns in many areas. Many senior managers left the company. BT came joint last (with Macquarie Bank) among the top ten fund managers in terms of its overall performance in the five years to 2001. Worse still, the group suffered the indignity of rating as the single worst fund manager in the year to June 2001, when it recorded overall returns of −0.2 per cent — a return that is seen as unforgivable by many investors, when the majority of funds performed profitably.

The following year, in 2002, BT was bought by Westpac and began its long climb back into favour. By 2008, BT, which manages Westpac's wealth-management arm, handled one in three investment dollars in Australia, mostly through its superannuation and pension products.

Steering Clear of the Duds

The worst funds are those that are launched by people who don't have expertise in the fund's supposed area of specialisation. Fund managers often launch funds not because they're good at managing investments in a certain area but because the investing public is looking for funds in this category.

At present, fund managers who know nothing, or very little, are opening hedge funds and emerging-market funds. In 2000, the same people were launching technology funds.

Fund managers that have no track record are always a risky investment. Overseas investment houses regularly open funds in Australia with a lot of fanfare, but they can rarely keep the most talented people. Soon, the funds are no longer run by the people who started them and things can go wrong very quickly from that point on. Very small funds — with less than $10 million under management — can also be undependable because they have no clout in the market. Once again, performance is everything in managed funds — you have to watch the prices of your fund against its competition and check its star ratings (refer to the preceding section).

Chapter 14

Buying, Selling and Ditching Managed Funds

*Y*ou want to make as much money as possible, as soon as possible and for as little risk as possible. Who doesn't? But when you choose managed funds, you make a pact with your fund manager — for better or worse — as you hand the management of your money to a third party. You put your cards on the table and you commit for the long term.

Somewhere in every fund's management *prospectus* (the document that details what's on offer from the fund manager) is a discreet warning — the fund manager says the fund is 'best suited to investors with at least a five-year investment timeframe'.

Managed funds are not a business for daytraders; they don't move as quickly as shares. A managed fund specialising in mining stocks never increases or decreases in price as fast as an individual mining stock, for a range of reasons — primarily because the fund manager has administration costs and regulations that slow things down.

Investing in managed funds is all about picking the right fund with the right fund manager and sticking with your strategy. Unless a fund is in deep trouble, and performing well below its peers, the five-year timetable makes sense.

As the Australian funds-management scene grows larger, the opportunity for specialisation in managed funds is increasing all the time. In recent years, a string of funds dedicated to Chinese stocks or to global property have sprung up in the market.

Managed funds are also becoming more complex, with hedge funds and private-equity funds that were once only on offer to the wealthiest individuals now on the investment menu of your local superannuation fund. Many of these so-called 'sophisticated' financial products were at the eye of the financial storm that engulfed Australia and the rest of the developed world in 2008. In fact, some of these funds were so 'sophisticated' that not even their creators and marketers understood them. The lesson for investors was, as always, if you don't understand it, then don't put your money in it.

In this chapter, we guide you through buying, selling and switching funds, including keeping an eye on fees and reinvesting your profits. We also take a look at new trends coming down the line in the managed-funds market.

Keeping Those Pesky Fees under Control

Dealing in managed funds means paying a variety of fees. The more funds you invest in, the more fees you pay. And, more importantly, if you continually switch between funds you can never get the full benefits of the fees you hand over to any one manager. (We discuss the usual elements that make up management fees in Chapter 12.)

Fees can make a big difference to the returns you put in your pocket, especially at times of low growth — when returns are low, you get less value from the fees you pay. We don't expect to see many returns from fund managers in excess of 10 per cent for the next few years, following the turmoil of the 2007–08 global financial crisis.

Think of the effect of fees on your annual return in this way: Assuming your total entry fees on a $10,000 investment are at least 4 per cent, then that means a $400 deduction from your investment. During the years prior to 2007, the fund may easily have returned 10 per cent a year, which means a return of $1,000. But things have changed: Assume again you put $10,000 in a fund and this time your fees are still 4 per cent, or $400, but the fund posts a negative return of –10 per cent, a fairly typical result in 2008, which means you lost $1,000.

Compare the two scenarios — when you make 10 per cent, a $400 fee on a $1,000 return appears pretty good. When you lose money, a $400 fee on a loss of $1,000 adds insult to injury. Your net return (inclusive of fees) drops from $600 ($1,000 minus $400) to –$1,400 (a $1,000 loss and an additional slug of $400 for the fee).

Prospectus Points to Ponder

As soon as you decide which fund manager you want to deal with and the type of fund that best suits your requirements (refer to Chapters 12 and 13 for more information), you can plunge ahead and make a purchase.

To purchase units in the fund you want, get your hands on a *prospectus*, which is the legal document where the fund manager sets out the range of funds on offer and the terms of their sale. Any fund manager will mail a prospectus to you for free. Alternatively, you can often download a prospectus from the fund manager's website.

When you get a prospectus, make sure you have the most up-to-date version. The 'use-by date' of the offer is on the cover. A prospectus has a relatively short shelf life of about 12 months.

A prospectus can be a daunting document, due to the complexity of some managed funds. Fund managers are making an effort to simplify the format, often using one prospectus for all their funds, but wading through the detail is still a chore.

What a prospectus can and can't tell you

The prospectus can tell you just about everything you need to know about a fund, except future performance — such a pity, as fortune telling could make wealth creation so much easier! Ensure you find out about the following:

- ✔ **Details of funds:** What funds are on offer from the manager? Is there a fund that suits your purposes? What are the fees?

- ✔ **Interests of each fund:** Includes key investments of an individual fund, some of its biggest stock holdings and the amount the fund holds in cash.

- ✔ **Aim of the fund:** What is the stated objective of the fund? Does this objective reconcile with your objectives?

- ✔ **Weightings of the fund:** The *weightings* of a fund show where the investments are spread around. If the fund is 'weighted 70 per cent' into industrial shares, this means the manager keeps about 70 per cent of the fund's investments in industrial shares.

- ✔ **Risks:** The prospectus must set out the risks involved in the fund and its underlying investments.

Checking on performance and fees

The prospectus is the best piece of information you can get from your fund manager on any particular fund. After you read a prospectus, you can fill out the form on the back pages and apply for the number of units that suits you. But, before you sign up, look for the following:

- **Previous performance record:** Look for the track record of the fund, which shows the annual return of the fund in percentage terms over the previous five years (where possible).

- **Age of the fund:** When did the fund commence trading? You're often safer with funds that have an established track record.

- **Size of the fund:** A fund that has less than $50 million on the books is small and has more risk due to its lack of scale.

- **Breakdown of performance:** A good fund prospectus also breaks up the annual return into two component parts — income and growth. In a *balanced* fund, the income and growth components are about the same. In an *income-based* fund, the income component dominates; in a *growth* fund, the growth component dominates. Some fund managers now also show returns *net of fees* (after fees have been extracted).

- **Entry fee:** Expect to pay an entry fee of up to 4 per cent for your managed funds, but the amount you pay will depend on how you choose to invest. Most online brokers rebate all or most of the entry fee. If you invest through a financial planner, you may also be able to negotiate a discount, or a rebate in the form of additional units in the fund, depending how much money you have invested with the financial-planning firm.

- **MER (management-expense ratio):** The industry standard MER is about 2 per cent. Funds that have little risk (for example, cash and fixed-interest funds) usually have a lower MER — around 1.5 per cent. (Refer to the section on fees in Chapter 12 for more information on a fund's MER.)

Apart from the explicit fees that your fund manager may charge, a built-in charge is the gap or 'spread' between the buy price of the fund and the sell price of the fund. The *spread* is the difference between the price at which the fund manager will sell you units — the sell price — and the price at which the fund manager will buy units from you — the buy price. The sell price is always higher than the buy price and the gap between the two prices is called the *buy–sell spread*. (Refer to Chapter 12 for a section on spreads.)

'Fee-free' funds: Know them for what they are

As you know, free lunches are anything but 'free' and, similarly, the concept of fee-free managed funds is also a furphy.

Trying to lure investors any way they can, fund managers are trying all sorts of promotional stunts to get people to hand over their money. One of the most common offers is a *no-load*, or *nil-entry-fee, fund* where no fee is charged.

Instead, you're charged more in terms of ongoing fees. A manager in this situation may also charge an *exit fee* (ouch!), which is, in effect, a fine for allowing you to leave.

The fee structure shows in the management-expense ratio (MER) for your fund. In general,

a no-load fund has an MER of around 2.5 per cent, against 2 per cent for most other funds.

Where exit fees are also charged, the system normally works on a sliding scale. Exit fees generally apply if you take money out of a no-load fund within three years. For example, the exit fee can be 2 per cent of your 'withdrawn amount' if you take money out in the first year, 1.5 per cent in the second year and 1 per cent in the third year.

Our advice on these funds is not to bother with them unless you're convinced the returns compensate the high fees.

Deciding It's Time to Sell

Investing in managed funds means sticking with your choice. If you pick the right fund at the start, hopefully selling out isn't going to be necessary for many years. But you do have to consider selling your units in a fund if the fund isn't performing or if you find your investment style needs to change.

Unlike brokers, fund managers never, ever say 'sell' because the most likely effect on them is that you leave their account completely. Funds are great if you keep yourself informed not just about the fund, but about the health of the fund-management company you're in. (To monitor your fund against the rest of the industry to see if you're ready to jump ship refer to Chapter 13.)

Buying and selling funds regularly is a worse mistake than trading shares too often, because the fees you pay on funds are much higher than any broking fees you incur on shares.

If you're selling a fund, here are the things to watch for:

- ✔ **Distribution deadline:** Check the date of the next distribution from the fund. If the deadline is coming up within a few weeks, try to hold on — for the money. Distributions are normally only twice a year, which means selling your fund and missing the distributions is a needless waste of your potential return. This caution is relevant only for *unlisted funds* (funds that aren't listed on the stock market). The price of *listed funds* (funds that are on the stock market) will already have these factors built into the price and the risk of losing money on your transaction is greatly reduced.

- ✔ **Exit fees:** Make sure you're aware of any exit fees the fund manager may include. Contact the fund manager and find out about the fee if you're concerned.

- ✔ **Desperation:** Don't sell because the market is low — if the market is tough, every fund manager is doing it tough. Only sell if your fund manager is clearly not performing as well as can be expected.

- ✔ **Strategy:** Make sure you have something else in mind for the money you raise from selling your fund. Until now, someone else has been managing that money; if you sell, the responsibility is in your hands.

Switching from Fund to Fund

Almost all fund managers allow you to switch between their range of funds for 'free'. This offer is all very well but, of course, nothing is free in the investment markets and fund switching has a distinct cost.

When you switch out of one fund and move to another, the fund manager treats your exit from the first fund as a *redemption* (or sale of your units). The money you raise is then treated as fresh money going into the fund you wish to switch to. As a result, you get the exit price (always lower) for the units you sell and the entry price (always higher) for the units you buy. You're stuck with a considerable expense in this exercise and you must recover that expense before your investments are back to where you started.

You may get an extra surprise, too. A capital gains tax (CGT) liability may apply when you switch funds (refer to Chapters 3 and 5 for more on tax). Because the fund manager deals with the switch as an exercise where you're selling units and buying units, then the tax office wants to see tax paid on any gains you make on your 'sale'.

Switching funds is a welcome facility but make sure you understand that it isn't free. When making a switch, ask yourself, 'Is the time right to get out of this fund-management company altogether?' After all, expecting a good fund-management company to match your investor expectations is a reasonable ask, whatever fund you choose to be in.

Reinvesting What You've Made

Reinvesting your distributions from a fund is a good idea because you're efficiently using what can be a small amount of money and most funds don't charge fees to reinvest the money back into the fund.

Dividend-reinvestment plans (DRPs) are becoming quite rare in the sharemarket because companies find them too expensive to administer. However, the schemes are standard in the funds-management industry — good news for you, the early investor.

When you buy into a managed fund, you fill out a sale document (or prospectus) giving the basic details of how many units you wish to buy. You also need to indicate if you wish to receive the dividends paid by the fund, or the fund *distributions*, in cash or in the form of units reinvested in the fund. Our advice is to go for the reinvestment option.

Our general rule on funds is that, if they're good enough to invest in, they're good enough to reinvest in.

Buy right . . . hold tight.

—*John (Jack) Bogle, investor and founder of Vanguard Investments*

Following Fashion: New Trends in Managed-Fund Investing

Australians have seen an explosion in the diversity of managed funds available over the past decade. In fact, Australia has more funds per head of population than does the US, the home of the managed-funds industry.

The market is now at a point where you can find a fund — if not an entire sector — that deals with every imaginable form of investment. Worried about global warming and dwindling supplies of potable water?

Sick of paying tolls to drive around the city? Get even, and invest in an infrastructure fund specialising in toll roads. Want to diversify your property investments? Look for a property trust that invests in car parks or aged-care accommodation. Now that's what you call a diversified market.

The Australian market is quickly becoming as diversified as any market in the world, and investors are clearly interested in diversifying their investments within the managed-funds sector. Here are some of the key trends emerging in managed funds:

- **Investing overseas:** Until very recently, buying units in overseas-based funds was very difficult. You had to be very rich and well connected to get into this market. These days, investors are willing to invest overseas primarily through international funds. In the space of a few years, these funds have become very diversified. They offer everything from sector-specific funds, such as funds devoted only to water-related stocks, or global funds devoted to one stream of activity, such as international ethical funds.

- **Foreign-registered trusts:** These trusts are overseas-based funds that you can buy inside Australia. Some of the hedge funds (refer to Chapter 13) are in this category. These 'offshore' funds offer a replica of their core products to Australian investors, tailored to Australian taxation and regulatory requirements.

- **No-load funds:** Funds that don't charge an entry fee have proliferated in recent years as online brokers and investment websites offer fee-free access to a wide range of managed funds to their subscribers. (However, check our caution in the sidebar '"Fee-free" funds: Know them for what they are' earlier in this chapter.)

- **Index funds:** These funds, which mirror certain stock indices (refer to Chapter 13 for details) are also set to become more popular because they offer an alternative investment principle and they have low fees.

- **Ethical funds:** Funds that avoid investing in nasty stuff like tobacco or gambling, and actively seek out sustainable companies, are becoming more popular. (See the sidebar 'Ethical funds: Green, greener, greenest'.) These funds have done surprisingly well in recent times.

- **Private-equity funds:** These funds invest in companies in their early years or in the lead-up to a stock market float. The principle behind all these funds is that investing in early-stage companies can be risky but very rewarding. Superannuation funds have been among the most enthusiastic investors in private equity in recent years. If the investment markets remain subdued in the coming years, these funds are unlikely to be as popular and some of them may close down.

Ethical funds: Green, greener, greenest

Ethical investment has come in from the cold, thanks to global warming and a period of sizzling returns. Ten years ago, ethical investment was regarded as a fringe sector for tofu-eating environmentalists, but Al Gore put an end to all that. The tipping point for ethical funds — or socially responsible investment (SRI) funds, as they are more often called these days — came in 2007, when Al Gore's film, *An Inconvenient Truth*, pushed the environment to the top of the national agenda. Australia's worst drought in 100 years, the drying up of the Murray–Darling river system, and the political furore over a proposed pulp mill in Tasmania's Tamar Valley did the rest.

In 2007, ethical funds grew at three times the rate of mainstream funds in terms of their funds under management. The acceptance of ethical funds in Australia followed the trend in Europe, where climate change and demand for action on renewable energy had already filtered through to the investment industry. That year was also when institutional investors began to integrate environmental, social and governance issues into their stock selection and their voting behaviour at annual general meetings of the companies they invest in.

Ethical investment is a broad church, so it's important to understand what you're investing in. Some funds are greener, and holier, than others:

- **Light green funds** screen out companies that are harmful to people, animals or the environment. They're sometimes called a *negative screen*, or a 'do-no-harm' approach to stock selection. Hunter Hall is the best-known example of the light green approach.

- **Dark green funds** seek out companies that are actively doing good. This approach is called *positive screening*. A typical investment may be medical research companies such as bionic ear manufacturer Cochlear and blood serum group CSL — companies that aim to improve health and wellbeing. Australian Ethical is Australia's best-known dark green fund.

- **Best-of-sector funds** invest in the most socially responsible companies in each market sector, regardless of what that sector is. Dark green investors criticise best-of-sector funds for including companies that deal in alcohol, tobacco, gambling or uranium on the grounds that they're the best of a bad lot. Best-of-sector funds argue that they encourage sinners to adopt more saintly behaviour, and there is evidence that big mining companies such as BHP Billiton are taking note and beginning to clean up their act. BT offers best-of-sector funds and funds that combine both positive and negative screens, screening out the nasties as well as screening for the goodies, and AMP also sits in the middle of the ethical range.

(continued)

(continued)

In recent years, the big ethical funds have added global equity funds to their product range. Another trend is the embrace of themed funds by heavyweight financial institutions better known for their ruthless pursuit of profit than for doing good. J.P. Morgan, Macquarie Bank and Credit Suisse are among the heavy hitters offering themed investment funds in renewable energy and water to Australian investors.

If you're a member of a superannuation fund, then the chances are that your fund includes ethical investment managers as part of its investment menu. One super fund, Christian Super, aims to invest in accordance with biblical principles, and offers a 100 per cent ethical investment option as its default option. Now that's really taking a holier-than-thou stand!

Ethical investment has come of age in the last ten years, but this has as much to do with the colour of money as the greening of the investment community. In the year to June 2008, according to figures compiled by *Ethical Investor* magazine, ethical Australian share funds out-performed similar mainstream funds over three- and five-year periods, returning 15.85 per cent a year over the previous five years compared with 14.68 per cent for mainstream funds. Ethical global share funds out-performed their mainstream rivals over one-, three- and five-year periods by an even bigger margin, due largely to the dominance of Hunter Hall, which has an excellent track record in the global shares sector.

Chapter 15

Elegant Bonds and Vulgar Cash

- -

In This Chapter

▶ Investing in bonds (and we don't mean underwear)

▶ Understanding how bonds work

▶ Distinguishing between types of bonds

▶ Delving into bond funds

▶ Looking at bonds and interest rates

▶ Reviewing your cash-management options

- -

*T*he bond markets — sometimes called the fixed-interest markets — are something of a byword for all that is boring and bland in financial markets. Once upon a time, bond traders were often genteel chaps who couldn't be expected to get a job anywhere else.

Today, the bond markets still lack the colour of the stock markets and you may even see the occasional genteel type hiding behind a computer screen. But don't let that stop you getting an understanding of the bond market because, after cash (and excluding property, which is much less liquid), bonds are the safest place you can put your money. Some years bonds surprise everyone. In 2008, a year when the global financial crisis turned the financial markets on their heads, Australian bonds were the best performing asset class for the first time since 1992!

> *Gentlemen prefer bonds.*
>
> —*Andrew Mellon, US financier*

A balanced investment portfolio includes cash and bonds. To balance your portfolio, put between 20 per cent and 40 per cent of your funds in bonds and cash.

Of course, if you put too much in bonds, you risk making very little money — low risk means low returns. The low returns from bonds are unattractive when the stock market is roaring ahead, but the low risk associated with bonds looks very attractive indeed when the stock market tanks. A balanced investor can sleep well at night in all market conditions.

For example, in 2008, the best cash rates offered by banks for term deposits were around 8 per cent. Those cash rates were comfortably ahead of an inflation rate that peaked at 5 per cent, which means the investments of those who put everything in cash were safe, but their returns were an unspectacular 3 per cent. Australian bond market returns of 6 per cent midway through 2008 weren't looking any better, until the global financial crisis sent stock markets plunging. At the end of 2008, Australian shares, as measured by the All Ordinaries Index, were down close to 50 per cent from their all-time high of 6,873 points on 1 November 2007. Australian government bonds were the best performing asset class of 2008, up 15 per cent. Boring old bonds had never looked so good!

You can have as much as 40 per cent of your portfolio in cash and bonds — if you think the international financial markets are well and truly doomed. Some professional investors move all their money into cash when the sharemarket looks set for a crash, but such extreme behaviour isn't recommended for beginners. More commonly, long-term investors have between 10 per cent and 20 per cent in cash and bonds.

This chapter describes the options you have when considering investing in the fixed-interest markets. We look at types of bonds, bond funds and how to check the credit quality of a bond, and we also examine cash-management and sweep accounts.

Why Keep Bonds in Your Investment Drawer?

We're pretty sure that when people in financial markets use terms without ever explaining them you're infuriated. Like, what are bonds? In the way that *equities* means shares or any spin-off investments linked with public companies, *bonds* generally means any investments that promise a set rate of return.

Strictly speaking, a bond is a legal contract in which an issuer promises to pay bondholders a specific rate (or a set formula for a rate) of interest and *redeem* (or buy back) the contract for its *face value* (the original price). In other words, a bond is a legal promise on paper from the issuer to whoever may buy the bonds (known as *bondholders*). For example, if the National Australia Bank sold bonds to investors, then NAB would be the issuer, and the investors who invested in the bonds would be the bondholders.

When you invest in a bond, you're letting other people manage your money; you're actually giving the money managers a loan. In return, they're giving you

- ✔ The promise that you're able to redeem, or sell, the bond back to the issuer.
- ✔ The promise that you're going to get a set amount regularly as the reward for lending the money.

Creating, or *raising*, a bond is a way for people to accumulate a block of money for a certain purpose, like building a bridge or extending an airport. For the state authority or company issuing the bond, the cost of paying you the set rate of reward is cheaper than going to a bank and asking for a straight-out loan.

When bond managers are trying to decide how much the bond should pay you in terms of reward (or interest), they take a bearing from *official government rates*. You'll see many different official rates but the one that matters — the *benchmark rate* — is the official cash rate. Most other rates are set at a level higher than the cash rate. Assuming official interest rates are 5 per cent — generally regarded as the 'neutral' setting, not too high, not too low — the bond manager may agree to pay you 7 per cent if you invest in the bond. This cost is still cheaper for the company than going to a bank or another lender, who would most likely charge more than 7 per cent for the same money. The bond issuer must consider their worthiness to issue bonds, as this influences their credit rating.

The bond manager wants to attract as many investors (or lenders) as possible, so they may place the bond on the market to allow investors to buy and sell the bond. This practice allows for the bond to *trade*, and it may go up or down in price. If the bond trades on the market, your return may include not only the rate of interest but also the change in the bond's price since you first bought it.

Understanding bonds is important because the bond (or fixed-interest) markets will steadily become a more important part of your investment portfolio as times goes on. As you get older (and no doubt richer and wiser), you'll probably want to take fewer risks. You'll want to know in advance what returns you'll be getting from a larger portion of your investment.

How Bonds Fare as an Investment

In recent history, if you look at the market since 1979, Australian bonds offered higher returns than Australian shares 12 times in 30 years. Over that same period, bonds returned 9.8 per cent a year, on average, whereas shares returned 16.2 per cent a year.

Bond markets did well in 2007–08, as global sharemarkets, and the US housing market, faltered then crashed. In 2008, bond markets offered better returns than any other investment category. Prior to that, bond markets had not had a year in the sun since the grim early years of the 1990s, when the Gulf War rocked financial markets.

As an investment, bonds are similar to putting money in a bank account and getting interest for your efforts. When you put $1,000 in a bank account term deposit, the bank may offer 5 per cent per year. In other words, the bank pays you 5 per cent for lending it your money, and returns the original amount you lent (the principal). With bonds the structure is similar. The bond issuer offers to pay a set percentage to anyone who lends them money and guarantees to return the principal.

The key difference between term deposits and bonds is that bonds are traded. They aren't static like term deposits. So, as well as a set rate of return on your investment, the bond can go up and down in price. As a result, your overall return from the bond can be higher or lower because, although your promised interest rate remains unchanged, the price of the bond may have gone higher or lower.

All the Bonds You Can Buy

In the United States, private investors enjoy a tradition of buying bonds directly. For example, private investors can directly buy bonds in their local power station or local authority housing corporation.

Australia has not come to that point yet — the bond market hasn't developed in the same fashion as in the United States and is a lot smaller. Here, your access to the bond market is primarily through other products, like term deposits, cash-management trusts and bond managed funds.

Knowing the basics of the bond market is still worthwhile so that you can understand where the fund managers and bankers put your money when they offer you a fixed rate of return.

Among the most popular bonds available to direct bond investors such as banks and fund managers are:

✔ **Government-backed bonds:** Both the federal government and state governments issue these bonds. They carry an explicit government guarantee. Commonwealth securities are among the most popular of these bonds.

✔ **Semi-government bonds:** Government-funded agencies or statutory bodies can offer bonds in their own right. They're not explicitly guaranteed, but they're *implicitly guaranteed* (which means the government is highly unlikely to allow the issuers to *default on* — or not pay — their promised rate of return).

✔ **Corporate bonds:** Very big companies can issue bonds to raise money for commercial projects. Corporate bonds aren't as safe as government or semi-government bonds — they don't carry any form of government guarantee. They pay higher rates of return to reflect this higher risk.

Taking the Plunge Into a Bond Fund

Buying bonds through a *bond fund* is an increasingly popular alternative to leaving money in a bank. In mid-2008, Australian superannuation investors who chose their fund's balanced option had about $97 billion invested in cash and bond funds — almost 26 per cent of the total invested. You can invest relatively small amounts, such as $1,000, into bond funds and have your money invested in a variety of different bonds.

The most popular bond products in the Australian markets are from banks and fund managers. Separately, *insurance bonds*, which are issued by life insurance companies, are a variation on bond funds. The objective of insurance bonds is to achieve regular income from a fund with investments in the bond market.

If you're willing to accept the fees charged by fund managers, then you can choose between two main bond funds:

✔ **Actively managed bond funds:** These funds strive to get the best returns from the bond market. Although bonds move in a more predictable manner than shares, the range of performance in the bond market can be great. For example, the variation in returns in the 12 months to June 2008 from the leading Australian fixed-interest funds ranged from –1.9 per cent to 7.1 per cent.

✔ **Indexed bonds:** If you buy these funds, you're buying a fund that aims to achieve the exact same performance as a bond index, such as the UBS Warburg Australian Composite Bond Index. In the 12 months to June 2008, for example, the index was up 4.4 per cent, better than the majority of actively managed funds.

If you want to invest in the bond market through managed funds, then indexed funds may be a good option because they have much lower fees. In this situation — where you know returns can be relatively low — indexed funds may have an advantage. Actively managed funds tend to have good years and bad years. An index fund removes the temptation to switch funds every time your fund manager has a bad year.

Keeping a Tab on Your Bonds

Bonds are much easier to track than shares because they more or less move in the same direction. The main difference is the variation in that movement. For the bankers and fund managers that invest your money in bonds, the two main issues to monitor are credit quality and interest rate movements.

Checking bond credit quality

The credit quality of bonds is the main factor in dictating their popularity with investors. So, the business of detecting bond quality is now a fine art.

Fund managers get the term *triple A* (meaning the very best quality bonds) from classification tables prepared by rating agencies. Rating agencies are companies like Standard & Poor's that monitor the credit quality of bonds (as shown in Table 15-1). Classification tables also define *junk bonds* (which, officially, are bonds with a rating of less than BBB). Junk bonds pay very high rates because they're a high-risk investment.

Interesting links between rates and bonds

The worst thing that can happen to a bond is the bond issuer defaults and can't pay the rate of return promised on the bond. Although this occurrence is rare in Australia (and unknown in government or semi-government markets), it is possible with corporate bonds. The second-worst thing that can happen is interest rates go up — if this happens, your bond automatically falls in price.

Bond prices and interest rates always move in opposite directions. If rates go up, bond prices go down; if rates go down, bond prices go up — the interest on your bond normally stays the same.

For example, assuming that a bond — the Highway to Heaven Bond — is offering a fixed rate of return, the main driver of your total investment return is movement in interest rates.

How does interest rate movement affect your return? Assume that your bond pays 7 per cent per annum and assume official interest rates are 5 per cent. When your bond originally issues, the people behind it decide that any bond they issue is to be 2 per cent above official interest rates.

Table 15-1	Standard & Poor's Bond Ratings
Rating	*Definition**
AAA	Capacity to meet its financial commitment is EXTREMELY STRONG.
AA	Capacity to meet its financial commitment is VERY STRONG.
A	Capacity to meet its financial commitment is STRONG.
BBB	Exhibits ADEQUATE protection parameters.
BB	LESS VULNERABLE to non-payment than other speculative issues.
B	MORE VULNERABLE to non-payment than obligations rated 'BB'.
CCC	CURRENTLY VULNERABLE to non-payment and is dependent upon favourable conditions to meet commitment.
CC	Currently HIGHLY VULNERABLE to non-payment.
C	Covers a situation where a bankruptcy petition has been filed or similar action has been taken, but payments are being continued.
R	Under regulatory supervision owing to its financial condition.
SD	Has failed to pay one or more of its financial obligations.
D	Will generally default on its obligations.
r	Attached to the ratings of instruments with significant non-credit risks.
N.R.	Not rated.

*Extracts of definitions provided. For full details, go to the Resource Centre at Standard & Poor's website at www.standardandpoors.com.au. *Ratings from AA to CCC may be modified by the addition of a plus or minus sign to show their relative standing within the major rating categories.*

Now, imagine if official rates move from 5 per cent to 6 per cent. The Highway to Heaven Bond doesn't look quite so good. In fact, the bond only offers 1 per cent above the new official interest rate of 6 per cent. The next time anybody tries to sell one of your bonds in the market, they'll sell for less — the price will almost certainly fall to a new level that reflects the new setting of interest rates.

Being Clever with Your Cash

You always need to have 'cash on hand' for a variety of reasons, especially if you're faced with unexpected bills. Cash also serves as the safest of all investments because, even though your return may always be relatively low, it is predictable. And, more importantly, when things are terrible everywhere else, cash investments shine. For example, back in 1990, cash was returning 18.5 per cent — a better return than any other investment in that desperate year!

When the world came to a standstill after the 11 September 2001 attack on the World Trade Center in New York, investors rushed into cash once more. In September 2001, Australian shares fell by 6.4 per cent, international shares fell by 8.9 per cent but cash inched ahead by 0.4 per cent.

More recently, when global sharemarkets capitulated in October 2008, Australian shares fell more than 16 per cent in just one week but cash was returning around 7 per cent.

Traditionally, people often used to keep cash in banks either in day-to-day *transaction accounts* like cheque or savings accounts or in *term deposit accounts* where the money is left alone for a fixed period, such as three months. The problem with transaction accounts is that banks pay little or no interest. By the time you pay account-keeping and transaction fees, your transaction account actually costs you money.

In a recession, cash is king. The problem is, nobody has any cash. Australians are finally seeing some innovations to the old workhorse transaction accounts. In 2008, some banks were paying more than 8 per cent on high-interest savings accounts — a very attractive rate of return when financial markets are in turmoil.

Cash-management accounts and online savings accounts (which we discuss next) both try to offer a full-function account with high interest rates.

Why a cash-management account?

With a cash-management account (CMA), you can leave funds that you may wish to keep as cash in a special account that pays a higher rate than ordinary cash accounts offered by banks. Unlike term deposits, which offer a specified return, CMAs have tiered rates of return depending on your account balance. Low balances may only earn low interest rates.

Cash-management trusts (CMTs) are slightly different to cash-management accounts. CMTs offer a single rate of interest — often higher than the rates for CMAs — and some offer the ability to withdraw and deposit funds on 24 hours' notice, plus chequebook and debit facilities. Most CMTs charge management fees of 1–2 per cent and access hurdles may be more restricted for higher rates of interest.

CMAs also offer cheque facilities; you can use them for standing orders and carry out transactions at an ATM. Most require a large minimum opening balance and you can only withdraw funds in set multiples, such as $500 at a time, and many charge an account-keeping fee.

Consider cash rates, like all investment rates, in the light of inflation. Inflation of 4 per cent means an 8 per cent return is really only 4 per cent. The top rate of interest often only applies to balances of $100,000 and higher, making them suitable for wealthier individuals. These days you may find a higher rate of interest on an online savings account for much lower balances.

One disadvantage of CMTs is that they may demand you keep a minimum amount in the account, normally about $10,000. These accounts require you to fill out a prospectus because technically you're investing in a managed fund or trust that specialises in cash.

Keeping a cash-management account with a major financial institution can offer extra benefits. For example, the stockbroking arm of the institution may regularly invite you to participate in initial public offerings (IPOs) that are only being offered to clients of the financial institution.

In recent years, there has been an explosion in the number and type of high-interest accounts on offer from the major banks, as well as smaller financial institutions. Ratings group Cannex (www.cannex.com.au) evaluates more than 100 CMAs and more than 80 online savings accounts.

Cashing in on internet banking

If you think the bond market is dry, take a look at the cash markets. If you don't wear your tie straight in that business, they think you're eccentric!

In the extremely conservative world of cash management, new ideas don't exactly come bouncing across the desks every morning. But the internet has changed the shape of business in cash markets as surely as it has changed all financial markets.

Online savings accounts — or high-yield savings accounts — pay some of the highest interest rates in the market, with some beating the official cash rate. At the time of writing, the official cash rate set by the Reserve Bank is 3.25 per cent, while the highest interest rate available for online savings is 6 per cent for a balance as low as $1,000.

High-yield savings accounts have been driven by smaller, aggressive financial institutions keen to snatch market share from the big banks. BankWest's TeleNet Saver is the trendsetter, with the highest headline-grabbing rates. St.George's Dragondirect, ING DIRECT and HSBC's Serious Saver Account are also serious competitors.

Although term deposits may offer a higher rate of interest, especially for longer term savings, online savings accounts have the advantage of providing instant access to your cash. Online savings accounts generally don't require a minimum balance and most don't charge an account-keeping fee.

Despite their obvious appeal, online savings accounts are not without their traps and pitfalls. Few offer transaction facilities, and you can generally only access your savings via a linked transaction account. Customers must also check the terms and conditions attached to the highest rates.

For example, some online accounts offer an introductory rate for a limited time only; some offer bonus rates but only if you make no withdrawals for a month or make a minimum deposit each month. Even so, online savings accounts are a breath of fresh air in the stuffy world of banking and look set to keep the big banks on their toes.

Part IV
Property and Collectibles

Glenn Lumsden

'Of course, in his younger days he was known as Bill the Property Investor.'

In this part ...

Whether home ownership means buying a house to live in, owning an apartment in another part of town or even in another city, Australians love property investment. No wonder! Property investing has had a safe and satisfying track record for many generations of Australians. But times change. The conditions for property investment in Australia are no longer so good that you're virtually guaranteed to make money. However, with the right strategy you can maximise your opportunities.

In this part, we introduce you to the basic steps towards purchasing a home or an investment property and help you learn some key lessons from the property market. We also offer a basic guide to investing in art and collectibles.

Chapter 16

Land: They're Not Making It Anymore

*Y*ou may find it hard to believe, but in many countries outside Australia the property market isn't that exciting — the whole process happens very slowly. For example, in the Irish country town James grew up in, selling a house can easily take a year — people move house once in their lives, if they move at all. Property development remains strictly for professionals. In Australia, the property scene is very different — property is like a game and is followed like the footy. Results are posted in the papers, auctions are held on the front lawn. This homegrown passion for property isn't the norm (which is not to say that this passion doesn't occur elsewhere in the world). However, the intense interest here sure makes for an exciting property market.

Because some Australians view the property market as a game, the market has developed speculative aspects that can challenge even the most seasoned investor. *Buying off the plan* (where investors buy properties before they're even built) is common and the practice of *dummy bidding* (where people associated with the vendor pretend to bid at auctions) is common, despite attempts by state governments to stamp it out.

Australians still love to own their own houses — in 2006, 70 per cent of households in Australia either owned or had a mortgage over the house they occupied. (However, only 34 per cent of households owned their home outright in 2006, compared with 41 per cent a decade earlier.)

Australia's property market has consistently shown strong returns for generations, because this is a 'new world' economy and immigration from the 'old world' has constantly pushed up property prices. Even in tough economic times, such as the global financial crisis of 2008, the steady flow of new migrants ensures a constant demand for new housing and cushions any weakness in house prices. Since the early 1990s, superannuation has become a major investment issue but, until that time, for the vast majority of Australians, their home was their only investment asset.

Interestingly, governments traditionally like to see everybody owning their own homes. As a result, successive governments offer generous tax incentives for buying homes.

Over the last two decades, the Australian property market has been influenced by these key factors:

- ✔ **Immigration:** The immigration rate hit an all-time high in 2008, with a net gain of 200,000 overseas migrants arriving on our shores in the year to March. Migration is the fuel that drives property prices as new arrivals look for a place to call home. In the 1950s, Australia's population grew at 3 per cent a year; today, it's closer to 2 per cent due to the lower birth rate.

- ✔ **Urban–rural differences:** The differences between regional property markets have become more marked as urban and rural Australia show varying rates of economic growth.

- ✔ **Regional differences:** The resources boom of the noughties put a rocket under housing prices in the mineral-rich states of Western Australia, Queensland and the Northern Territory, while house price growth in the old-economy states stalled.

- ✔ **Inner-city living:** More people are living within five kilometres of city centres — a trend that has totally reshaped inner-city property markets.

- ✔ **Seachangers and treechangers:** Cashed-up baby-boomers are leaving the city for the more relaxed lifestyle offered by small coastal towns and rural hamlets. Retirees and families with young children are joining the flight from the big cities in search of cheaper property as well as a better lifestyle.

Even inside our largest cities, the markets are splitting as never before, where values in seaside, riverside and bayside suburbs can increase dramatically and prices in outer suburbs can actually decline over the same period.

Outer suburbs show very small price increases — or declines in some cases — because the cost of the land is minimal. Property developers hold huge banks of land in these areas and the development costs are no more than the cost of subdividing the land. This subdivision may include drainage and other services but the land values barely change each year because, as soon as you get to the edge of the city, only government planning regulations limit the amount of land available.

Putting all these factors together creates a property market that is much more complex than it used to be. This mix of forces also offers plenty of investment opportunities to the wise investor. But property isn't necessarily the ideal investment for everyone. In this chapter, first we ask you to think about whether property investment is right for you. We also look at the role of real estate agents and take you through the golden rules of property investing, including location, timing, financing and choosing your investment.

Purchasing Property as an Investment

Is buying property suitable for everyone? For the vast majority of people, investing in property, including the family home, is a good long-term investment. In the following chapters, we deal separately with the three key areas of property investment:

- ✔ **Home investment:** Buying your own home is normally the first step most people take in the property market (see Chapter 17).
- ✔ **Residential investment:** Purchasing residential properties to rent is a way of both receiving income and accumulating capital wealth (see Chapter 18).
- ✔ **Commercial investment:** You can invest in property via the commercial markets or, more commonly, through property syndicates and managed funds that specialise in the property market (see Chapter 19).

Why property investing isn't for everyone

Judging whether or not property is a good investment for you is an important decision. Here are some of the situations where property investment may not be appropriate.

- ✔ **The uncommitted couple:** Short-term couples who jointly enter the long-term world of property investment are the perennial victims of the property market. If a couple breaks up shortly after purchasing a property — say, within three years — they can face an uphill battle to recoup their joint investment after paying all the fees involved in selling the property. Worse still, they're likely to disagree on the terms of any sale.

- ✔ **The uncommitted migrant:** People who like to work in different cities or different countries are badly suited to the property market because they buy or sell properties at the wrong time in the cycle. They may also hold the property for too short a time to make a profit.

- ✔ **The over-extender:** Coming to the crunch, you have to be able to afford a property even with today's generous mortgage facilities. If, for example, a buyer overextends in purchasing a property, meeting mortgage payments can turn into a tightrope act. Any major changes in the buyer's economic conditions — a mortgage rate increase, for example — can force them onto the ropes. The property has to be sold and most likely at a loss after fees are included.

What's proper about property

When you buy property you enter the oldest way known of accumulating wealth. The investment is that reliable! You can make mistakes, of course, but, by following some basic rules, the result is more likely to be a question of just how much profit you make.

Purchasing shares — as you can see in Part II — can be the best long-term investment of all. But picking the right shares is a much harder business than picking the right property. Put simply, your chances of picking a real loser are slimmer in property investing than in shares.

More importantly, the sharemarket changes every day. In contrast, trends in the property market are much more durable — if you pick the right property on day one, the chances are it remains the right property to sell five years later.

The greatest security offered by property is known as the *underlying asset* — meaning that the asset has an undisputed rock-bottom value. In theory, your house is always worth at least the cost of its reconstruction and the land underneath always has a value to someone. This concept was tested during the global financial crisis of 2008, when banks in the United States were unable to give away houses they had earlier repossessed, even for a dollar! Sanity will undoubtedly return to the housing market, but that will be small comfort for people who lost their homes. The lesson here is that a financial asset, be it a parcel of shares or your family home, is only worth what someone else is prepared to pay for it.

Shares offer the best returns over a long period. The problem is, though, which shares? Property is a less complex business; the vast majority of properties increase in price over time. Property is also a bigger single investment than a parcel of shares, so investors are less likely to buy and sell property based on a knee-jerk reaction to the latest piece of bad news in the market. Property investors tend to be very practical people who like to be able to control and even 'touch' their investments. Although you may like to associate property investors with heavy borrowing, don't forget that virtually every company on the stock market has borrowings, too. However, unlike share investors, who have no control over the amount that listed companies may borrow, property investors can at least decide the level of borrowing they wish to retain.

In choosing between property and stock market investment, don't let a fear of borrowing affect your decision. You can't avoid borrowing, or *gearing*, in the investment market. Stock market companies borrow all the time — and they risk shareholder money in their activities.

Property is the most direct investment you can make with your money. You can take advantage of this direct connection by influencing the way the investment is managed (for example, you can choose to cut the costs of managing the property by doing things yourself). We give you some tips on this aspect of property investing in Chapter 18.

If you're the type of investor who has big-picture ambitions — maybe even dynastic ambitions, where you don't just want to be wealthy but you want to see your family wealthy for generations — then property is also the most suitable investment for you because it's the ultimate long-term investment.

Arguments over which is the best investment — shares or property — have raged for years, and the debate will continue for years to come. We both worked as reporters on the *Australian Financial Review* (James as a property reporter and Barbara as a sharemarket reporter) and learned some invaluable lessons in the process. In the 1980s, we met a generation of immigrants who had come to Australia from Eastern Europe. These exiles from post-war Hungary and Poland built their first fortunes in textiles, fashion and retailing. In almost every case, they put the profits from their

Property-investment seminars: A wealth warning!

What we say here doesn't apply to all property seminars. Some seminars are reasonably informative and the promoters make great efforts to explain the property market. However, the quality of seminars is generally low and the 'sucker rate' is high.

The property-investment seminar business harbours some of the worst nonsense, fantasy and downright exploitation you're ever likely to see in Australian business (a bold statement, indeed!).

Three powerful forces are at work. First, the knowledge that property investment over the long term is a proven way to build wealth. Second, the desire to be taught in an 'educational' setting. And, third, the even deeper desire to be among the successful elite of the community who have become genuinely wealthy through property investment.

Inside the property market is a long history of high-pressure selling to people who don't know the ropes. Even though you see the stories in the papers and the reports on television, still the scams happen year after year.

The real problem with investment-seminar gangsters isn't their ability to fleece you of $50 or $75 for turning up to their special presentations. That ability to lure you into their company is only the tip of the iceberg. The serious exploitation goes on when the companies behind the seminars work on the people who attend them and lure them into buying property. These are not random properties; they're often properties owned by the very companies that are running the seminars.

Think about it. These guys run seminars with names like 'Recession-Proof Property Investment', when they should be called 'How to Pay Us Money to Find Out How to Buy Our Properties'.

Each property boom produces a new generation of predators and cautionary tales. The collapse of Westpoint Corporation in 2006 marked the end of the last Australian property boom. For years, Westpoint seduced thousands of ordinary Australians with promises of safe, secure, 'capital-guaranteed' property investments paying a fixed return of up to 12 per cent a year. One arm of Westpoint developed apartment complexes, mostly in Sydney and Melbourne, while another arm raised the funds to build the apartments. The property-development juggernaut depended on people paying high prices for city apartments.

When the market for Westpoint's apartments dried up, the company could no longer pay its investors. People soon realised that the guarantees they'd been promised weren't worth the paper they were written on because the securities they held were unsecured. Up to 90,000 people lost more than $300 million, or an average of $90,000 each. Many investors had mortgaged their homes to take advantage of the high returns Westpoint offered, often at the urging of financial advisers. The only people who got rich in this particular scheme were the financial planners who earned commissions of up to 10 per cent for every client they signed up.

What can we say about property promoters and property-investment seminars being conducted every week? Don't go there. Don't bother. Don't waste your time and your money.

core business activities into property to ensure long-term wealth. This group was always trotting out folksy wisdom about property: 'Buy land, they're not making it anymore,' was one of the most popular.

For decades the *BRW* Rich List was dotted with family names such as the Lowys, Gandels, Roths, Liebermans and Perons. It's a very long list and one where the family histories are remarkably similar.

Over the years, as business journalists, we also met a generation of economists who had come through the ranks in the exciting years of deregulation. They would argue property was a poor investment, saying, 'It's local, it's too slow, it's illiquid.'

We still see these economists around the traps — they still put forward the same arguments, they're all still working to pay off their mortgages, to put their kids through school and save for retirement. They just have greyer beards and thicker spectacles. Meanwhile, the property-laden families of the Rich List get richer ever year. Few Australians are ever likely to get as far as the Lowy family, but still the security of property investment is a very attractive proposition for anyone. And you know the saying is true; they're not making land anymore, especially in the middle of Sydney or Melbourne.

Oh, Those Real Estate Agents!

Dealing in the property market means dealing with real estate agents. We can't think of any other industry where the middleman is so powerful. At the bigger end of the property market, the power of the real estate agents fades slightly as parties sometimes deal directly with each other.

For example, in 2001, controversial tycoon John Elliot sold his home in Toorak, Melbourne, to a stockbroker for $11 million. Elliot did the deal himself with no real estate agents involved. But, for most Australians, real estate agents rule the roost.

Good agents can do almost anything with a standard property — they can increase or decrease the selling price, they can flush out a string of prospective acquirers, and they can make your property seem more desirable than you ever thought possible.

A bad agent can lose your money almost as easily — by not getting the best price for a property or by getting the wrong kind of tenant, or failing to get any tenant, into an investment property.

As soon as you enter the property market, you have to deal successfully with agents. As a group, their reputation is less than flattering — down there with politicians, lawyers, car salesmen (and journalists!).

Analysing real estate agents as a group (we deal with them in Chapter 17), it would appear that their most negative quality is their ability to exaggerate how the property market is going to perform in the future (see the sidebar 'Telling it like it isn't' later in this chapter).

Real estate agents can break your heart. They can use you as cannon fodder at auctions by luring you into bidding for a house that you can never hope to afford. They can encourage you to have false expectations on price when you're selling.

On the other hand, you're equally able to develop a soft spot for the agent that sells your property for a very good price. A friend of James recently went through a nail-biting auction of her inner-city property. The house was a difficult property in that it was semi-detached with a curious 1980s design, and situated near the corner of a busy street.

On a wet Saturday morning before a damp crowd of grim-faced bidders, the agent — a veteran who knew the neighbourhood inside out — managed to lift the price a full 20 per cent more than she had ever expected. When the auction was over, he came back into the house and said: 'There you are. I hope I never have to do that again ... I've sold this bloody house three times now and I still hate it; it just takes too much out of me.' That's the best and worst of real estate agents. You want guys like him to sell your house; the problem is, you may just meet them when you're buying a house, too.

The Golden Rules of Property Investing

Property is a very practical business and is a relatively easy-to-understand investment market. However, you need different talents inside each area of the property market. For example, the investor in inner-city apartments has to be finely tuned to fashion trends. The investor in pastoral properties need not worry about fashions; instead, what matters are commodity prices.

Despite these variations in regional markets, certain rules do stand the test of time in any property market. The following sections detail the seven golden rules to be mindful of when investing in the property market.

Your location

What are the three most important words in the property market? Location, location and location. Location is one aspect of a property that you can't change if you get it wrong.

The location of a property matters most when you're dealing with inner-city property, where every detail, such as the width of the street or the number of the postcode, can make a huge difference to perceptions of its value.

Proximity to schools, public transport, shops and services can turn a humble shack into a desirable residence. In some cases, families will insist on purchasing a home within the catchment area for a top public school.

Your timing

Property prices are driven by supply and demand — when the market is strong, people pay beyond good value for property. When the market is weak, people simply don't pay fair value for almost any property. In either scenario, the property can be unchanged — in fact, the property in question can be no more than three-quarters of an acre of grass in the middle of a suburb!

Timing isn't a perfect science. You can't expect to get it exactly right but you must make every effort to avoid buying at the top of the market and selling at the bottom. Property investors who get caught at the top (buying) or at the bottom (selling) can take years to recoup the extra costs they incur from bad timing.

Your financing

Just how much you're paying on a mortgage can make a big difference to your success or failure in property investing.

With interest rates constantly changing and a substantial variation in mortgage rates charged by financial institutions (especially if you go outside the 'big four' banks), conservative financing is an essential art to master. (We discuss mortgages and lenders in Chapter 17.)

Your piece of land

You can do almost anything with a property, but it's hard to reshape or extend the land itself. When purchasing a property, remember that, apart from location, the land it sits on is its most important physical aspect, especially in the city, where values are high.

Your house is worth nothing; it's the land underneath that holds the value.

—Property developer maxim

Telling it like it isn't

Maybe the worst thing about real estate agents is that many of them actually believe their nonsense. After all, they're in a business where you really need to be confident. You need to get up in the morning and convince people that any property on your books is worth buying. Convincing yourself first is a powerful driver in convincing others.

Agents are likely to exaggerate the advantages of any property to a buyer — it's only human nature. They can also exaggerate trends that stimulate property prices. When you're talking to real estate agents, it seems as if interest rates are always about to go up and long-term trends like the move towards the inner city and bayside suburbs take on a sudden urgency. (Keep cool … loads of houses are out there!)

So many clichés exist in the real estate market that picking a favourite isn't easy, but the old refrain 'a once-in-a-lifetime opportunity' must come pretty close to the best example. You can hear this piece of real estate nonsense trotted out a thousand times on any Saturday morning on the streets of Australia's biggest cities.

The relentless optimism of real estate agents can be tiresome. In their defence, most of them are so gung-ho by nature that they're genuinely surprised when things don't work out as planned.

In October 2008, global financial markets were in freefall and most economists believed Australia was headed for recession, along with the rest of the developed world, and that unemployment was set to rise. The federal government doubled the First Home Owner Grant to stimulate housing activity, but auction clearance rates remained stubbornly low. The most pessimistic forecasters said Australian residential property was overvalued and due for a fall of 30–40 per cent. Even optimistic forecasters predicted flat property prices, yet real estate agents were still spruiking property 'hotspots' in the real estate liftouts of the nation's newspapers.

The message is this: Take everything real estate agents say with a pinch of salt. Real estate agents are in the business of selling property, in fair economic weather or foul. Often they believe their own clichés — confidence is, after all, the name of their game.

Your local knowledge

Property is a local business that requires knowing all about the exact values of property in a particular location.

If you ever lived in one spot for five years, think of how differently you viewed your residence after five years compared with the first year. Perhaps, during the second year, you noticed an advantage like a terrific shopping strip five minutes away in the car. Or maybe a few months went by before you noticed a big disadvantage like the rattle of freight trains that you heard only at night.

You probably know most about the neighbourhoods you've lived in — consider these neighbourhoods first when making your first property investment.

Your renovation budget

The profit you make on a property is due to the improved value of the land (which you can't influence) and the improved value of the property (where you can make a difference).

The secret is to only spend on renovations and repairs in proportion to the improved value of the property. If house prices in your area are falling (as they were in parts of Sydney in 2008), spending large amounts on renovations isn't sensible. Keep the renovation budget in line with the property price patterns in your area.

Your five-year timeframe

If you buy a property as an investment with the aim of renting it for income and selling it for a profit, then you should have a timeframe in mind.

Inside the property industry, the general rule of thumb for landlords who buy new properties is to sell them after five years — because five years is about the limit before major maintenance jobs rear their ugly heads.

The five-year mark is generally seen as the time when everything from pipes to electrical fittings suddenly starts to deteriorate. From a financing point of view, too, this timeframe is also the end of the best period for taking advantage of tax strategies. (We discuss ways to minimise tax in Chapter 18.)

Chapter 17

Buying Your Home, Paying for It and Selling It

- -

In This Chapter

▶ Working through the pros and cons of owning your own home

▶ Buying your dream home

▶ Choosing your real estate agent, carefully

▶ Facing up to mortgage fun

▶ Counting the costs of buying

▶ Moving on: Time to sell

- -

*T*here you are on the morning of the auction. Today is the day you're going to bid for a home! You've one arm propped against a telephone pole with the property brochure in your hand. The perspiration is running down your face. The auction crowd seems enormous (where did all these people come from ... they weren't at the inspections!). The auctioneer is taking bids ... you've waited weeks for this moment.

And then real estate reality dawns on you: You haven't a chance. A quiet man in dark glasses has just put in a bid of $25,000 more than you think the house (or apartment) is worth. The bid is $20,000 more than the highest price you can afford — and the auction isn't even over yet. The time has come to go back to your rented home-sweet-home and start again.

 The big difference between investing in property and investing in other assets is commitment. You have to do your homework. You have to make sure that, when you settle on a target property, you have a very good chance of getting it at the price you think is fair value.

One of life's tough calls is the fact that your family home is probably the biggest single investment you're ever likely to make. But, hey, life is full of challenges. The secret is to make your investment a successful investment.

At least you can be consoled by the fact that home purchase is also the safest and most tax-efficient investment you're likely to make in your lifetime.

The Real Estate Institute of Australia says residential property values moved ahead by between 1 per cent and 3 per cent above inflation throughout the last century. (Figure 17-1 reveals the upward trend in house prices in Australia's capital cities.) In other words, most people make a profit from home investment most of the time. The chances are that you too will make a tidy profit from your investments in property. This chapter shows you how to get started. We look at finding your perfect residence, dealing with agents and how to structure your mortgage. We also delve into the costs of buying and selling your home.

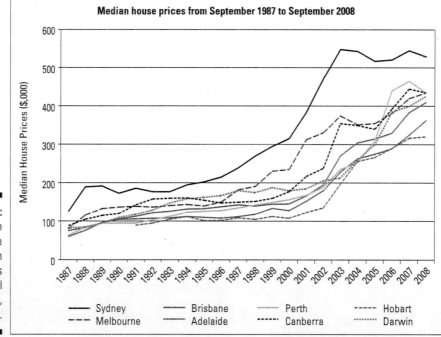

Figure 17-1: Median house prices in Australia's capital cities, 1987–2008.

Note: Statistics for Hobart available only from 1991.
Source: © Real Estate Institute of Australia.

Why Bother Buying Your Own Home?

We're sceptical about a much-vaunted 'trend' away from home ownership. Home ownership has remained steady at around 70 per cent of the population for decades. Our best guess is that declining affordability, a long property boom and a period of rising interest rates followed by the global financial crisis means the under-35s are putting off buying property until later. In fact, these days younger people do everything later — they get married later, they have their kids later.

Like many trends in real estate, although the move away from home ownership may be genuine, it is greatly exaggerated by real estate agents. All of the major cities are now dotted with high-rise apartment blocks; real estate agents need to sell these apartments to investors and they, in turn, need to rent them to tenants. A substantial slab of the real estate industry depends on people believing that the family home is out of fashion.

But the owner-occupied home isn't going out of fashion and remains the best and safest investment open to you. Here are the best and worst aspects of owning your own home.

The good bits about buying a home

The stock market is more profitable over the long run than property — but property investors sleep easier in their beds. Here's why:

- ✔ **You rarely go wrong:** Property prices increase on rising demand linked to rising population. Property studies show falling population is highly unusual in urban areas. Rural areas are a different matter; rural populations can fall regularly.

- ✔ **You can understand your investment:** You may never fully come to grips with the stock market but you can come to understand every feature of your property and your neighbourhood.

- ✔ **You can improve your investment:** If a share or managed fund is falling in value, you can't do much about it. If property prices soften, however, you can always make your property more valuable by making improvements. (As long as you don't overcapitalise; refer to Chapter 16.)

- ✔ **You enjoy tax breaks:** The sale of your primary residence is tax-free (or, to be more precise, free of *capital gains tax* — the key tax on all commercial profits; refer to Chapter 5 and see Chapter 18 for more on tax and investment property). Of course, you may still have to pay other taxes, such as stamp duty, if you're purchasing a home. The taxes you pay, and any waivers for first-home buyers, depend on the state you live in.

- ✔ **You're forced to save:** Nothing else exists like a weekly mortgage payment to make you save. You must transfer the money to the bank. If you plan to invest in other areas, such as shares, you rarely have the same compelling need to invest your money on a regular basis.

First-time home buyers can take advantage of the Commonwealth Government's First Home Owner Grant (FHOG) when buying a new or established house, home unit, flat or other type of self-contained fixed dwelling. In 2008, the grant received a boost to $14,000 towards the purchase of an existing home and $21,000 towards the cost of a newly built home. Things can change, however, so check the website at www.firsthome.gov.au for more information.

In October 2008, the Commonwealth Government also introduced new First Home Saver Accounts (FHSAs) in response to the dramatic fall in housing affordability. The government contributes 17 per cent of the first $5,000 of contributions you make to your FHSA each year, up to an overall balance cap of $75,000. Investment earnings — or interest on your account — is taxed at a discount rate of 15 per cent instead of at your marginal tax rate. When you're ready to dip a toe in the housing market, withdrawals from your FHSA are tax-free provided you use the money to buy your first home and live in it. You can find more information at www.homesaver.treasury.gov.au.

The scary stuff about owning a home

Investing in property demands a big commitment on an investment — if you choose badly, you pay a big price. Here's the bad news about investing in your own home:

- ✔ **You must have money already:** Property investors are advised to have a minimum 10 per cent deposit. Even with a 100 per cent mortgage, you must be able to pay all fees on purchasing a property. Property investment requires you to have the necessary up-front funds. Fees relating to the acquisition of a property can be about 5 per cent (around $25,000 on a $500,000 home) of its value.

- ✔ **You can't move your home:** Location is the most important factor in property. If you buy a house in the wrong place, no amount of improvement to the property can overcome this disadvantage.

- ✔ **You can't sell your property fast:** Property is an 'illiquid' investment. You can't sell one room at a time when you need extra cash and it can take a long time to sell a property in a depressed market. Generally, selling a property at auction can take you six weeks.

- ✔ **You can't expect very high returns:** If you mortgage your home, the money you pay isn't tax deductible, even though you've 'geared'. As a result, you have to include all mortgage payments in any calculation of the 'profit' you may finally make when you sell the property.

✔ **Your home isn't a pure investment:** Technically, your own home isn't taken very seriously as an investment. After all, you can only extract the cash from this asset if you sell the house, and you always need somewhere to live. If you ever get rich enough to deal with a private bank, they like to see around $2 million in pure investment assets when you open an account — and they don't count your family home as an investment asset. You can, however, use the equity in your home to borrow additional funds to invest in property, shares or other assets.

Hunting for the Perfect Cave

Buying a home is up there with the most stressful events in your life, like changing your job or choosing who you sit next to at your employer's Christmas lunch! Yet, Australians like to move house regularly — homeowners sell their house and move on every seven years or so, on average.

Selecting a new property is never simple, but the process has become much easier in recent years because the distribution of property information has improved dramatically.

Acquiring a new house or apartment calls for research skills: You need to find the right property and the right financing package. In this section we show you how.

Finding a place to call home

Are you looking for the perfect home? That might take an eternity. You're better off looking for a place that suits your needs (and with some extra work can suit you perfectly). This practical approach is the secret to finding the right place.

You're really looking for the property on the market that most closely matches your requirements. If you wait ten years, your ideal home may come on the market, but even then you may not get it at a reasonable price.

Every personal-investment book warns against putting too much emphasis on your family home. This warning makes absolute sense. Ideally, you need to have a diversified portfolio of investments — your family home should not be your most important asset, but it is still an investment. The success of that investment comes back to your ability to find the right place.

Selecting the best area for you

Don't go driving around the city aimlessly looking at attractive homes in different suburbs. Pick one region and then select an area within that region where you want to live. Eliminate the parts of the selected area you choose not to live in (maybe on a highway or next to an all-night supermarket) and then get down to the finer details of your househunting strategy.

The further out from the city you wish to live, the larger your selected area needs to be. In the inner city you can select a relatively tight area such as a square kilometre, because city districts have high property turnover rates. In inner Sydney, for example, you may decide to hunt within a square kilometre of Bondi Junction.

On the other hand, if you're interested in an outer suburb such as bayside Melbourne, you can draw a line between the Nepean Highway and any two roads that connect the highway with Port Phillip Bay.

The most important financial factor is the recent history of house or apartment prices in your area. Inner-city suburbs can have quite volatile prices linked with short-term fashions; as you move out through middle and outer suburbs, price patterns become more reliable.

Consider the following external factors when selecting your desired area:

- ✔ **Distance from the CBD:** The current trend is to move in towards the city or central business district (CBD). If you're further than five kilometres from Australia's major cities, you may be cutting yourself off from a portion of the buying market.

- ✔ **Location of good schools:** Many smart investors now focus on suburbs that boast state schools with strong academic records. They hope their children can get into local state schools that don't charge exorbitant school fees.

- ✔ **Distance from the beach:** You may never go to the beach, but proximity to a beach is built into the price of any house in all of Australia's capital cities (except Canberra, of course, though prices on the New South Wales south coast may well be affected by its proximity to the ACT).

- ✔ **Distance from the airport:** Airports can move property prices up or down. Nobody wants to be on a flight path or beside an airport, but many professionals like to be within easy reach of one. Regional centres with an airport are also a drawcard for seachangers and treechangers.

✔ **Distance from public transport:** Areas without good transport develop in a different fashion to suburbs close to main roads and public transport. Well-serviced areas tend to be more densely populated. In contrast, areas with poor transport links tend to have fewer townhouses and apartment blocks. These lightly populated areas also show a lower turnover of properties.

What kind of home do you really want?

Decide what you want in advance; don't let a real estate agent decide for you. Establish in your mind what features you most require in a property.

In a high-density area, try looking for a house on a corner. All other properties will potentially have up to five neighbouring properties, counting those they share a corner fencepost with — and that means five potential problems. With a corner house, you can have only up to three neighbours.

You can't expect any single house or apartment to provide all of the features you want to find, or be without those you want to avoid. The best thing to do is to make a checklist before you go on property inspections. You need to make your mind up in advance on certain issues that arise in the course of househunting. Here are some internal factors to ponder when considering your options:

✔ Would you live in a weatherboard home?

✔ Would you consider a two-storeyed home?

✔ Are you comfortable with a semi-detached house or a house in a terrace?

✔ Is a swimming pool an advantage to you or an unnecessary expense?

✔ Does your home have to be a free-standing house on a quarter-acre block? What about a unit or a townhouse?

✔ How thoroughly are you prepared to renovate? Would you be prepared to live with big-time renovations like replacing ceilings and floors or reblocking (where the wooden supports of a house are replaced)?

✔ Are you willing to trade off a big living area for a smaller garden?

✔ Are you prepared to park in the street or is off-street parking important to you?

✔ Are you able to put up with noise from traffic or railway lines or flight paths? If you're willing to take these distractions on board, you can get a discount on house prices. For any suburb, houses on busy roads always bring a discount.

✔ Are you willing to buy a house with legal or other limitations? Legal restrictions can include easements (patches of land where you can't build) or covenants (set rules for the future development of the house, such as a height limitation). Other limitations can include a heritage listing. (Don't worry about National Trust listings on the Gold Coast ... not for another century at least!)

Your solicitor must examine property title documents for easements (such as sewers) or covenants (for example, guidelines that rule out certain developments such as treefelling). Such details can affect the value of any house.

Sooner or later, you're going to settle on a place in a location that you think suits you. The next step is to investigate whether it's worth buying. Assuming you don't plan to demolish it, your main aim is to evaluate whether the place is in working order.

If you're inspecting a property and the owners have left all the lights on, turn them off and have a look around with only natural light. This trick can reveal whether the level of natural lighting is adequate and if the place has dark areas that may pinpoint areas of dampness.

The inspection stage in the home-buying process is terribly practical. You can find out whether existing features of the property are working properly and whether the property can accommodate your long-term plans.

Don't be distracted by sentiment. While you may like a certain tree or a certain stained-glass window on the property, keep your mind focused on what matters: What is the standard of the property? How much work is absolutely necessary for you to do if you move in?

Weeding out the weaknesses

If you're not a technical person, having the property inspected by a professional is a good idea. An inspection by a local builder or an architect can reveal any serious problems to you.

People jumping on floors to test their firmness during property inspections are unlikely to know much about property investment. Floors, windows, doors and other surface details have little relevance to the overall value of the property, especially in high-value areas. Characteristics that can make a difference, though, are signs of structural weakness or dampness.

You can't depend too much on an architect's inspection. The first time James had a house inspected by an architect, the architect fell through the roof of the outhouse. He recovered but James took a little longer to regain his faith in an architect's ability to spot weaknesses in buildings.

Architects or builders can only make a calculated guess on the condition of your property; you can't expect them to make a decision for you.

The best service architects or builders can offer is the ability to warn you off buying a property. (They can never so confidently recommend that you go ahead and acquire a property.) An inspection often costs a few hundred dollars but it can save thousands.

If you've come across properties nearby that had a history of pests such as white ants (that like to chew away at people's front doors or back stairs), then consider getting a pest inspection. Of course, don't believe pest inspectors are always 100 per cent correct. James' cousin was selling her house in Manly during the late 1980s property boom. She knew there was a problem with white ants that had made a nest under the back bedroom. The pest inspector came to the house and very quickly checked out the most likely trouble spots.

Out in the back garden he finally came to the back bedroom rear wall. The back part of the house had sagged over the years and there was no room to crawl underneath the boards and do a proper inspection. The inspector stood in the garden for a few moments considering the situation. Then he squatted and aimed his torch under the house for about 30 seconds. Standing up, he turned and proclaimed to James' stunned cousin: 'It looks all right in there.'

Five minutes later, he handed her a certificate saying the property was free of problem pests. The white ants munched onwards, the inspector drove off with another hard job avoided and James' very guilty (but plainly pragmatic) cousin went ahead and sold her house (complete with pest certificates).

Like architects or other building experts, pest inspectors are far from perfect. The greatest service you can get from a pest inspector is advice about when a problem is extreme and you're warned off buying the property.

Using a buyer's advocate

Who is that woman at the auction driving the auctioneer crazy with her endless questions? She's a buyer's advocate, the new breed of property professional paid to help real estate buyers.

Mostly, buyer's advocates are real estate agents themselves and they know all the tricks of the trade. Buyer's advocates represent you at the auction, call your bids and deal with the auctioneer. You can simply sit and watch, or even stay at home if you like.

The advantage of using a buyer's advocate is that you don't have to go through the stressful process of buying a house at auction. What's more, the advocate may purchase the house for you at a cheaper price than you expected.

Of course, nothing is free. Buyer's advocates charge hefty fees and they're always keen that you win the auction, even if you end up paying more than you had planned. The fees charged by buyer's advocates vary widely and depend on the depth of service they offer. Some advocates will simply represent you at auction; others will handle the entire process from searching for the right house to clinching a deal.

Buyer's advocates' fees range from a few hundred dollars to about 2 per cent of the purchase price of the house, depending on the extent of the service they offer you. If you end up paying $20,000 (that is, 2 per cent) on a $1 million property, you have to ask yourself whether the fee was good value for money.

At their worst, buyer's advocates are seriously troublesome failed agents who spend their weekends making life difficult for their former colleagues. One flare-up between a Melbourne buyer's advocate and a real estate agent ended up in court as the real estate agent sued for defamation (the real estate agent lost). Buyer's advocates are useful if you're very new to the property market, too busy to look for yourself, you live interstate or overseas, or you want a certain property at all costs. Otherwise, think seriously about the fees you have to pay.

Remember, though, that fees paid to buyer's advocates on the purchase of investment properties are tax deductible. They're not, however, tax deductible on properties to be used as a family home.

Dealing with Real Estate Agents

For most Australians, real estate agents *are* the real estate market, and how successfully you deal with them can determine the success of your property investment. Real estate agents hold nearly all the cards in the residential property market. Unlike the commercial property market, where they regularly meet their peers, home buyers can be easy pickings.

You may not appreciate them at the time, but real estate agents do perform a vital service in what can be a very messy transaction process. But the standards of that service are widely variable. If you have doubts about a real estate agent, you should enquire if the agent is a member of the REIA (the Real Estate Institute of Australia).

The effective way to deal with a real estate agent is to keep your own targets in mind. Listen to what the agent says and ignore extreme comments. If the agent's estimate of a property value sounds too high or too low, it probably is just that! Keep in mind always that the real estate agent works for the seller; often what the agent says doesn't make sense to you, but, if you view the exercise from the seller's perspective, you can see the scenario often makes sense at the time.

The agent will always act in the seller's best interests; don't expect any special attention if you're the buyer.

Tough luck

A friend of James — let's call her Sally — spent many months searching for a house in the Floreat district of Perth. Eventually she found the ideal property and, because the house was for private sale (it wasn't planned to auction the property), she asked the agent for some guidance on how she might acquire the property.

Weeks passed and, after a series of successive offers, Sally was told the vendors were willing to sell her the property. The price the vendor wanted was $285,000. Sally and her partner finally made a deal for $280,000 over the phone to the agent. They were asked to pay a deposit of $28,000 and the agent said he would bring papers over to their flat on Sunday afternoon to clinch the deal. That weekend they signed the contract papers and handed over the cheque for $28,000. On Sunday night they went out to dinner, delighted with their purchase, and began making plans for a new life in a new home.

On Monday morning the agent rang. He said another buyer had appeared and was offering $295,000 for the property. Sally, in her innocence, thought the agent was merely letting her know how lucky she was to have struck a deal at $280,000.

But that's not how this story goes. The agent announced that the vendor had not actually signed his part of the contract so the contract didn't exist yet. Besides, her cheque was only a deposit, which was refundable — the sale process was, in fact, not yet over. Dismayed and bitterly disappointed, Sally told the agent she simply couldn't raise another cent for the house; she'd reached her maximum bid.

The agent said the seller would take the higher offer. Sally's cheque was put in the bin and she was back where she started. This train of events isn't unusual and is perfectly legal.

Real estate is a tough game. The only thing that matters is money. Don't ever think you've clinched a property deal until the title to the property is in your name. Thousands of stories exist about people who felt they got a raw deal from agents. But agents act for the seller. If Sally had been the seller, she would have been impressed that the agent had lifted her sale price by $15,000.

All About Mortgages

Tracking down the right mortgage package is a lot harder than it used to be. Once upon a time, the majority of mortgages were variable (they changed with official interest rates) and they came from one of the 'big four' banks. These four banks — ANZ, Commonwealth Bank, National Australia Bank and Westpac — still control about 65 per cent of the mortgage market. When smaller banks are added, the banks' share of the mortgage sector rises to 90 per cent, with the remainder financed by non-bank lenders. Today, the problem for the home purchaser is the tyranny of choice.

Rating the various mortgage packages

Around 80 per cent of all mortgages are variable-rate loans (especially if you include honeymoon mortgages that offer a low-cost introductory rate). However, the number of people choosing mortgages with a fixed rate over an extended period of time increases dramatically when they expect interest rates are about to rise.

With a variable-rate mortgage, your repayments are dependent on movements in interest rates. If you take a fixed-rate mortgage, you 'lock in' to a gamble that rates are going to move in a direction that benefits you. This move is a big gamble, as your home mortgage is probably your biggest financial commitment.

No-one can give you a secret recipe for the right mortgage — you need to get the package that suits your circumstance from the best lender. The main decision to make is how closely you wish to hitch your stars to the official interest rates. When official government rates move, so do variable rates charged by home lenders. Here are the main choices in the mortgage market:

- ✔ **Standard variable rate:** This traditional 'plain vanilla' mortgage is the simplest and most popular form. If you get one of these mortgages, you're likely to always be reading the newspaper headlines to see if interest rates are moving.

- ✔ **Fixed-rate mortgages:** The most common fixed-rate mortgages are generally fixed for periods of three years or five years. These mortgages can suit two types of people: Those who are reassured by knowing in advance what their rate is going to be for the next few years, and those who believe the fixed rates offered today are going to look like very good value in the coming years.

✔ **Split-rate mortgages:** This type of loan is a 'six of one, half a dozen of the other' option. A split-rate loan allows you to 'fix' a portion of your mortgage and take the variable option for the rest. These loans suit people who like the security of a fixed rate but believe they have some extra cash to throw at reducing their mortgage in the coming years. Split loans can be complicated, and the fees on these mortgages can ultimately be quite expensive if you pay fees on both portions of the loan.

✔ **Honeymoon loans:** When honeymoon loans first came on the scene, senior bankers would often smile and privately joke that these loans were for 'absolute beginners'. A honeymoon loan offers a very low first-year rate on your mortgage and then the mortgage reverts to a variable rate, often with strings attached. Before taking out this type of loan, check the details, because in some banks the honeymoon borrowers end up paying a higher rate than standard variable rates.

A mortgage is for at least five years, not just for one! Think of a five-year term when you assess honeymoon loans. The first cost of taking a honeymoon loan is that you effectively rule out the possibility of fixing at the rates on offer at the time. And, more importantly, you can pay a higher rate than most people after one year under the terms of the 'honeymoon' package.

Leaving it up to a mortgage broker

Mortgage brokers — agents who find you the best mortgage for a fee — have exploded on the scene over the last decade. As bank branches become a thing of the past, and non-bank lenders proliferate, close to half of all new mortgages are now sold through mortgage brokers.

The number of mortgage brokers fell during the credit crunch of 2008, as borrowers fled to the security of the big four banks and the banks squeezed out the mortgage-broking middlemen. Even so, mortgage brokers are here to stay. The biggest mortgage broker in Australia is Mortgage Choice (www.mortgagechoice.com.au), but a number of online mortgage service companies exist that help you decide which home loans suit you and then charge the lending institution you choose for your business.

This boom in the number of mortgage brokers is enough to tell you to tread carefully with them: The standards and qualifications in this industry are very mixed indeed.

The most important point to establish with mortgage brokers is which banks are on their 'panel of lenders'. You rarely find that any broker has all four of the big banks on the books. For example, Mortgage Choice has

23 lenders on its panel, but not National Australia Bank. As a result of this limitation, you're not actually getting the results of a hunt through every available bank for the best mortgage, but a selection from the mortgage broker's panel of lenders.

Ask a mortgage broker which of the big four banks — ANZ, Commonwealth, NAB and Westpac — are on their panel of lenders. If any of these banks is missing, then you're not getting the full story on all your options.

Nevertheless, mortgage brokers provide a very useful service because they can give you a quote on a mortgage from a lender that you may not have considered in the first place.

The best way to deal with a mortgage broker is to see them as someone who may have the best loan for you — but not as someone whose job it is to find the best loan.

Home-Buying Costs (Sure Does ...)

Buying a property means facing a range of fees. You have to add these fees to the price of the house because you can't seal the purchase of any property unless you cover these fees. The biggest fee of this type is stamp duty.

Be careful you don't underestimate the cost of buying a house. If you don't have enough to cover the total costs, you may have to get a short-term loan to carry you through. If that has to happen, you end up owing money on two loans — your mortgage and your short-term loan.

Stamp duty is a tax that is levied by state governments on legal documents. In this case, the conveyancing documents are taxed. In general, stamp duty is in the vicinity of 2.5 per cent of the purchase price, although rates vary from state to state. In late 2008, stamp duty rates for buyers of average homes in Sydney, where the median home price was $554,000, was around $20,420. Most states offer a concessional rate of stamp duty for first-home buyers — New South Wales, Queensland and Western Australia charge no stamp duty on first-home purchases up to $500,000.

Don't forget stamp duty in your calculations — after the cost of the property, it's the biggest cost you face. (Overall, buying a house is dearer than selling a house, due to stamp duty.) You can find a guide to stamp duty in your state on the Real Estate Institute of Australia website (www.reia.com.au).

Apart from stamp duty costs, the other costs you're likely to face when buying a house are:

- **Legal fees:** The legal process of passing a property from one owner to another is called *conveyancing*. As a rough guide, legal costs on a standard house purchase range from around $600 to $2,500.

- **Government fees:** Apart from the standard property-based stamp duty, some states charge stamp duty on the actual amount of your mortgage. Mortgage stamp duty fees have been reduced or abolished in most states, but New South Wales and South Australia still charge a reduced amount.

- **Inspection fees:** A builder or architect inspection on a property can cost you between $500 and $700. (Unlike other fees, you may end up paying this fee without ever owning the property.)

- **Lender's mortgage insurance (LMI):** If you borrow more than 80 per cent of the purchase cost of your home, you're charged lender's mortgage insurance. For example, lender's mortgage insurance on a $450,000 mortgage for a home priced at $500,000 is around $6,000.

Selling Up

Why does everyone pay so much attention to buying property instead of selling property? Two reasons exist:

- First, a lot of the factors that affect the outcome of your sale are actually sealed when you first buy the property. For example, when you want to sell, you can't change the location or the land it sits on.

- Second, a huge element of luck is involved if you achieve more than a reasonable price. If you get two or more bidders who are willing to fight for your property, the ensuing bidding war is more valuable to you than any physical improvement to the property.

Preparing your house for sale

Selling a property is a process that normally takes about six weeks. The timeframe may sound long but is actually quite brief when you think of all the marketing and hustling that is done in that period of time.

In general, the amount of work you put into preparing a house for sale needs to be linked to the location of the property. We believe, for example, that the further out from a city centre your property is located, the more important the physical condition of the house becomes.

Closer to the city, properties (unless they're in a terrace or are semi-detached) are primarily viewed as 'areas to be considered for property development'. Remember the maxim, 'Your house is worth nothing; it's the land underneath that holds the value.'

Allowing for the fact that luck plays a key role in selling a property — and that, in the inner city or high-income areas, half the potential buyers are considering pulling down your house for a new property development — be careful you don't spend too much money to make a house look its best during property inspections.

Here are some low-cost tips for making a property look its best:

- **Paint it:** No cheaper way exists when you want to improve the attractions of a property.
- **Empty it:** Take out everything but the minimum amount of furniture. Remove all clutter. The emptier the house becomes, the bigger it looks.
- **Create a garden:** If the garden is terrible, buy some plants and get the grass cut.
- **Cover the walls:** In an older property, where walls can be in bad condition, cover the walls in paintings, posters and anything else you can lay your hands on.
- **Fix ugliness:** Don't bother with big structural repairs or putting in a new airconditioning system, because you're too late for that. But fixing broken windows or drooping drainpipes can make a big improvement.
- **Replace handles:** Often small items that get a lot of use can make a house look tired. A new handle on an old door can spruce up an entire corner of a room. New cupboard handles and taps are a cheap way of making a cosmetic improvement.

Here are four extra tips that we find work very well during private viewing or on auction day, and cost almost nothing:

- Take one last look through the house for screaming embarrassments. You can sometimes leave behind stuff like underwear or that half-finished bottle of tequila from early this morning!
- Play an easy-listening 'ambient-style' CD on repeat for the duration of your open periods.

✔ Strategically place a vase of flowers and bowls of fruit to add to the aesthetic appeal of the living room and kitchen.

✔ Brew very strong coffee a half-hour before opening to counter any unpleasant odours and encourage that homely feeling.

Getting a handle on house-selling costs

Selling a house isn't as expensive as buying a house (unless you want to put a price on stress!). The biggest costs you incur relate to your real estate agent and any other work you choose to do in marketing the property or improving its physical condition.

Real estate agent fees for residential property tend to be fairly standard across the country. As a general rule, you can expect to pay 2 per cent to 2.5 per cent of the sale value of the property as fees.

Though agency fees may be standard, the amount you spend on marketing the property through advertisements in local papers and other media is up to you. Real estate agents encourage you to market the property far and wide. Keep marketing costs in proportion to the price of the property.

You may decide that, apart from the sign outside your property, a well-placed ad in the local paper does the trick.

The biggest selling cost you can face is the price of overcapitalisation. If you spend too much on renovations on a property in the wrong location, you don't get your money back when auction day arrives.

To move from one house to another can cost more than $40,000. Property purchase fees for agents, lawyers and other services can come to around $25,000. Selling a house can cost about $15,000. In other words, you have to make $40,000 if you want to avoid losing money during your transfer from one home to another.

Bearing the transition costs in mind, you really need to stay in any home for five years in order to allow your property to appreciate well beyond the costs you incur in selling the property and buying another.

You also incur the cost of legal fees when you sell your house. However, the transaction of selling is relatively simple compared with purchasing a property — no stamp duty issues and you don't pay capital gains tax on the sale of your primary residence.

Choosing a real estate agent with integrity and ability (hmm ...)

Property is an incredibly local business. A good real estate agent knows the local patch intimately. In most towns or suburbs a handful of big-name agents that operate nationwide compete with a group of independent agents that specialise in the local area.

The major real estate agents have excellent resources and their greatest advantage is the ability to find you a buyer for your property. The problem with these agents is getting them to devote sufficient time to your sale. On the other hand, the local independent agents are more likely to help you in preparing your property for sale, but they don't have the network of potential buyers.

Choosing the right agent is important. Ask friends and relatives for recommendations. If you have the time, visit the offices of local agents, watch the staff of these agents in action at local auctions and observe the quality of their sales campaigns. After you feel you know who's who in the area's real estate business, ask three different agents to visit you and make their pitch to sell the property.

Chapter 18

So, You Want to Be a Landlord?

*I*nvesting in the residential property market is a very different business from buying your own home. For a start, many people feel that owning their own home is the right thing to do for a variety of reasons — and not all those reasons are connected with investment or profit.

On the other hand, investing in residential property is a pure investment activity — the idea is to make a profit or a regular income and to spend a lot less than you earn. A simple concept perhaps, but worth bearing in mind for when we deal later in this chapter with negative gearing and tax.

Buying investment property also takes guts, because you're taking a big plunge. Unlike managed funds or shares, where you may have a block of money spread over a range of individual investments, a residential property puts a lot of your money into one single investment.

The fear of borrowing money also looms. The amount of money you borrow is up to you. But you can't escape the presence of borrowed money in the property market — indeed the entire industry (and these chapters on property work on the presumption that you borrow to buy your properties).

Everyone borrows money, not just property investors. If you're investing in shares, the listed company you choose has borrowings; if you're investing in managed funds, the fund manager has borrowings; even your superannuation fund has borrowings.

No pets allowed!

James' friend — let's call her Jane — rented out her house in Richmond, Melbourne, while she lived in London. Before she left, the managing agents told her they had found tenants for her house. According to the agent, a married couple with no kids wished to rent the property. The only issue was that these tenants had pets — two dogs, two cats and a guinea pig. Without a second thought, Jane, a pet lover herself, agreed to rent the property.

Every now and then, Jane called the agent from London to see how her investment was faring. After about six months, the agent became increasingly unavailable — time after time when she called he would be unable to come to the phone. However, the rent kept coming through to London so she didn't worry.

Then, one night in London, she was called by the Australian Federal Police to be told her house was the headquarters of a radical group of animal liberationists and the police needed her permission to make a raid! After the raid, the tenants left the house — with rent fully paid and up to date — but the clean-up required was nothing short of heroic. Jane still rents the house but, guess what? No Pets Allowed!

We're sure you've heard horror stories about investors who've had nightmare tenants. Perhaps you know first-hand of investors who have had flats wrecked, burned or even partly demolished by tenants.

However, the experience of renting property is, if never trouble-free, invariably profitable. Moreover, although your property returns a regular amount in rent, you do find comfort in your capital investment appreciating faster than inflation.

Traditionally, residential property investors buy houses, especially in the inner city, as investment properties. More recently, apartments and townhouses have emerged as a very popular form of investment, especially close to, or inside, the central business districts (CBDs) of the major cities and on the Gold Coast.

Don't be distracted! As a residential property investor, your concern is only with the attractions of a property as an investment — the short-term potential for income and the long-term potential for capital growth are your primary concerns.

Investing in residential property has something in common with investing in the sharemarket or managed funds. First, you have to grapple with and understand the 'big picture' of the market. As soon as you have a grip on the basic trends in property, you can then strike out and make your own entry into the market. We show you how in this chapter. We look at the popular areas of investment in each state and we show you how to keep a check on prices. We also go into more detail on financing and managing an investment property, and making the most of the tax system.

The Residential Property Market: The Basics

When you enter the property market as an investor rather than as an owner-occupier, you want to make the most money you can from your investment. Your criteria when assessing the market compared with those of a home buyer are different.

Over the last decade, a few very important changes have been taking place that could influence the profitability of your property investment. The ongoing urbanisation of Australia and the new ways that the finance industry sells mortgages have combined to reshape the market. Here are the major features of the market in the 2000s:

- **Inner city:** More people are living in major cities in apartments. Inner-city populations are growing for the first time since early in the last century. Each year, the number of people living in inner-ring suburbs of our capital cities increases.

- **Seaside:** Apart from within the five- to ten-kilometre 'ring' around the major cities, the other area where capital cities show strong price increases is coastal locations. This trend is most obvious in the population increases recorded on the Gold Coast, the Sunshine Coast and the New South Wales Central Coast. More than 80 per cent of Australians live within 50 kilometres of the sea.

- **Second-hand homes:** In the 1970s, everyone wanted a new house. In 1977, 50 per cent of all houses sold were new. In 2000, that figure had fallen to 20 per cent — people are happy to buy older houses or older apartments in good locations.

- **House moving:** The average Australian homeowner moves house every five years.

- **Mortgage turnover time:** As banks try harder to win customers with special deals, more people change their mortgages. The average life of a mortgage dropped from seven years in 1995 to five years in 2000, where it remains today.

These trends are some of the key changes that can influence your property investments in the coming years. Some of these trends may change; for example, if the economy has a long period of low growth, homeowners may choose to stay put longer.

However, the key trend of more people living in the city and by the sea is likely to remain a reliable pattern for the future (especially if those real estate agents have their way!).

Hot Property in Australia

The Australian property market is splitting into distinct sub-markets that have very little to do with each other. Price movements in harbourside Sydney are very different from those of the south-west and the Blue Mountains, and price movements in Adelaide's garden suburbs have little in common with the prices achieved in Bordertown or Mount Gambier.

In general, the price of houses in every mainland capital city has increased strongly over the last decade — at least doubling in most cities and more than tripling in Brisbane, Adelaide, Perth, Hobart and Canberra.

Price increases have been the most spectacular in the resource-rich states of Western Australia and Queensland. Queensland has also benefited from the flight of people from southern states to the Sunshine State, in search of warmer weather and lower property prices. Although Brisbane property prices have soared, houses are still more affordable in the north than in Sydney or Melbourne.

If you can afford a small house, this choice of investment may be much better value than an apartment in the city. Houses may take more maintenance but a limited supply of them in inner-urban areas ensures their appeal — remember, developers can always build more apartments.

Nevertheless, some national patterns are emerging. Properties within five kilometres of the city centre and one kilometre of water appear to have a long-term attraction for all Australians, whether they're buying or renting.

The other reliable areas of property investment are *middle-ring* areas within ten kilometres of the city, including suburbs known as *sterling suburbs*. These are long-established suburbs like Mosman (Sydney), Camberwell (Melbourne) or Chelmer (Brisbane), where the land values appreciate steadily.

The extraordinary feature of the urban property market is that the enthusiasm for inner-ring locations near the city or near the sea gets stronger, regardless of what those suburbs currently look like. Older parts of Sydney and Melbourne that are dotted with factories, warehouses and even slaughteryards show a powerful performance year after year. Bayside locations cluttered with industrial estates or former dockside enterprises also move up in value with surprising speed.

The end of the property boom in Sydney and Melbourne, the seachange and treechange phenomenon and the resources boom in the north and west of the country means big city investors are looking further afield for hot property. In late 2008, some of the hottest property was in small coastal hamlets transformed by an influx of cashed-up baby-boomers. Here's a non-definitive list of 'hot' investment locations across Australia, gleaned from a variety of media sources.

Cosmopolitan Canberra

As a 'new city', Canberra has a unique property market. However, Canberra hasn't escaped the trend towards inner-city living and large comfortable apartments close to the city.

Politicians and public servants like to be close to the action, near the city or Parliament House, in suburbs such as Braddon, Campbell, Griffith and Reid. Academics and students are drawn to Acton, on the shores of Lake Burley Griffin and the Australian National University.

Not-So-New South Wales

Sydney is baring the brunt of the global financial crisis, but you can't keep a property-mad city like Sydney down for long. Sydney's population is edging towards five million as it continues to attract the lion's share of new overseas migrants. For this reason alone, inner-city apartments continue to attract investors and new residents.

Sydney property hotspots include Chippendale — west of the CBD and next-door to the University of Sydney — as well as the inner-city precincts of Haymarket, The Rocks, McMahons Point and Surry Hills.

As new migrants fill the city's apartments, baby-boomers and young families continue to move up and down the coast in search of affordable housing and a more relaxed lifestyle. Hotspots include Ballina and Yamba, coastal towns that share the lifestyle of their northern neighbour, Byron Bay, at a fraction of the cost.

Terrific Northern Territory

Darwin is on a roll as money and people pour into town to service the resources boom and the armed forces. Houses are still affordable and rental yields are the best of any capital city in the nation.

Houses close to the harbour are the pick of the crop. Hotspots include Larrakeyah, the Cullen Bay marina estate and Myilly Point.

Quirky Queensland

Some of the hottest property in Queensland is on the coast, in the whale-watching mecca of Hervey Bay and the holiday playground of Magnetic Island.

Unlike other capital cities, Brisbane has a less industrial landscape; the city spread to the hills and the coast has occurred in a much more spacious fashion.

Moreover, the city is quite decentralised, and the presence of the Gold Coast nearby also creates a pull from the immediate confines of the city centre. Experts advise investors to look within ten kilometres of the city centre or outer suburbs with good transport links. The Redcliffe Peninsula on the city's outer fringe is a current favourite.

Subtle South Australia

Prices in Adelaide are traditionally less volatile than in other capital cities across the country. Le Fevre Peninsula is a relatively affordable corner of Adelaide, on the Gulf St Vincent and just 15 kilometres from the CBD.

However, the town most likely to prosper is reportedly Ceduna, an isolated regional centre in the west of the state, rich in agriculture, aquaculture and mining operations.

Traditional Tasmania

As the smallest of our capital cities, Hobart has a modestly priced property market. You can find pockets of relatively strong growth in historic areas of the inner city and around the wharves.

For a cheaper entry into the Hobart property market, new opportunities are opening up east of the city centre, where a large retail precinct is being built near the airport. Suburbs best placed to cash in on the new development are Cambridge, Seven Mile Beach, Mornington and Warrane.

Venerable Victoria

Over the last decade, Melbourne's inner city has come alive. Inner-ring suburbs to the north of the CBD offer investment opportunities in apartments. Hotspots include Ascot Vale, Flemington, Carlton and Clifton Hill.

Outside Melbourne, the Latrobe Valley offers employment growth and good transport links to Melbourne. Towns such as Traralgon and Morwell offer good entry-level investment opportunities. Gippsland's Lakes Region is also attracting buyers' attention.

Wild Western Australia

The Western Australian property market is cooling its heels after several years of extraordinary growth. At one stage, Perth was almost as expensive as Sydney. An influx of workers for the resources industry and related services sent rents sky-high in Perth and outlying mining towns alike.

Perth is no longer cheap, but suburbs such as Withers, College Grove and Carey Park, south of the CBD and a few minutes from the beach, still offer affordable housing.

The regional city of Geraldton is close to the mining action and the beach, and still offers value for money. South of Perth, the coastal town of Bunbury has good transport links to Perth.

Picking Falling Price Trends

Do residential property prices ever drop? Oh yes, they do — a lot more often than many people realise. The long-term pattern for residential property prices is ever upwards, but prices can drop in regional pockets (Sydney, Melbourne, Canberra, Perth and Hobart in 2008) or across the country (in 1990).

Sydney has a particularly volatile market. Median home prices in Sydney jumped from $103,000 in 1987 to $210,000 in 1989; by 1991, they were back at $170,000. By the end of 2001, they were riding high again at $400,000 and, by the end of 2007, they reached $555,000 before retreating to $542,000 in mid-2008 as the credit crisis took hold.

Buying in holiday locations

As a rich sunny country with a huge coastline, Australia has more than its share of holiday locations compared with, say, Poland. Globalisation has the effect of pulling the population into the bigger cities, and that means regional locations desperately need economic development through tourism. Putting these two factors together, you get a property-development market in holiday locations that runs way ahead of itself during every property cycle.

Remember that holiday locations rarely suffer from a lack of space — and lack of space is a force that drives up property values. (Of course, exceptions do exist, for example, at headlands like Palm Beach in New South Wales or Portsea in Victoria.) In general, prices of holiday homes are very volatile — they increase dramatically in good times; they fall dramatically when things are slow.

But holiday locations have an allure. The Gold Coast, the Sunshine Coast, the New South Wales Central Coast, Victoria's Great Ocean Road, and the beaches south of Perth and west of Adelaide have all won the hearts of millions. But does that allure make them good investment potential?

The short answer is no. Even in very good times for property, like 2006, demand for coastal property, in terms of potential investors and tenants, falls short of demand for well-located city property. The outlook is better in regional growth centres, where investors can attract local tenants rather than seasonal holiday-makers.

Buying a property in a holiday location isn't good sense as an investment. Such a property may delight the family — and the many friends you suddenly realise your teenage son or daughter has found in recent years — and may even create solid long-term capital appreciation. But a holiday-home investment is very unlikely to beat the returns from a flat in the centre of any major city.

Why? Because the property is more than likely to be empty five days a week, at least for 40 weeks of the year. And having different people there every weekend means a string of different tenants with all the attendant complications like keys, cleaning, directions and maintenance. A holiday home as an investment rarely makes sense.

Isolated regional drops in price tend to occur in two ways:

- ✔ **Rural areas:** When the population of an area is actually decreasing, as happened in 120 rural areas in 1999, prices fall too.

- ✔ **Outer suburbs:** Suburbs located in the outer reaches of Australian major cities that have no distinguishing physical feature, such as a bay, a river or mountains, can fall while the rest of the city shows an average price increase. This result is the downside of the rush to invest in the inner city and bayside properties. Major decreases in home prices occurred in 2008 in some of Sydney's outer south-western suburbs.

Playing the Property Game

The approach to purchasing or selling an investment property can be the same as the principles that we spell out in Chapter 17 for buying and selling your own home. Narrow your search down by region and by suburb, and then refine it further to within a set area, perhaps bounded by a number of streets.

Unlike the family home, you have much more control over when you purchase an investment property or when you sell it. You can use this freedom of timing to ensure your financing of the property takes best advantage of market conditions.

The key difference with investing in residential property compared with owner-occupied property is that you can stay emotionally detached from the process. You can have very strict self-made rules on investment properties, such as location and price limits, and you should have no trouble keeping to them.

Everything you look for in your home purchase, you should also aim to find in an investment property. Here's a checklist for your assessment of an investment property:

- ✔ Is the house or apartment rentable 12 months a year?
- ✔ Has the property been rented previously and what is its rental record?
- ✔ Is the area known as a popular location for renting property?
- ✔ Is the property secure? (You can't be there to protect it yourself.)
- ✔ Does it have a low-maintenance yard and durable interiors?
- ✔ Does it offer off-street parking? (Some tenants don't like to leave their cars on the street.)
- ✔ Does it offer all key urban amenities (shops, public transport services and proximity to restaurants and cafés)?

When you're buying the family home, you have to try to satisfy everyone in the family; when you're buying an investment property, you only have to satisfy your own investment criteria.

Finding the Dough to Finance Your Investment Property

Property investors are treated differently than owner-occupiers. These days, though, most banks and non-bank lenders offer the same interest rates to investors and owner-occupiers. Investors in property normally go for a variable-rate mortgage with interest-only repayments, because only the interest component of your investment loan repayments are tax deductible. Fixed mortgages are rare among property investors because, in most cases, the property owner isn't seeking the sort of security offered by a family home. Rather, the investor is looking to maximise profits.

Choosing investment finance

Looking for a mortgage for your investment property is a different experience than when seeking finance for your home. Like the majority of property investors, you most likely already have a mortgage on your home, so the lender views you as both a sophisticated borrower and someone who is a slightly higher risk.

The *default rate* on investment mortgages (the rate at which people are unable to make their repayments) is always higher than the default rate on owner-occupied homes.

As a residential investor you're faced with a large selection of mortgage options, but industry figures show that the vast majority of investors in residential property opt for a standard variable rate — you're likely to do the same as a way of optimising your possible profit.

Don't be negative about negative gearing

Whether you like it or not, negative gearing is the fuel that drives the investment property market. In recent years some income tax reductions have made negative gearing less attractive in some circumstances but, for most people, most of the time, this investor's tool is worth investigating.

Negative gearing is a tax strategy. Don't invest for tax reasons. Invest to make money — saving on tax should always be a secondary consideration.

Here's how negative gearing works. *Negative gearing* allows you to receive a tax reduction based on the pure costs of owning an investment property. The benefit of this process is that you can claim a tax deduction on the cost to you of an investment after you subtract any income (or rent received) from that property.

For example, you buy a small apartment for $240,000, with a mortgage of $200,000 at 8 per cent interest. (The average mortgage rate in Australia over the last 15 years is around 8 per cent; Figure 18-1 shows how the interest rate has changed over this period.)

The rental on your property is $240 a week and your total annual expenses (excluding interest) are $2,370. The $2,370 comprises: Bills for rates and other utility costs at $700; insurance at $120; real estate agency fees for managing the property at $550; and other fees, including maintenance (such as fees for the *body corporate*, the owners' co-op that manages the apartment block), which comes to $1,000.

The higher the costs associated with your rental property, the better the negative gearing becomes. The total rental income is $11,520 per annum, allowing for four weeks' vacancy (48 weeks × $240).

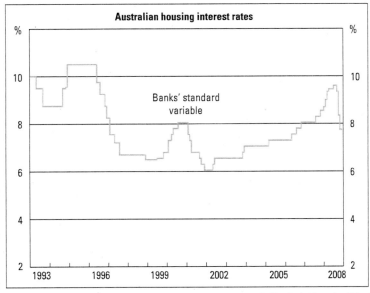

Figure 18-1: Fifteen years of mortgage rates.

Source: Reserve Bank of Australia Chart Pack, 3 December 2008.

Your mortgage costs per annum are $18,500 ($200,000 at 8 per cent for a year). Your expenses related to keeping the investment are $2,370. So your total ongoing costs relating to the investment are a total of $20,870.

However, your total income is $11,520 and, as a result, your pure out-of-pocket costs relating to this investment are $20,870 less $11,520, which equals $9,350. Under the negative-gearing system, you can make this $9,350 tax deductible on your tax bill.

The beauty of the negative-gearing system is that, while you get your tax deduction, the value of your investment property is — with a little luck and careful property selection — increasing all the time. In five years' time you can likely sell the property at a profit if you need to.

Negative gearing really only makes sense if

- ✔ You're on one of the two top tax rates of 41.5 per cent or 46.5 per cent.
- ✔ Your expenses on the property exceed your income.
- ✔ The property investment appreciates in value.

Don't assume your apartment is going to be rented 12 months of the year — it's wise to allow for a one-month vacancy.

The whole project assumes you get a payback through *capital appreciation* (that is, more than anything else, you aim to achieve an increase in the value of the property). If you don't get that capital appreciation, you make a loss on your investment and, worse still, you actually borrowed to achieve that loss!

As with all complex tax-based projects, talk to a financial or tax adviser (refer to Chapter 5) before making decisions relating to negative gearing.

Appreciating depreciation

Depreciation is the amount that the value of your assets decreases by over time and through wear and tear. Apart from negative gearing, depreciation is the other major factor to take into account before you enter the investment property market.

For example, if you buy a refrigerator, it deteriorates every year. Under the tax system, the government decides by how much it deteriorates and gives a tax deduction according to that calculation. The government also decides the *effective life* of the refrigerator, after which time it is worthless (for depreciation purposes) as far as the tax office is concerned.

In the same way that negative gearing makes buying a property with borrowed money very attractive, depreciation can make buying a newer property very attractive. You can get tax deductions for the depreciation of your property and all its various bits and pieces (known as *chattels*) like refrigerators, lawn mowers and sink plugs. (Yes, some poor schmuck in the tax office actually sits down and works out depreciation rates for sink plugs ... and you thought those types of jobs were long gone!)

The main thing to understand about depreciation is that a brand new building has more to depreciate. If you want to get big tax deductions, buy a new building or a new apartment and depreciate in the fastest way possible. If you don't need the tax deductions, consider older properties.

We suggest you consult with your financial or tax adviser (refer to Chapter 5) when making decisions relating to depreciation.

Paying Off Property Pronto

From little things, big things grow. Earlier we dealt with the wonder of compound interest (refer to Chapter 3). A modest amount of money swells to a very big amount of money over a long period (if you can earn more than the fees charged to you by banks). The process by which a small amount of money earning interest can steadily grow into a large amount is called *compounding* or *compound interest*.

You can also have a compound effect as a property investor by regularly paying a tiny bit extra off your mortgage earlier. The secret is to make this saving after all other costs have been considered. In other words, do your calculations on how much your investment property costs to manage. Then, when you're finished, add another $20 a week to throw at your mortgage.

Even that tiny amount of $20 a week over and above your initial budget that you spend on paying out the mortgage results in huge savings over the long term. For example, if your mortgage is $100,000 and you pay an additional $20 a week, you'll finish with the mortgage faster, as shown in Figure 18-2.

One successful property investor put it this way: 'You'll notice the reduction in your mortgage but you'd never have known where the $20 went anyway.'

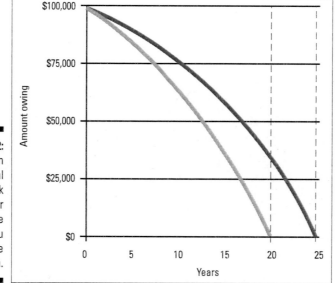

Figure 18-2:
An additional $20 a week off your mortgage saves you heaps in the long run.

Can You Manage on Your Own?

For many people, owning a residential investment property is their first foray into the business world, and some nasty surprises can be just around that new investment front door. For example, people who seem quite reasonable at first meeting now want more money — or they want you to fix something they broke. (And that's just the real estate agents!)

Renting a property can be very frustrating, especially if your first tenants turn out to be hardened criminals who insist on parking their motorbikes in the kitchen. (Only kidding, your first tenants are bound to be better than that — they leave their motorbikes tidily in the bedroom along with the drugs!)

But, seriously, unless you lay down some ground rules for yourself, your tenants and anyone else in the loop, such as the managing agent (if you decide to use a managing agent), the entire process of property rental can get out of control very easily.

For many people, owning an investment property is considerably more challenging than other forms of investment. Paying an agent to manage the property can be a valuable move and less stressful for you because you're not personally involved with the tenants.

You can, however, decide to manage the property yourself. Some people manage to rent properties for years to a succession of friends and acquaintances, but many more people find direct management hell.

We recommend hiring a managing agent; then you only have to have one successful working relationship (with the agent) to make the investment work. Here's why:

- A managing agent knows the market and knows precisely the amount of rent you can charge at any given time.
- A good managing agent also helps you find and select tenants.
- A managing agent will conduct regular property inspections and deal with tenants on an ongoing basis.

The main job for you then is to pick a good managing agent who charges reasonable commission. In most inner-city areas, the competition between managing agents is strong, so make sure you visit several agents before making a decision.

Choosing a managing agent isn't unlike choosing an agent for selling a property (refer to Chapter 17). The difference is that your relationship with this particular agent is long term — so keep things cordial at all times.

A managing agent generally charges between 6 per cent and 9 per cent of your weekly rental income, plus one week's rent each time they let the property.

Here are some useful tips for effectively managing your residential investment property:

- **Don't expect too much of your managing agent.** The primary aim is to ensure someone is in the apartment or house 11 months of the year paying a reasonable rent.
- **Don't bother meeting your tenants; the relationship is commercial.** What is there to talk about? Only repairs and improvements. Let the agent deal with tenants. A relationship with a tenant can only cost you money.
- **Expect your tenants to damage the property.** Almost certainly, you can't escape regular outbreaks of damage to rented properties. Accept in advance the likelihood of floods, fires, break-ins and parties. (You're likely to feel a lot better when it happens!)

✔ **If you've bought an apartment in an apartment block, go to body corporate meetings.** Most importantly, go to the first meeting of a body corporate in a new block, or at least the first meeting held after you've bought into an older block. If you're not at the meetings, you can't keep up with planned developments for the property.

✔ **Don't believe in rental guarantees.** A *rental guarantee* (where property developers promise a 'guaranteed' rate of return on your investment) is only as good as the person or company that offers the guarantee. A rental guarantee is not a reliable way to invest. If a property-development company goes belly up six months after offering you a rental guarantee, that guarantee is worthless.

Making Money Out of an Investment Property

Property isn't a complicated business, compared with, say, investing in carbon credits. You have costs and you have income — your power to make a profit depends on cutting costs and raising income.

Rent levels tend to be set by the market — you may get a top rental but there is an upper limit to what you can charge. Therefore, your income from rent is fixed. On the other hand, you're the one who has real control of the costs relating to an investment property. Keep costs to a minimum. The less you spend on your property, the more valuable your investment becomes.

In urban areas, especially in waterfront, inner-city and middle-ring suburbs, the asset is the land, not the building.

On the basis that your rental income is fixed by the market and the land value is where you get capital appreciation, then money spent on the property on anything other than emergency repairs is a total waste.

Keep maintenance to a minimum and don't bother with renovations. Renovations are for owner-occupiers and repairs are for tenants.

Property developers talk about the *merging principle*. If a rented property is too valuable, it decreases the land value because demolition costs are too high. If a rented property is in extremely bad repair, you have to spend money to fix it. A house where the value of the land is least affected by the condition of the house has 'merged' with the land value and is the ideal residential investment property.

Taking tax to task

A clear tax strategy is very important when investing in property, and we don't just mean negative gearing. As the owner of an investment property, you're going to face a number of new taxes that you probably avoided previously. The main taxes to be aware of are:

- **Capital gains tax (CGT):** You become liable for CGT on the capital appreciation of all investment property when you sell. For all property bought after 21 September 1999, you pay tax on half the profit at your top marginal tax rate.

- **Pay as you go (PAYG) tax:** You must pay tax on your rental income at your marginal tax rate. The good news is that you can offset this tax by claiming deductions for expenses incurred on the property, depreciation and negative gearing.

- **Goods and services tax (GST):** GST isn't applicable to investors in residential property in the vast majority of situations. However, GST can be applicable in a mixed-use development (that is, where commercial units such as shops and residential units such as apartments are in the one complex).

- **Land tax:** Land tax is a state-based tax on the value of land (not buildings) held by you for investment purposes. The tax is applied at different rates in different states and usually has a generous threshold for when it kicks in.

Tax tricks for young players

Our tax system never stops changing. So, the information we give you about tax is only as good as the publication date at the front of this book. (For more on tax advice, refer to Chapter 5.)

Perhaps the greatest secret tax benefit for investors in property — or anyone 'gearing' into any investment — is a piece of tax law called *PAYG income tax withholding variation*. If you own an investment property and you borrow to finance the property, then you can get the tax deduction prepaid in relation to any negative gearing.

Instead of waiting until you file your tax return each year to benefit from the tax deduction, you can actually spread the deduction over the previous 12 months by having it subtracted from the tax you owe on your salary each week. PAYG income tax withholding variation is an almost unbelievable piece of tax law and makes so much sense that we can't see how it sits with the rest of Australia's crazy tax system!

Say you're fairly sure you're going to get a tax deduction of $9,350 at the end of the year, then a withholding variation lets you get that tax deduction applied immediately to your weekly, fortnightly or monthly income, instead of waiting until the end of the year for a 12-month deduction. In this example you get a $179 reduction on your taxable income each week.

PAYG income tax withholding variation allows you to get money in your pocket rather than paying tax up-front on your property investment, and is one of the best ways to gain money from the tax system.

Chapter 19

Casting About for Commercial Property

In This Chapter

▶ Investing directly in commercial property

▶ Buying into shopping centres or industrial property

▶ Owning property through property trusts

*W*ho owns all those building on the main street of your city? If you take the time to look at a register of properties in your local council offices, you can see a list of all building owners. In almost every case a financial institution or a private investor owns the building.

The same goes for any industrial estate or shopping strip — some form of commercial property investor owns every factory, shop and warehouse in your town.

The council register, or the privately published *Cityscope* guide, is a terrific way of finding out about property ownership in any urban district of Australia. If you have even the mildest tendency towards snooping and private investigation, you can find out who owns any building for the price of a subscription.

As a property reporter on the *Australian Financial Review*, James had great fun digging names out of the *Cityscope* guides and calling them for stories — if he noticed these investors had taken control of expensive buildings. A lot of people thought he was a clever reporter tracking down these investors. Of course, all he was doing was reading names from a guide and locating those names in the phonebook!

Less than 30 years ago, private investment in commercial property was strictly for millionaires. Like many other areas of investment, smaller investors now have easier access to the market through new 'products', especially over the last three decades. These products have been created by property developers and financial institutions.

Nevertheless, getting started in commercial property is still a lot trickier than residential property investment. And, with different leases and tenant arrangements, it's a very different business.

Commercial property isn't for the faint-hearted. Usually, the stakes are higher but the rewards are greater.

If you're already comfortable with the residential market, then this chapter gives you a basic guide to the commercial property market. We look at the pros and cons of commercial property, and examine retail and industrial options. We also explain some of the finer points of strata titling, property syndicates and real estate investment trusts (REITs).

Going Commercial

Everything in commercial property is bigger — the prices are higher, the leases are longer. In short, this style of investing is the big league.

The *yield* on a property is a general indicator of its 'rentability'. Strictly speaking, a property's yield is the ratio of its income to its value. For example, if you pay $200,000 for an apartment and the tenant in that apartment pays an annual rent of $20,000, then the gross yield — the percentage return on your investment you can expect per annum — is 10 per cent. The net yield is the return you get after deducting expenses.

First the good news

You don't have to be a genius to make a success of commercial property but you need a bit of luck at the start to keep your costs within your budget. Here are some of the advantages of commercial property investment:

> ✔ **Higher rents:** The rent you get for a commercial property is much higher than for a residential building, but the capital gain is much lower. As a general rule of thumb, the *rental yield* — that is, the return on your money per annum — in commercial property is usually

between 7 per cent and 10 per cent, with average annual capital gains of around 3 per cent to 4 per cent. In residential property, returns are reversed — rental yield is only 3 per cent to 6 per cent but average annual capital gains can be as much as 10 per cent or higher.

- ✔ **Longer leases:** Commercial leases are reassuringly long, with about three years minimum in industrial units and up to five years for shops. In contrast, the minimum lease on an apartment is usually only six months.

- ✔ **Faster ownership:** Because you make a higher rent on a commercial property, you can pay out a mortgage faster and ultimately you get to own the property more quickly.

- ✔ **Less maintenance:** Most commercial buildings (especially industrial units) simply have fewer things to break or damage.

- ✔ **Fewer complications:** In practical terms, commercial tenants have fewer complications because the arrangement with you, the landlord, is strictly commercial.

Commercial property tends to have a slower increase in value than residential property but the rental rates are better. Always check whether an advertised yield is a gross or a net yield. The net yield can be up to 40 per cent lower than the gross yield.

Now the not-so-good news

Doing your homework becomes more important than ever in commercial property investment. The biggest issue after your property location is the nature of your tenant. Sure, your tenant might wear a suit, but some very expensive 'suits' went bust at the height of the 2008 credit squeeze. The chances that your tenant won't pay rent, is likely to go bankrupt or may treat you ruthlessly are considerably higher than in residential property. Here's the worst of commercial property investment:

- ✔ **Slower capital appreciation:** Nobody ever goes crazy at a commercial property auction and starts bidding extravagantly to get the factory of their dreams. Acting like a very sober business, property price rises are steady and predictable.

- ✔ **Higher risk of non-payment:** When commercial tenants go bad, they really go bad. More than half of all small companies end in business failure ... and business failures don't pay the rent.

- ✔ **Extended empty periods:** Commercial tenants are often very slow to get out of or to move into a building. A million things always need sorting out. As a result, vacant periods can run for months, although they're unlikely to occur as often as they do in residential properties.

- ✔ **Higher legal and advisory costs:** Because the stakes are higher in commercial property, you'll have to seek expert legal and financial advice with uptown prices.

- ✔ **Exposure to big business:** In a way that never occurs in residential property, you may be totally snookered by bigger players. A major property group can create a building site beside you, thus making entry to your property almost impossible for a year. Or a supermarket can open at the end of your shopping strip that spells doom for the butcher who is your tenant. Commercial property is business with gloves off — be ready for anything.

Getting a Foot in the Commercial Property Door

Traditionally, commercial property investment was strictly for the big end of town — to be taken seriously you needed a bank manager in your back pocket and a gold-plated Rolls Royce. (Well, at least you had to look like you had that sort of spending power.)

Now the scene is changing and you can enter the commercial market via a dozen ways, ranging from slow and sensible to absolutely dangerous (refer to Chapter 16 for a warning on property-investment seminars).

Commercial property is largely a game for professionals. Unless you're an experienced investor or you're in a special position to view the market — that is, when you have existing business relationships in the district where the property is located — you're more likely to be in safer territory in the residential property market or a listed property trust with a diversified portfolio.

As a general rule, the more direct your investment is in property the more likely you are to make a better profit. This is because there are fewer middlemen to take their cut and you make decisions that are always in your best interest. In this section, we describe the main ways to get into the commercial property business.

Going shopping

Shops have the longest leases of all forms of property — at least three years, but often as long as six years. As a business, shops are also relatively easy to understand. The main issue with a shop is ensuring that your tenant's business is complementary to the other shops in the neighbourhood.

In 2008, the rental yield on shops ranged from 5 per cent to around 15 per cent, depending on the type, size and location of the retail outlet. The big danger is that shopping areas can go in and out of fashion — too little choice for consumers and the shops are quiet, too much choice and the traffic goes out of control. The most attractive option is probably a settled tenant in a middle-ring suburb (a *middle-ring* suburb or area is generally taken to mean within ten kilometres of a city centre) with a long-established business.

Looking at industrial units

Small industrial units (sometimes known as *factoryettes*) have the advantage of being very easy to manage with minimum maintenance. Industrial prices move very slowly compared with residential prices but the compensation is that rental yields can be between 7 per cent and 10 per cent. With interest rates at their lowest since the 1960s, and the economic cycle at or near its low point, the next few years may be a very good time to examine industrial property.

The toughest part of getting into the industrial market is judging the quality of industrial locations. You can either build up expertise by studying a certain area or receive advice from a trusted adviser in the property industry.

With commercial property, a lot of importance is attached to vacancy rates. *Vacancy rates* are an indication of how much free space is available in a certain district. The lower the rate, the higher rentals and prices tend to become. In the late 1980s, CBD vacancy rates in Australian cities fell as low as 2 per cent. At the peak of the recession in the early 1990s, they were almost 20 per cent. In 2008, vacancy rates in all capital cities are back in single figures. At one end of the scale, Melbourne vacancy rates are at a record low of 3.1 per cent, while Gold Coast vacancy rates are 8.1 per cent and likely to move into double digits in 2009.

Separating into strata titles

The business of *strata titling* came into fashion in the 1970s property boom and has stayed ever since. This property-development idea is very simple and effective — a building is split into separate parts and sold to separate owners. The most common way to strata title a building is by offering separate titles or strata lots for each storey (or strata) on, say, a ten-storey building.

The term strata titling is common but, legally, the process of splitting up a property for investment purposes is now called *subdividing*. Getting into a strata title investment allows you to get those big rents that are common in commercial property without needing the funds to buy an entire building.

Strata title properties offer rental yields well in excess of the 3 per cent or 6 per cent you can expect from a residential property.

Strata title property, like all commercial property, offers very strong rental income but slower capital growth compared with residential property. Assuming you have a mortgage on the investment, you don't make as much money on the property, but you do own it sooner.

Joining the syndicate club

The property-syndication business bounced out of the 1980s property boom when everybody wanted to get into property as prices skyrocketed across the nation.

In fact, syndicates have always been around but traditionally they were genuine collections of like-minded businesspeople. Maybe four top Sydney surgeons buy an office block together or a group of property developers combine to buy a hotel. Today's *managed syndicates* can be much bigger, less clubby affairs where very little connection — or very little trust — between partners need exist.

Syndicates allow you to buy a slice of the action in properties that you don't have access to otherwise, such as office towers, shopping centres or apartment developments. You can get involved in property syndicates with an investment of about $10,000.

Over the last decade, property syndicates have lost market share to open-ended property trusts. Unlike a syndicate, which invests in properties for a certain length of time, open-ended trusts allow investors to add properties to their portfolio over time.

In a property syndicate, you're very far away from your money — other people manage your investment for you. This disconnection is the very opposite of the best advantage of property investment — the direct connection. At their worst, large syndicates do what they like with your money as soon as they have it in the bag. The same problem exists with all managed funds (which we discuss in Part III).

Property syndicates regularly show strong returns, and almost always enjoy good rental incomes. If you're thinking of entering a syndicate, remember, property is a long-term game. In a syndicate, your money is locked into a fixed structure for a set period, such as five or ten years. You may find getting your money out is very hard unless the other syndicate members agree with your ideas.

Are Property Trusts Trustworthy?

Property trusts are managed funds that specialise in investment property. The trusts have a structure like most other managed funds (see Chapter 13) but they have a special attraction to property investors because you can invest in the property market with little of the property market's typical complications, like real estate agents and lawyers!

Property trusts allow you to diversify your portfolio. You don't have to make the one big single bet on a property. Instead, you can spread your investment funds across a range of properties, managers and geographic regions.

More importantly, property trusts manage to overcome one of the great drawbacks of the property market — liquidity. Because you're able to buy and sell units in property trusts for as little as $1,000 at a time, the property trust market allows you to move money in and out relatively easily.

At their best, property trusts reflect the solid and predictable returns available in the property market. In good times, the trusts can also offer a safe place for investment funds. In the ten years to June 2008, listed property returned 8.5 per cent a year on average, second only to Australian shares (11.3 per cent a year).

Of course, all this convenience and flexibility has a price, mostly made up of the fees charged by fund managers.

Two main types of property trusts exist:

- **Listed trusts:** These trusts — called *real estate investment trusts*, or *REITs* — are listed on the stock market.
- **Unlisted trusts:** A fund manager runs such trusts and the fund manager controls the market, selling and buying units in the trust.

Over the past ten years, pressure from investors for higher yields has seen many property groups shifting their focus away from traditional rental income to property development and funds management. While this strategy boosted income, it also resulted in higher levels of debt. When global credit began to dry up in 2007, highly leveraged REITs were unable to refinance short-term debt. Investors fled the listed property sector in 2007–08, sending prices plummeting.

In the 12 months to June 2008, returns from listed property plunged 36 per cent compared with a 17 per cent fall for Australian shares over the same period. If there is a silver lining in such a steep fall in prices, it is that yields on listed property shot up to around 10 per cent in the same period.

The big names in the property trust world are a mixture of financial institutions like Colonial First State and property specialists like Westfield Group.

Real estate investment trusts

The easiest way to buy and sell interests in property has to be through listed property trusts — officially known as real estate investment trusts, or REITs. You can buy units in a listed trust in the exact same way that you can buy any other shares. Fees relating to buying shares in a listed property trust can be as little as $20 through an online broker.

Because they're 'on the stock market', listed property trusts bounce around in price in tandem with the rest of the market. This can be good and bad. A good day on Wall Street is likely to lift your investment in a listed property trust; a war in Afghanistan can reduce its value just as quickly. As you can see, the value of property trusts can be influenced by things that have nothing at all to do with the property held by the trusts.

If you like the sharemarket and like the way it works for you, then you can consider investing in listed property trusts.

Listed property trust prices are driven by factors that have as much to do with the stock market as with the properties they represent.

The listed property trust business harbours some of the biggest names in property — and some of the biggest slabs of money held anywhere in the country, as shown in Table 19-1. The Westfield Group (run by the Lowy family) had assets of more than $50 billion in 2008, and controls many of the nation's — and the world's — biggest shopping centres.

Table 19-1	Listed Property Trusts
Name of Fund	*Gross Asset Value, 2008 (A$ billion)*
Westfield Group	50.80
GPT Group	13.97
Stockland	13.70
Goodman Group	9.61
DEXUS Property Group	9.01
Centro Properties Group	8.00
Mirvac Group	7.66
CFS Retail Property Trust	7.31
Macquarie Office Trust	6.96
ING Industrial Fund	6.00

Source: Property Investment Research.

Unlisted property trusts

If you invest in unlisted property trusts, you have to do a little more work than you would buying sharemarket-listed property trusts. You have to obtain a prospectus and pay fund managers' fees in the usual fashion. Entry fees are on the high side, at between 4 per cent and 5 per cent of the value of your investment.

But unlisted property trusts are a closer link with the real world of property investment. In a sharemarket downturn, these trusts are likely to hold up better than their listed counterparts.

In sheer numerical terms, unlisted property trusts are the biggest category in the property trust market. In 2008, around 70 property trusts were listed but hundreds more were unlisted. However, listed property trusts far outweigh their unlisted counterparts in terms of the net value of their total assets.

In common with other managed funds, the manager runs unlisted property trusts. The manager of the trusts sells and buys units in the trust. (We discuss managed funds and property trusts in Chapter 13.)

The main danger with unlisted trusts is that many of them are just too small. If a trust has an interest in only one building (which isn't uncommon), then you don't get diversity and you may have trouble getting money out if the building runs into major problems.

Chapter 20

The Arty Side of Investing

*W*hen James was a kid, his grandfather showed young James his favourite ornament — a teapot that sat on the mantelpiece in the main room of his house. He turned the teapot upside down to point out a marking underneath that read 'EPNS'.

'When you see that mark, that's a sign of very good silver,' he said, gazing at that piece of ornate 'Irish silver'.

Many years later James and a friend who edited an antiques magazine got to talking about items of silver. 'EPNS ... that's all I remember. It's the mark that's placed on the best silver as far as I know,' said James, proud to reveal a little bit of understanding of the subject.

'Not quite,' said his friend. 'If you see "EPNS" on something it means it's made from electroplate silver on nickel base — in other words the mark actually tells you it's not the best. The best is sterling silver, I thought you'd know that.'

The big problem with art and antiques is that the level of understanding you need to invest successfully is very high ... much higher than the level you require to invest in shares or property.

A little learning is a dangerous thing.

—*Alexander Pope (not necessarily talking about collecting but making a crucial point all the same)*

More importantly, investing in art is really the dizzy end of the investment market. You may notice that very few articles about investing in art and antiques appear in financial publications. Finding books on investing in this area, apart from price guides, is also almost impossible. Why? Because investing in art and collectibles is a very tricky business. It can bring very strong returns but generally it is an inferior investment because prices are unstable and the market is *illiquid* (you can't always buy or sell these goods quickly).

Investing in art, antiques, wine, stamps and any other collectible is very unreliable. Many financial advisers don't even regard spending money in this area as a genuine investment activity.

But investing in collectibles is always fun and is often more interesting than other markets, as well as being occasionally lucrative, too.

If you're making every effort to build a diversified investment portfolio, you may easily decide to spend around 5 per cent of your funds on art, antiques or other collectibles.

The guideline of 5 per cent comes from financial advisers who recommend that investors don't spend more than 5 per cent of their funds on 'alternative' assets. In other words, if you do dabble in art, make sure you have enough money invested in mainstream assets such as shares, property and bonds to finance your retirement. If you spend your money on a beautiful work of art, you may not want to sell it when you need some cash. You're less likely to feel emotionally attached to your Woolworths shares or your term deposit.

In this chapter we take a bit of a hard-nosed approach to investing in art and collectibles, dealing with some of the crucial points for each category, and we give you the lowdown on buying and selling at auction.

Focus or Be Fleeced

The most likely way to make money in the art market is to focus on a single area of activity. By a single area, we don't simply mean Australian artists; we mean something much more precise, like Aboriginal art.

If you're collecting antiques, then you can choose to concentrate on English Victorian sterling silver; with stamps your choice can be a certain genre of stamps such as British Colonial Islands stamps.

Read everything you can on your chosen subject and become an expert before you become an investor.

Many business and political figures are specialist collectors. Former prime minister Paul Keating famously enjoyed antique French 'Empire' clocks. The disgraced former premier of Western Australia, Brian Burke, knew a thing or two about stamps — the 'WA Inc.' Royal Commission discovered that Burke had no less than $87,000 worth of stamps in the boom years of the late 1980s.

Investing in art and antiques isn't an exact science. You can't get accurate estimates of market value and, worst of all, you can't get regular income in the way of dividends from art investment. Your investment is an all-or-nothing gamble on capital appreciation. Most analysis of art investment makes one key point ... go for quality and aim for long-term returns.

As the art and collectibles market gets bigger with each passing year — and the number of pieces in circulation accelerates thanks to internet-based auction houses — the trend is for prices to rise for higher quality items and drop for lower quality items. In other words, rarity and quality are more highly valued each passing year.

Is Art Really an Investment?

The answer is yes. Art prices jump around dramatically and art collectors are notorious for blowing hot and cold on various fashions but, overall, evidence exists to suggest that, on average, quality art is going to appreciate in value over time.

That last sentence is cautionary: It really means that some top-quality art, antiques and collectibles are going to increase strongly in price over time at the expense of many low-quality items.

The nearest thing to an index of the international art market is the Artprice Index (www.artprice.com). Art has proved a more reliable investment than shares or property over the last decade. In the three years to January 2008, international art prices rose by 48.9 per cent (67 per cent in the United States). Then, in the first ten months of 2008, art prices fell by 14.5 per cent. It seems that not even the rarefied world of art is immune to a global credit squeeze and a collapse in buyer confidence.

The art market might not be immune to a global financial crisis, but, as a rule, art prices move in an entirely different rhythm to shares and property. In some ways, art and collectibles add diversity to a balanced investment portfolio. But, as soon as you start adding in the huge commissions (of up to 20 per cent) that you must pay for buying or selling works of art, not to mention the cost of insuring works of art while you keep them in your possession, then art as a collectible begins to look like a weak investment against shares.

Of course, art isn't a typical investment — most Australians would much rather look at a masterpiece painting than a collection of share receipts! What price do you put on the pleasure of owning art? The choice is yours.

Dealing with Antique Dealers

What a lovely way to make a living. Sitting in a pretty shop, surrounded by pretty things and making precious little pretty money! This low-profit business presents a dilemma for most antique dealers. The 'holding costs' of keeping those antiques in the shop for months on end are just too high for most dealers to make a good profit.

So, for you, the potential collector, knowing that most of the dealers don't make big profits is an important angle — in fact, the business is notorious for sending people into bankruptcy. This doesn't mean you should drive a hard bargain; instead, be reasonable with a dealer, because people dealing in genuine antiques are rarely focused exclusively on profit.

Few antique dealers manage to stay in the business for more than ten years; the trade attracts more sellers than buyers. So try to deal with established dealers with a track record of successful trading: They're likely to still be in business if you need to go back to the shop for any reason.

In Australia, the antiques trade is unusual by international standards because it's heavily dependent on imports. Many of the biggest dealers travel to Europe and Asia on a regular basis and fill containers with antiques for shipment to Australia. This process means the dealers control the market fairly tightly and the chances that you can pick up genuine antiques outside the dealer network are pretty slim.

It is the hunt as much as the finding of a work of art that gives the pleasure. For me ownership is a secondary quality.

—*Lord Alistair McAlpine, renowned collector*

Although generalising about antiques isn't possible, since every piece is different, a number of common investment rules do stand the test of time:

- ✔ **Buy what you like:** Sounds simple but collectibles is a high-risk market; you may never be able to sell the item you purchase ... make sure you like it!

- ✔ **Make sure of the age:** An antique must be at least 100 years old — no exceptions.

✔ **Get quality:** The three most important words in the antique trade are condition, condition and condition.

✔ **Get a detailed receipt:** Every purchase should be accompanied by a detailed description of the item purchased.

✔ **Keep records:** Some day you're going to have to pay capital gains tax on your investment (if you're lucky enough to make a profit).

✔ **Use reputable dealers:** Many of the best dealers are members of their state-based Antique Dealers Association.

Painting a Picture of the Market

The art market is a world within a world. Fashion trends are every bit as important as technical standards when considering investment returns.

Understanding the art market isn't easy, but clearly supply and demand ultimately dictate price in this type of market. These market forces are most obvious when a famous artist dies and the artist's family moves to control the release of any unsold works — they know that if all the works hit the market at the same time, the prices drop.

Art works, antiques and other collectibles such as stamps can be free of capital gains tax if they're bought or sold for less than $500.

Just because an artist is famous, every painting by that person isn't necessarily going to reach the same level of value. Some artists are more valued for their landscapes than their portraits — or the other way around.

In general, you can purchase sketches, even by very famous artists, for much less than paintings by the same artists. This discount for sketches is because paintings take much longer to produce than sketches.

You can purchase and hold art as an asset inside a self-managed, or DIY, superannuation fund, in some circumstances. (Part V of this book deals with superannuation.)

Unlike the stock market or the property market, keeping track of the art market by using the mainstream media is often difficult. With the exception of the *Australian Financial Review*, few publications seriously track financial activity in the art market.

Apart from looking at specialist collector magazines, your best way of getting a grip on this market is to watch for vital signs such as clearance rates and record prices.

Keeping abreast of clearance rates

The clearance rate at auctions is a very useful signpost to the overall health of the art market. When things are booming, the *clearance rate* (representing the total percentage of items sold) is high; when things are slow, the rate is low.

The Australian art market peaked in 2007 — a record $176 million worth of art was traded and clearance rates were around 80 per cent — thanks to bevies of buyers who had grown rich in the sharemarket boom.

If you look back over the last 20 years, the clearance rates were around 80 per cent in the art boom years of the late 1980s. In the early 1990s, clearance rates were averaging around 60 per cent as the art market recovered from the excesses of the 1980s. By the year 2000, the rates had inched back up towards 70 per cent.

Clearance rates can be seriously influenced by two factors:

✔ **Unrealistic expectations:** Like the property market, where sellers have too high an expectation and have set a high reserve price, the clearance rate is forced lower.

✔ **Cheap lots:** When auctioneers aim for volume over quality and are happy to sell almost anything, from tea sets to worn-out sofas, the clearance rate may be pushed higher.

Buried treasure

All art lovers dream of finding a lost masterpiece in a garage sale or hidden under decades of memories in Great-Aunt Martha's attic. In 2008, not one, but two Texan women did just that, discovering paintings by two famous Australian artists in their local stores.

In August 2008, a woman bought a painting of wildflowers with white coral at her local antique market in Texas for US$25. The painting, by Grace Cossington Smith, was later valued by Sotheby's Australia at up to A$45,000!

Three months later, another Texan was rummaging in her local second-hand store, where she found an interesting abstract painting. She paid US$45 and took it home, where she displayed it with her collection of modern pottery. Out of curiosity, she Googled the name written on the back of the painting, John Coburn, and discovered that he was a famous Australian artist. She contacted an Australian art expert who recognised the work as a genuine Coburn and valued it at A$20,000.

So, the next time you go to a local garage sale, dig deep. Buried treasure can and does surface in the most unlikely places.

Knowing your record-breaking artists

Keeping track of record prices is a useful, if limited, measure of the art market. Rather than giving an indication of the overall health of the market, records tend to highlight which artists are 'hot' at any given time. Table 20-1 lists the ten highest prices achieved at auction for Australian art over the ten years to 2008.

In recent years, Modernist and Aboriginal art has been in fashion, while abstract art and traditional landscape painting has not been as popular.

Table 20-1	Ten Highest Prices at Auction 1998–2008		
Price ($m)	*Year of Sale*	*Artist*	*Title*
3.48	2007	Brett Whiteley	*The Olgas for Ernest Giles, 1985*
3.36	2007	John Brack	*The Old Time*
3.12	2006	John Brack	*The Bar*
2.88	2007	Brett Whiteley	*Opera House*
2.31	1998	Frederick McCubbin	*Bush Idyll*
2.04	2007	John Brack	*Backs and Fronts 1969*
2.04	2006	Brett Whiteley	*'Frangipani and Humming Bird' — Japanese: Summer*
1.98	1999	Brett Whiteley	*The Jacaranda Tree (On Sydney Harbour), 1977*
1.92	2007	Frederick McCubbin	*Childhood Fancies, 1905*
1.92	2007	Brett Whiteley	*Orange Fiji Fruit Dove, c.1983*

Source: Compiled from Australian Art Sales Digest *(www.aasd.com.au).*

As one fashionable artist is breaking records, another's works may be falling in value. For example, the works of Brett Whiteley, who died in 1992 aged only 53, are fetching record prices, while those of a currently unfashionable artist like Rupert Bunny fail to appreciate.

Sometimes you see stories about 'crazy auction prices' where, for example, a Charles Conder or Ian Fairweather painting sold for twice as much as the auctioneer had expected.

The angle to remember about these stories is that they're just isolated reports and hype, except in record years such as 2007. Auctions every week in every city in Australia never hit the headlines. Only the record-breakers get noticed.

The vast majority of art investors don't make spectacular returns. The major auction houses claim that good-quality art, antiques, wine and stamps increase in price faster than inflation over a long period. This claim is certainly true for quality artworks. Just remember that we're talking about *average* figures.

> *If art is appreciated, it will appreciate in value.*
>
> —*Roger McIlroy, former Managing Director, Christie's Australia*

Buying and Selling at Auction

If you like property auctions, you're almost certain to love art and antique auctions. Better still, you have a real chance of picking up a bargain at an antique auction because the auctioneers generally have hundreds of lots (or items) they wish to sell in a single session. If you're lucky, you may find you're the only bidder on a certain lot — a time when the auction process works for you.

Buying or selling at auction takes a bit of nerve because you're charged high fees by the auctioneer, especially if you're selling. You carry the additional risk, too, that the market can reject your artwork in a very public fashion.

If you're planning to sell through an auction house, remember you're going to face fees of 10 per cent to 20 per cent of the value of the items sold for you by the auctioneer — called a *buyer's premium*.

Among the leading auction houses that operate in Australia are:

- Bonhams and Goodman (www.bonhamsandgoodman.com.au)
- Christie's (www.christies.com)
- Deutscher and Hackett (www.deutscherandhackett.com)
- Leonard Joel (http://leonardjoel.com.au)
- Shapiro Auctioneers (www.shapiroauctioneers.com.au)
- Sotheby's (www.sothebys.com) — click on About Us and go to Locations Worldwide for Australian auctions

If you're selling goods, the fee is usually a straight percentage, of around 20 per cent, so the fee charged depends on the value of the goods you're selling. Even if you're selling an item worth only $1,000, you can pay a commission of up to $200.

Fine Wine and Stamps of Approval

Sitting somewhere between the reasonably predictable world of art and antiques and the highly unpredictable world of collectibles (which we discuss in the next section) are wine and stamps.

As a general rule, wine and stamps attract highly specialised investors and have a reputation for being able to keep ahead of inflation as an investment.

The most highly valued wine and stamps are clearly good investments for specialist collectors. These investments are illiquid (yes, even wine) and they often require a major outlay of cash to get started. Even after you've bought them, you must be prepared to spend whatever is necessary to keep them in good condition. For example, wine needs cellaring in a controlled environment. Usually, unless you're prepared to commit a lot of time and money to such investments, they can be more trouble than they're worth.

Collecting Collectibles

You're cleaning out the attic and there it is — the classic Pink Floyd album with the 'gatefold' sleeve. 'It's bound to be worth something,' says your partner. (Guys always say the most obvious things!)

Don't depend on it! Remember the album probably sold a few million copies at the time. The same goes for your Uncle Fred's quaint 1940s cast-iron 'Kookaburra' oven or anything else that was mass-produced and is unlikely to ever become genuinely rare.

For most investors, collectibles are probably the most interesting and accessible of all potential investments but, sad to say, this category is the single most unreliable area of investment activity.

A working definition of a collectible is any article over 50 years old. The quality or rarity of 50-year-old collectibles can never match art or antiques, and their price tags can never match them either.

We all love vintage beer glasses, Toby jugs or gatefold albums of progressive rock bands, but they have little if any real value in the open market.

Of course, exceptions can always be found. Online auction sites are transforming the market for what can only be called rubbish. Who can forget the ten-year-old grilled cheese sandwich with a charred image of the Virgin Mary that sold on eBay in 2004 for US$28,000? Or the so-called Nun Bun (a cinnamon bun with a striking resemblance to Mother Teresa)?

At the very bottom of the collectibles ladder are 'ready-made' collectibles like 'limited edition' photographs of your favourite football team pictured with this year's league prize. Don't be fooled — you don't 'invest' in collectibles, you just spend money on them. If some day you can sell a collectible for more than you paid for it, Lady Luck is smiling on you.

Does this taste good to you?

One of the problems with 'marginal' investments like wine, stamps or even thoroughbred racehorses is that outstanding winners are trotted through the media as if their success was the norm.

Of course you, the wise investor, know that all that glitters is not gold. Only exceptional stamps, wine or horses make the headlines. Among these exceptions there is no better example than Grange Hermitage, the wine from the Penfolds Vineyard (now part of the Foster's group) that seems to rise in price year after year.

Penfolds Grange Hermitage is 'the great Australian red wine' and it was first produced in the 1950s by winemaker Max Schubert in the Barossa Valley, South Australia.

In the more than half a century since its first vintage in 1951, Penfolds Grange Hermitage has displayed an amazing ability to gain in price. Back in the 1980s, a bottle of 1951 Grange sold for $8,800, a record price at that time. In August 2008, a bottle of the same wine from the same vintage sold at auction for $53,936.

Grange is now so popular among wine lovers and investors alike that a string of attempts to produce fake versions of the wine have even been made. For example, in 1998, wine auction house Langton's Fine Wine Auctions reported attempts in the Australian market to distribute fake versions of the 1990 vintage. Later that year, Penfolds introduced tighter security measures for the wine, including laser-etchings on bottles of the real thing.

Langton's Managing Director, Stewart Langton, speaking at the August 2008 auction, said the 1951 vintage was seen by some observers as wine's equivalent to powered flight! We'll take him at his word for that, because neither of us is ever likely to taste a drop of the stuff.

Just don't forget, though, that this result is one of the best returns anyone, anywhere, has managed in the Australian wine-collecting market.

Part V
Your Nest Egg: Superannuation

Glenn Lumsden

*'I'm not really wise. I'm only up here
because I never had a super fund.'*

In this part ...

Superannuation is a much more attractive word than pensions, don't you think? And superannuation is a much more attractive way for you to finance your retirement. The government has created some generous tax advantages for anyone willing to make an investment in their own retirement nest egg ... the trick is to get a basic picture of the system and how it works. In this part, we spell out the basic features of our superannuation system and how you can profit from opportunities on offer from the superannuation industry.

Chapter 21

Super: You Gotta Have It

* *

In This Chapter

▶ Learning why super is a necessity

▶ Answering common questions about super

▶ Shopping for a superannuation package

▶ Checking out super choice and consolidation

▶ Rolling into retirement

* *

*H*ere's the news (hot from the history department): Since time began, people have had to look after themselves when they got old. Then for about a hundred years — say from 1880 to 1980 — governments in some western countries began to pay people a pension when they reached retirement age. However, if you're hitting retirement soon, you'll know that the splendid practice of handing out money to anyone over 65 has become a lot more complicated.

Why are governments trying to reduce dependence on age pensions? Because people are living a lot longer and because the first of the baby-boomers (those born in the late 1940s and the 1950s) are starting to ease into retirement and, in a few years, will place an enormous strain on government resources unless they're able to pay their own way.

In addition, government has become *smaller*. If you think back 20 years ago, state and federal governments owned water, electricity, airlines, railways, buses and trams. Governments were richer in those days. Today, however, Australia has more aged people needing more money from smaller government funds.

Whichever way you look at superannuation, there's going to be too many snouts at the pension trough. In 1993, Australia had 5.3 workers to support each non-working Australian. In 2007, the figure was four working Australians for every retiree and, by projection, in 2031, that figure will be 2.6 workers. Put simply, you can't depend on a government-funded pension any longer.

Companies, too, have less money for pensions. Charles Handy, the management guru, recalls that, when he joined Shell Oil in 1956, the company handed him his pension book on his very first day's work. Back then, big companies assumed they would employ people for a lifetime, and employees assumed the same thing.

Of course, as Handy explains, statistics in the 1950s indicated that, on average, employees would only live for 18 months in retirement. Statistics today indicate that retirees are likely to be pensioners for between 20 and 30 years.

So, unless your family owns the local bank or your partner is heir to the local casino, you're going to need to at least partially fund your own 'superannuation package'. In this chapter, we guide you through the main features of investing in superannuation in Australia. We look at how the super system works and ways you can top up your employer's super payments. We also answer some of the common questions about super. And we check out your options for managing your super and how you get paid from your super in retirement.

There are few ways a man can be more innocently employed than in the getting of money.

—*Samuel Johnson, 18th-century British author and occasional superannuation consultant*

Understanding This Thing Called 'Superannuation'

Superannuation is money accumulated for your retirement. Saving for superannuation is tax-effective because it isn't subject to the full rate of normal tax and is locked in — you can't (generally) access it until you retire.

Unfortunately, because successive governments keep trying to 'improve' the superannuation system, it's becoming even more bizarre in its overall design than the tax system. The trick for you is to concentrate on what really matters ... building your superannuation wealth the most efficient way.

The superannuation guarantee

The superannuation guarantee (SG) is a government-backed guarantee that means every employer in Australia must pay at least 9 per cent of your weekly earnings into a superannuation fund for you.

As a general rule, industry calculations suggest you're going to need 15 per cent of your weekly income invested in superannuation to fund a comfortable retirement lifestyle (by 'comfortable' we mean 60 per cent of your current income).

Assuming your employer puts in 9 per cent through the SG, your responsibility is to put in that extra 6 per cent of your income in the form of superannuation savings each week.

Pension penury or super survival

Less than $15,000 a year! This figure is all you have to remember if you doubt the value of superannuation. If you rely on the government pension, you receive (at the beginning of 2009) $14,612 a year to live on.

Government pensions are miserable. Australia is a rich country but single pensioners are expected to live on only $14,612 a year — that's $1,217 a month, $281 a week ... peanuts!

Meanwhile, the little perks of being a pensioner, like discounted travel fares or cheaper energy bills, are constantly under threat because utilities that were once owned by governments are now in private hands.

Luckily most people don't try to survive solely on the government pension; they have some savings or superannuation. In fact, Australia's superannuation assets more than doubled in the period 2002 to 2008, as shown in Figure 21-1. But a close look at the official statistics clearly shows that many age pensioners are barely scraping through. The Westpac ASFA Retirement Standard estimates that the average retiree couple needs about $27,151 a year for a modest lifestyle (against a government pension of $24,076) and the average single retiree needs around $19,300 (against the government pension of $14,612). (In Chapter 22, we help you work out how much you'll need in retirement.)

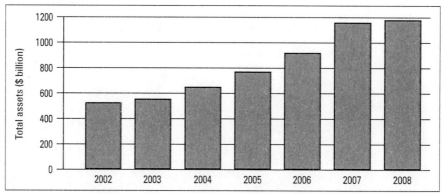

Figure 21-1:
Growth in total super-annuation assets.

Source: APRA (Australian Prudential Regulation Authority).

Getting Answers to Five Big Super Questions

You see the headline: 'Expert says you need millions of dollars to live comfortably in the future.' Funnily enough, these experts are always employed in the superannuation and financial-planning industries — they get a commission from the money you invest in retirement products.

You don't want a basic government pension of $14,612 a year and neither do you need to have $10 million — you need a reasonable and secure amount of money that allows you to live in *the style you regard as comfortable* for your entire lifetime.

The big problem with superannuation is that the industry is packed with jargon. By stripping away the jargon you can uncover the few key factors you need to know about the superannuation industry. In this section, we answer five of the most commonly asked questions.

Can I have a government pension and superannuation at the same time?

Yes, you can supplement your superannuation money with a government pension. The government has a list of really easy-to-understand (just joking!) formulas and calculations that allow you to get income from both sources.

The most important thing to concentrate on is the amount of income you can receive after paying all taxes. Many people find they can survive on relatively small incomes when they retire because those incomes are largely tax-free. For example, if you used to earn $100,000 a year, you may very well get along fine on $40,000 because you no longer have such high taxes and high expenses as when you were working. You can get information on superannuation and tax at the Australian Taxation Office (ATO) website at www.ato.gov.au/super.

Can I get money out of my superannuation before I retire?

Yes, but only in exceptional circumstances. If you're suffering severe hardship (as defined by the government) you can get money out of your super fund to pay major health bills or mortgage bills and other items. You can also get *unrestricted non-preserved superannuation* — money invested before 1999 that did not get a tax concession — out of the fund before you retire.

Should both partners have superannuation?

Yes. You may not stay with your partner forever and dividing up superannuation in a divorce settlement is very tricky. High-income earners can split their super with a low-earning or non-earning spouse. More importantly, you can access many of the tax advantages of superannuation twice if both you and your partner have separate superannuation accounts.

Does superannuation make sense if I'm self-employed?

Yes. More than 90 per cent of full-time employees have superannuation. Why treat yourself any differently? Only 72 per cent, though, of self-employed people have superannuation and 53 per cent have a superannuation balance of less than $40,000.

If you're self-employed, finding non-superannuation investments that can beat investments that are protected inside the superannuation system is very hard indeed. And, more importantly, money in superannuation is protected for your benefit no matter what happens to you or your business in the future.

Superannuation savings are protected from all claims — including any creditors claiming against a failed business.

Can superannuation funds lose money?

Unfortunately, yes. Superannuation funds invest in the same markets as everyone else and, if the markets reflect a bad year, superannuation funds have a bad year, too. As bad years go, they don't get much worse than 2008. The average balanced super fund fell by around 20 per cent in the 12 months to December 2008, the worst performance since the introduction of compulsory super in 1992.

Remember, though, that superannuation funds are generally well managed. If you choose your fund's balanced investment option, you're never totally exposed to one sector of the market.

Understanding Your Super Options

Sooner or later you're going to want to join a superannuation fund. If you're employed, the fund you join is most likely to be one that's offered by your employer.

These days, employers offer a choice of fund from a selection that includes industry funds, corporate funds and private providers such as AMP or BT. If you find the choices baffling, you can select the default option chosen by your employer or, if you do nothing, your employer will direct your superannuation guarantee payments into the default option.

If you're self-employed or if you receive payments from a wide variety of sources, getting a major financial institution or industry fund to manage your super for you is the best option.

Launching your own self-managed superannuation fund is also an option — if you have the time and patience to do all the administration yourself.

Having super managed for you

Most people get professionals to manage their superannuation. Two styles of superannuation fund are available in the market:

✔ **Defined-benefits fund:** A *defined-benefits fund* promises you on your retirement an amount based on a set formula. The formula is defined in advance; the performance of the investment markets at the time of your payout doesn't matter to your payment.

The public service and large traditional employers still offer defined-benefits funds but they're steadily going out of fashion.

✔ **Accumulation fund:** The final payout from an *accumulation fund* isn't defined in advance. You decide how much money you put into the fund, on top of any employer payments; what you get out when you retire depends on the performance of the investments you choose after fees and tax.

Accumulation funds are now the dominant form of superannuation offered to employees from most employers and to the self-employed by public-offer superannuation funds.

Managing super yourself

Organising your own superannuation, or with a small group of trusted friends and family, is an alternative to putting your money with the superannuation industry giants. These funds are called *DIY (Do It Yourself)* or *self-managed superannuation funds (SMSFs)*.

Until about ten years ago, the only people who had their own super funds were the very wealthy who were savvy and rich enough to use expensive consultants to get the best from the superannuation system.

However, the last decade has produced an explosion in the number of people doing their own funds — what is now known as the DIY sector. In 2008, more than 393,000 people in Australia have DIY funds and they control about 30 per cent of the superannuation assets in the local economy.

DIY is a relatively new form of superannuation. Why not consider this alternative to having your superannuation monies managed for you? As the fastest growing part of the superannuation industry, services for DIY members are getting better all the time.

DIY super is a world within a world and isn't for everyone. Seasoned DIY investors say that the main challenge for anyone game enough to run their own super fund isn't making money but filling out all the forms you must complete for the ATO and the government! You have to draw up a trust deed and an investment plan, and arrange for an annual independent audit, a tax return and business activity statements. Are you sure you're willing to do this sort of work?

The average annual cost of running your own fund is around $3,500 a year. Generally, superannuation funds will charge you about 2 per cent of your annual contributions as an annual 'administration fee'; these fees will rarely work out as high as the fees you'll face in DIY superannuation.

As a basic rule, industry experts suggest you should have a minimum of $200,000 in superannuation assets and a good working knowledge of investment markets before you dive into DIY.

Shopping for a fund

The superannuation industry is worth more than $1 trillion and, because Australia's going to have a relatively larger and older population in the near future, the industry is booming.

Looking around the superannuation sector, you can find dozens of superannuation products on the market aimed at almost every type of customer.

You're facing a tyranny of choice that is a bit like trying to buy a plain white loaf of bread or hoping to open a basic bank account — the wide choice of products these days is at once impressive and irritating!

The key is to search the market for a super fund that suits you and your circumstances — whether you're employed, self-employed, young or old. Figure 21-2 shows where superannuation funds were held in the Australian market in 2008.

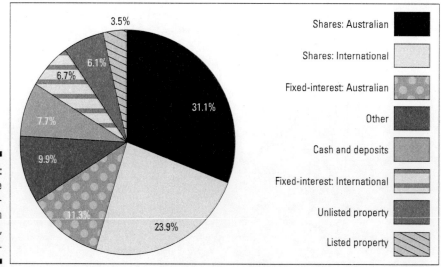

Figure 21-2: Where super-annuation was held, 2008.

Source: APRA (Australian Prudential Regulation Authority).

The main types of superannuation sellers, or funds, on the Australian market are as follows:

- **Corporate funds:** If you work for a big company like Qantas or Telstra the likelihood is that they offer an in-house superannuation fund. In the same way that you can have good or bad employers, you can just as easily have very good or very bad employer funds.

- **Industry funds:** Industry funds are run by industry associations, trade unions and industry representatives. Some of these funds, such as Australian Super, are among the biggest in Australia.

- **Master trusts and wrap accounts:** These are administration services that offer access to a wider range of investments and direct shares than other public-offer funds, under the umbrella of a single trustee, usually one of the big fund managers such as BT or Colonial. With a *master trust*, investors pool their money to invest in a wide range of managed funds at wholesale prices. These days, most people who invest in super via a financial adviser are offered a *wrap account*, which is similar to a master trust, except that it gives the investor ownership of the investments held within the wrap. Total fees for investment management, administration and advice may be high.

- **Public-sector funds:** The generous superannuation arrangements offered by the public service in funds such as the Commonwealth Superannuation Scheme are a major attraction for recruitment in this area. Public-sector funds are still powerful and one of the few areas where 'defined' funds are common (refer to the section 'Having super managed for you' earlier in this chapter).

- **Retail funds:** These funds are the monsters of the superannuation market — the open-to-everyone funds provided by the leading names in the industry such as AMP, BT and Colonial.

- **Retirement savings accounts (RSAs):** RSAs are a form of retail superannuation offered by banks for people needing to consolidate their super in one place. Intending to act as a safe haven for part-time workers and people with low incomes, RSAs haven't been very successful so far. RSAs have been disappointing because their conservative styles have produced low returns and little interest from the public.

Working with Your Super

In 2005, the right of employees to direct their employer's superannuation guarantee (SG) payments into the fund of their choice was enshrined in legislation. When you change jobs, you need to ask your new employer to pay your SG into your chosen fund.

Choice of fund

If you're self-employed, you get to choose how and where you invest your savings in super. If you're an employee, you're also entitled to nominate which fund will receive your compulsory super contributions, provided your employer offers choice of fund. Some public servants and people in defined-benefits funds may not have a choice of fund.

For those people who do have a choice of fund, choice doesn't end there. You can elect to change funds every 12 months, although frequent switching is not recommended because it can be time-consuming and costly. If you change jobs, your new employer must also give you the right to choose your super fund.

Think carefully before you switch funds. Other funds may produce bigger investment returns for a year or two, but super is a long-term investment so you need to look at returns over a period of at least three to five years. Investment returns are only one feature of a good fund — fees, insurance cover, service levels and communication with members are also extremely important features to note.

Consolidating your nest egg

Over your working life, especially if you change jobs frequently, you're likely to accumulate money in a number of super funds. Monitoring one fund is a chore for most people, let alone keeping abreast of a handful of funds. If you have more than one fund you're also paying more than one set of fees. Consolidating your super into one account is often the best way to keep an eye on your money, and cheaper than maintaining multiple accounts.

The average Australian holds three super accounts, which may help explain why more than five million accounts are on the government's Lost Super Register. If you think you may have some money wasting away in a long-forgotten super account, go to the ATO website at www.ato.gov.au/super and, from the dropdown menu for Your Super Essentials under Individuals, select Finding Your Lost Super. You may end up with a Christmas bonus!

Receiving Retirement Income

Getting your superannuation out of the system and into your pocket is a major challenge once you reach retirement age. Super is complex, but ultimately very rewarding. Under the 'simpler super' measures introduced in July 2007, Australians can now take their super in a lump sum or a pension from age 60, absolutely tax-free. That's a very persuasive reason for investing your retirement savings within the super system.

Making the transition to retirement successfully is pretty important. You're no longer accumulating — you're spending, or *drawing down*, your long-held superannuation. In the language of the superannuation industry, you're at the preservation age. (Maybe they mean the pickled age!)

Your *preservation age* — the age at which you can withdraw your superannuation money — depends on when you were born. People born before July 1960 — and that's the group of people planning for retirement now — can receive their super from age 55. Preservation age will be gradually lifted to age 60 for people born after June 1964.

Getting to this stage means that you have several options available for choosing how you receive the money you've been accumulating in superannuation.

Paying for your retirement

Most people nearing retirement age decide to keep at least some of their money within products designed for retirement income. If you take money out of the super system and blow it on new cars and overseas travel, the likelihood is that you won't have enough savings to go the distance. If you keep your money inside the retirement-income system, it retains special tax advantages and may allow you to claim some age pension.

Here are your main options:

- ✔ **Purchasing an allocated pension:** With an *allocated pension* you invest a set amount of money with a financial institution that in turn pays you an income. The difference between this type of pension and an annuity (see next) is that the return from an allocated pension isn't guaranteed in advance — your income may go up or down depending on what's happening in the markets.

> ✔ **Purchasing an annuity:** With an *annuity* you invest a set amount of money in an account with a financial institution (like an insurance company) and they guarantee you a set income over a set period of time. If you want to know exactly how much your pension will be each week (and take no further risks with your money), then an annuity pension is for you.

Allocated pensions are very flexible — you can withdraw different amounts at different times. If you're prepared to have your retirement income fluctuate in exchange for a higher income when the markets are strong, then allocated pensions will suit you.

The majority of *superannuants* (people receiving superannuation) looking for a regular income from their superannuation savings go for allocated pensions over annuities. Allocated pensions are popular because they're more flexible — you can enter or exit with less trouble than annuity schemes.

Transition to retirement

In the past, you had to retire before you could get your hands on your hard-earned super savings, even if you had reached the current preservation age of 55. Now you can withdraw part of your super when you reach preservation age and continue working full or part time as you ease your way into retirement.

With a transition-to-retirement allocated pension you can withdraw up to 10 per cent of your super balance each year. Baby-boomers are flocking to these pensions because they've discovered they can draw down a pension and salary-sacrifice (see Chapter 22) an equal amount, or more, back into super. By doing so, they're not only giving their nest eggs a final boost but gaining the tax advantages of salary-sacrificing pre-tax income. It's no wonder that the transition-to-retirement strategy is known as 'The Magic Pudding' — every time you cut a slice of your super pudding, it grows back again.

Chapter 22

Getting the Best From Superannuation

*W*hen you think about the biggest financial commitments of your lifetime, your home and your superannuation are likely to be the most important items. Financial commentators regularly detail the finer points of superannuation, but the first thing you need to do is to get a grip on managing your own basic superannuation requirements. How much superannuation will you want? And what is the best way to go about achieving this target? This chapter aims to help you through the super minefield to answer these questions and more. We also look into salary sacrificing and co-contributions, how to find a super fund that's right for you and where to go for further advice.

The State of Your Super

Behind all the coverage and comment on superannuation is the fact that most people just don't have enough superannuation.

Doing better than the average

Researchers from the Association of Superannuation Funds Australia (ASFA) have found that the average super balance for men nearing retirement is $126,000, and just $58,760 for women. Worse still, those figures are averages. In other words, a small number of people have generous super packages and the majority of people have very little (a lot less than $126,000 for men and $58,760 for women) to invest as a top-up to their government pension.

Unless you want to depend on a government pension of $14,612 a year, you need to start contributing a sufficient amount into a superannuation fund, on top of what your employer may be putting in, as soon as possible. Figure 22-1 shows the growth in annual contributions to super by both employees and employers from 1997 to 2006. The line in the chart illustrates the falling proportion of employer contributions. In other words, Australians contributed a bigger share of their superannuation in 2005 and 2006 as people began to appreciate the tax incentives for investing within super.

Many people, however, are simply depending on the 9 per cent of their salary that employers are legally required to put into a super fund for them. Worse still, employees are changing jobs and frittering away their superannuation payments. Some people are even losing track of their super completely — $13 billion currently sits in unclaimed superannuation accounts across the country!

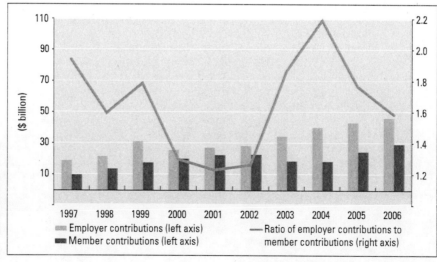

Figure 22-1: Growth in annual contributions to super.

Source: © APRA (Australian Prudential Regulation Authority).

The average Australian has three superannuation accounts. However, all that figure means is that many people have three or four accounts, whereas the smarter set have 'consolidated' their funds into one account. But the overall picture is grim — too little money in too many accounts.

Deciding how much is enough

How much superannuation should you have? Well ... how rich do you want to be in retirement?

Finding a one-size-fits-all answer isn't possible — each person has different needs and wants. To get a reasonable standard of living, such as 60 per cent of your annual income every year in your retirement, analysts suggest you need to be investing up to 15 per cent of your annual income in superannuation throughout your working life (over 40 years). Getting a more accurate picture of what you need in retirement depends on your age, your life expectancy, your current income and, most importantly, what you expect you're going to need to live on.

Most superannuation providers, like Australian Super and BT, or industry groups like the Association of Superannuation Funds Australia (ASFA), can provide you with an online calculator or set of tables that can help you estimate your retirement needs. Do this exercise at least once and then you can decide (approximately) how much superannuation you need. Check the Australian Securities and Investments Commission consumer website for their superannuation calculator at www.fido.gov.au. (Remember, superannuation sellers will never underestimate your needs.)

For example, if you're 30, on a salary of $75,000 a year, and you wish to have $45,000 a year in retirement, industry calculations suggest you need to save 6 per cent of your annual income over and above the 9 per cent superannuation guarantee (SG) to achieve that amount. (These figures assume you retire at 65 and your money makes an average of 7 per cent per annum after fees and tax, paying just 15 per cent on your earnings.)

Changing another variable, such as the age at which you begin investing for your retirement 'salary', the picture changes again. If you're 40 and have the same income and retirement aspirations as the person mentioned previously, you'd need to save an additional 14 per cent of your salary to achieve a retirement income of $45,000 a year. The later you start to save for retirement, the more you need to put aside each year.

Also, if you work until you're 70 rather than 65, the period of your retirement is five years shorter, and because you work five years longer you have more money to spend in retirement.

Take superannuation requirement calculations with a grain of salt. The people who create these tables are employed by the superannuation industry — an industry that wants to attract as much money as possible from you.

A practical way to arrive at a sensible calculation of what sort of superannuation income you'll need is to assume the worst-case scenario and then build from that point. For example, because of illness, you're forced to stop working at 60, and you're not going to make any extra income from then until for the pearly gates.

The fastest growing segment of the population, according to official statistics, is the over-80s. Everyone is living longer! You might as well assume that you're going to live for a long time. Strangely, the retirement age keeps falling while the length of time people live for (their *life expectancy*) keeps expanding. The average retirement age for Australians is now around 57, and they're likely to live up to another 30 years. A man of 65 today is expected to live until he's 83, and a 65-year-old woman until she's 86 years.

All you need is enough. Most industry calculations don't assume you get a government pension and they don't include the possibility that someday you may inherit money from someone.

Signing Up for the Long Haul

Superannuation is a long-term investment. Of course you're expected to view almost all investments as long term, but with super you have no choice, because generally you can't get your hands on the money until you reach retirement.

You may be a lifelong employee of a bank, an executive with a different job every four years or self-employed. Regardless of your employment profile, you can follow a few key strategies for maximising your super.

In the beginning ...

Superannuation is a lifetime investment — the earlier you start, the better. The problem for most people is that, when they're under 30, they believe they just have too little money to invest. (Of course, when the same people are in their 30s or 40s they feel the same way!)

Just do it! The smartest approach is to commit to putting a set percentage of your salary into superannuation and sticking to your plan. Building your superannuation takes time. Your superannuation returns depend primarily on two things — the length of time your money is invested and the level of return you achieve.

Start investing in a superannuation fund with good ongoing returns as early as possible — the miracle of compound interest takes time.

Sacrificing your salary (it's not that painful)

Salary sacrifice is a way you can put money into superannuation from your pre-tax salary. Salary sacrifice is one of the two great tax breaks in Australia (the other is the absence of capital gains tax on your primary residence).

Make your contributions weekly if possible, because you build up your superannuation investment faster as the years go by.

The beauty of salary sacrifice is that your contributions come from your gross salary, not your net salary. The benefit is two-fold. First, you reduce your taxable income in the course of investing. Second, your money is taxed at 15 per cent when it's in a superannuation fund rather than your marginal tax rate. Average wage earners pay 31.5 per cent (30 cents in the dollar, plus a 1.5 per cent Medicare levy), while someone earning $80,000 to $180,000 pays 41.5 per cent and top wage earners pay 46.5 per cent.

Salary sacrifice is one of the few genuine tax breaks open to you if you're on a standard salary package.

Making a co-contribution

The government is so keen for all Australians to save for their own retirement that it hands out money to boost the retirement savings of low-income earners. That's right, the government gives money away.

If you earn $30,342 or less (in the 2008–09 tax year), the government will contribute $1.50 tax-free for every dollar you invest up to a maximum co-contribution of $1,500. For example, if you contribute $1,000, the government will add $1,500 to your super account. If you can only muster $500, the government will come to the party with a $750 co-contribution.

The government co-contribution reduces for every dollar above $30,342 you earn until it cuts out completely at an income of $60,342. Grab it while you can — more than a million of your fellow citizens already do so.

Spreading your super — don't!

James has a friend who proudly boasts of having 'bits of superannuation all over the place'. His chum is labouring under the illusion that several superannuation accounts make her richer. They don't — they make you poorer. Big is beautiful with superannuation.

In other parts of this book, we recommended that you diversify your shares, managed funds and property. Superannuation is different. Superannuation is not an investment asset; it's simply a special type of account where you, hopefully, hold a diversified portfolio of investments. If you have your superannuation scattered in different accounts, you're paying an administration fee to each and every one of those fund managers.

Superannuation works best in one single account — don't diversify your super accounts. By putting your money into one fund, you pay fewer fees and you'll find it easier to keep track of your money.

Putting off retirement

Don't assume you have to stop working or investing as soon as you reach *preservation age* — the age when you can take money out of superannuation. Why should you stop getting wealthier? Superannuation is insurance for your later life; nobody says you must stop earning income.

These days you can draw on your super and continue working — and boost your super at the same time by taking advantage of salary sacrifice. (We look at this strategy, called 'transition to retirement', in Chapter 21.)

You can continue making contributions to super until you're 65, whether you're working or not. However, your employer is required to pay the super guarantee (SG) until you turn 70, if you're employed until then. If you want to make voluntary contributions between the ages of 65 and 74, you must work at least 40 hours within 30 consecutive days in that financial year. Self-employed people can claim a full deduction for super contributions until age 75.

If the tables issued by the superannuation companies suggest you're not going to have enough money in your superannuation account to pay for what you regard as a comfortable lifestyle, why not consider working a few years longer?

Why are Australians retiring earlier when they're living longer? The answer has more to do with people being forced out of jobs than any voluntary move towards retiring earlier, unfortunately.

If you wish to build a larger nest egg of superannuation, think about working those extra few years — that is, working until 70 rather than 65. (You don't have to keep your old job; just keep making money and keep contributing, and postpone withdrawing your savings.)

If you've contributed to super all your life and you're prepared to work a couple of extra years past the legal retirement age, a multiplier effect impacts on the final figure. For example, an extra two years in the workforce can finance an extra seven years in retirement.

Making sure you roll over

A *rollover* is a mechanism that allows you to switch, or roll over, your superannuation money from one place to another and still keep that money inside the superannuation system.

Most Australians change jobs up to six times in their lives. Each time they make a major change, they may waste, or even lose track of, their superannuation money. Don't let this scenario happen to you — when you change jobs, make sure you always roll over your superannuation money into a new fund or continue making contributions to your original super fund.

Picking the Super from the Not-So-Super Funds

Choice of fund legislation came into effect in 2005, giving most employees the right to direct their compulsory super payments into the fund of their choice. Choice is a good thing, but too much of a good thing — in this case, a bewildering array of superannuation funds — can paralyse the best-intentioned people into inaction. Choosing the best fund for your personal circumstances is a time-consuming chore, but well worth the effort. A difference of just one percentage point in your annual returns can add up to tens of thousands of dollars by the time you retire.

Picking a superannuation fund is similar to picking a managed fund. (Refer to Chapter 13 if you need help in this area.) Superannuation funds can have very similar fees and charges but very different returns, depending on their investment performance.

For most people, superannuation choice comes down to picking the default fund nominated by your employer, your company's own corporate fund or your industry (union-related) fund. These days, many industry funds are public-offer funds; that is, they're open to all-comers, not just employees of a particular industry. If you use the services of a financial planner, you probably invest in retail funds via a wrap account or master trust (refer to Chapter 21).

Choosing the fund for you can be a lengthy process, but it's worthwhile. A good place to start is one of the new online superannuation comparison sites, such as Chant West's AppleCheck (www.chantwest.com.au), SelectingSuper (www.selectingsuper.com.au) or SuperRatings (www.superratings.com.au). These sites allow you to compare the features and fee structures of two or three funds at a time. Here are some tips on what to look for:

- ✔ **Track record:** How has the fund performed in terms of its return, especially over the last five years? If the fund hasn't managed 7 per cent per annum, you should be asking questions. If the fund has managed more than 10 per cent, it has been doing very well. Check the returns of each fund against the average returns for similar types of funds and investment strategies.

- ✔ **Balance of the portfolio:** How is the portfolio balanced or structured? This question is crucial; you want to be comparing apples with apples. A fund should have higher returns if it takes higher risks; if the fund has a low return on high risks, then it's faring much worse than may be obvious at first glance.

- ✔ **Exposure to risk:** The best way to measure the risks a fund is taking is by checking the portions it has allotted to various levels of risk. For example, if one fund has 70 per cent of its money in 'aggressive' investments and 30 per cent in cash, then it's not fair to compare its returns with a fund that has 30 per cent of its money in 'aggressive' investments and 70 per cent in cash.

- ✔ **Fees:** How do fees compare? Over the long term, the level of fees you're paying on your superannuation can make a big difference to your returns, because the money you lose on the fees may have otherwise been compounding returns for an extended period. The best way to compare the fees charged by superannuation funds is by checking their MER (management-expense ratio) and administration fee percentages. Superannuation funds have fees similar to managed funds. (Refer to Chapter 12 for more information on fees.)

- ✔ **Life insurance cover:** How generous is the life insurance cover? Your life insurance needs to be as good as or better than what you might have had elsewhere. Insurance offered within super is often cheaper than insurance purchased from a retail fund, and you can have your premiums deducted from your super contributions. Look for a fund that offers binding death benefit nominations to make sure your super ends up in the right hands if you should die while you still have money in the kitty.

Decisions, Decisions: Your Options Inside a Super Fund

Traditionally, most superannuation funds simply told you once a year how they performed and you could do little about their performance one way or another.

Today, everything is different; most funds now offer a range of options within the fund. Boiling down these different options, you find they're mostly about risk — the lowest risk option is mostly cash, with little in bonds or shares. The highest risk option is mostly shares, with little in cash or bonds.

Modern-style funds also offer a variation on standard investment strategies called *ethical* or *socially responsible investing (SRI)*, where the fund manager steers your investment away from unsavoury investments such as tobacco or woodchip production.

Generally, funds that offer a range of investing options also have a default option, which your investment reverts to if you don't make a choice.

The *default option* in your superannuation fund is the investing option the fund imposes on you if you don't actively choose one of the options the fund offers you. The default option is usually the 'balanced' option, with something like 60 per cent of your money invested in shares and 40 per cent going into cash, fixed interest and alternative asset classes such as infrastructure and private equity.

In assessing which investment option you should take, remember that superannuation is a lifelong exercise rather than just another investment. You can afford to take risks you wouldn't normally consider and the younger you are, the more risks you can take.

Ultimately, make a choice that suits your own position as an investor. In making that choice, your decisions on how long you wish to work and what level of material comfort you want in your retirement will point you towards the right balance.

Getting More Advice

Superannuation isn't as glamorous as the sharemarket. When you look at the bookshelves or the magazine racks at your local newsagent, you can see that the popular coverage of super is very slight.

Until recently, super got a low billing in the financial markets but this profile is changing, thanks largely to the very attractive tax benefits and the growing army of Do It Yourself (DIY) superannuation savers. (Refer to Chapter 21 for more on managing your own super.)

Totally independent financial advice is hard to get, and superannuation is no exception. Keep in mind that nobody in the super business ever underestimates how much you should save in super.

Here are some useful organisations that can give you independent advice on your super options:

- ✔ **The Association of Superannuation Funds of Australia (ASFA)** is the key representative body of the superannuation industry. ASFA has a good website at www.superannuation.asn.au, which offers a range of educational material, and facts and figures to help you estimate your superannuation requirements.

- ✔ **The Australian Securities and Investments Commission (ASIC)** is a good source of plain-English information on superannuation and investment. Go to the ASIC consumer site at www.fido.gov.au and check out the superannuation calculator for the impact of fees, extra contributions, the co-contribution, switching funds and strategies for your final super benefit.

- ✔ **The Australian Taxation Office (ATO)** website offers substantial information on superannuation at www.ato.gov.au.

Part VI
The Part of Tens

Glenn Lumsden

'After years of research, we've finally identified the two factors that affect the stock market. Things we can see coming and things we can't . . .'

In this part ...

*H*ere we give you a couple of chapters full of canny
advice that's too important to leave out even
though it's really above and beyond the daily investing
scenario. Chapter 23 deals with issues in your life that
can affect your investing and can make you think hard
about where you channel your disposable income.
Chapter 24 looks a little more closely at the relationship
between you and your new best friend — your financial
adviser.

Chapter 23

Ten Life Lessons for Clever Investing

*Y*ou can't separate living and investing into two neat chambers. Partying till dawn, throwing caution to the wind in every part of your life and then sitting down and becoming a first-class investor is a way of living not all of us can manage. However, if you never take a risk in any aspect of your life, you may find building a fully diversified portfolio hard work.

Your life and your investments keep getting tangled up together, for better or worse. You reflect some of your best and worst habits in the decisions you make as an investor.

In this chapter, we summarise the most important investing lessons we've ever read, heard or experienced. True, exceptions exist here and there. But you can serve yourself and your financial status well if you choose to stick to some — if not all — of these suggestions.

Buying When You Can

Everyone over 50 in Australia has a story about the time they nearly bought that house in Manly or those six acres in the Snowy Mountains for a very reasonable price. If you're a careful investor, you rarely regret what you buy; instead, what you don't buy always hurts.

One of James' in-laws returned from Houston to Dublin in 1998 as a very successful bio-medical engineer. When he saw that prices in his chosen part of Dublin were up nearly 100 per cent since 1996, he said he'd rent for a year and 'wait for prices to drop'. The following year the prices in his target area of Dublin rose by another 50 per cent.

Lesson: If you can afford the investment ... do so. No-one knows what will happen to house prices in the future. If you buy the right house, in the right location, for the long term, then it won't matter in 10 or 20 years' time if you paid a little too much.

Making Your Moneymaking Efforts Count

Penny wise, pound foolish.

—Anonymous

We just love the phrase 'penny wise, pound foolish' because this smart comment takes a well-worn proverb ('a penny saved is a penny earned') and tells you something really worth hearing. Being mean may save you cents — for example, leaving a tiny tip to a struggling waiter — but leaving your investments with a fund manager who charges the highest fees in the market is simply wasting your investment return.

You can apply the 'penny wise, pound foolish' warning in a thousand ways across your investment portfolio. Don't sweat the small stuff. Forget about driving halfway across the city for a cheaper car park. Put your moneymaking efforts into what matters — your big investments, such as your house, managed funds, superannuation and property.

Lesson: If you get the big-dollar investments right, the pennies look after themselves.

Staying in Your Home

Moving house can cost at least $40,000 in fees, not to mention the hidden costs in a range of replacement goods and services. Selling your existing home can cost around $15,000 and purchase costs on your new home can easily add an additional $25,000.

The property market is pressuring you to keep moving all the time. Check out this plan: A modest flat after student days; a stylish apartment in your 20s; an inner-city house in your 30s; a sterling suburb in your 40s and 50s; back into the city for a townhouse in your 60s, and a retirement village by the sea in your 70s.

But don't be fooled by that plan — it was written by property developers. If you're happy where you are, stay where you are and make money rather than spend money.

The chances are that, in moving house, you make more money for all the hangers-on — the real estate agents, the removalists and the lawyers — than you do for yourself.

Lesson: If you want to avoid throwing money down the drain, stay in your home for at least five to seven years at a time.

Using Tax as an Opportunity

You might say tax is boring. Well, tax returns are rewarding and saving on tax is making money ... which is never boring!

Make sure you get advantages from the tax system. At the very minimum, salary-sacrifice into superannuation (refer to Chapter 22) and invest in your home (refer to Chapter 17).

With a 15 per cent tax on superannuation investments, you have a huge advantage for making healthy returns on your money.

Likewise, investing in your home puts the money in an enriching asset that is free from capital gains tax, and you get to enjoy the benefits of the investment every day.

Consider your annual tax return the biggest opportunity of the year to save money. Preparing your tax returns can be hard work, but very well paid work.

Lesson: Be aggressive — exploit the tax system, rather than allowing the tax system to exploit you.

Choosing Free School Education

Now this lifestyle topic is really testing whether you want to be rich or just look like you're rich. In a private school, what are you getting for $15,000 to $20,000 a year? 'A good education for my kids', you say in a miffed manner.

Sure, but you can get a good education in non-private schools. Once upon a time, private schools were elite institutions where your concept of a 'good education' meant strong academic skills coupled with a promise your child was entering an elite stream of society. But, with a huge proportion of kids going to private schools — around one-third of all high school students in most states, and more in affluent pockets of our major cities — what's elite about that statistic?

If you have more than one child in a private school, you're in for a long period of beans on toast unless you're a brain surgeon (or one of those guys who runs property-investment seminars!).

Seriously, private school fees at $15,000 to $20,000 a year in a country where the average adult earnings are $59,540 simply seems out of whack. Imagine for one moment how you can increase your family's wealth if you successfully invest even one $15,000 school fee for the six years of one child's secondary schooling. Even at a conservative return of 7 per cent per annum, you can be $21,037 richer than if you pay for that school.

Lesson: You don't have to pay for your kids' education. If you find a good local non-fee-paying school, make sure to use it.

Knowing Your Place

The rich are different.

—Anonymous

As a start-up investor, sometimes you can feel like a child in a toyshop. So many investments are close at hand to choose from! And some investments seem a lot more glamorous than others do. Shares in a French perfume company or a Spanish vineyard sound a lot more attractive than stock in a Geelong tile manufacturer. But the only question that matters is which investment is going to make you the most money for the least risk?

If you have a large diversified portfolio, you can begin to take bigger risks. As soon as you have a truly diversified portfolio of strong investments, then you can go out on a limb and buy shares in a Spanish vineyard. But making exotic investments before you have a plain-vanilla portfolio of investments under your belt isn't smart.

Knowing your place in the investment markets means doing the right thing at the right time. Commencing a superannuation plan at 25 is an excellent idea, but commencing a superannuation plan at 65 makes no sense. Using a private bank (and paying its fees) is useful if you're a millionaire, but doing so when you're struggling to pay off your credit card each month makes no sense.

Lesson: Matching investment products to your needs means knowing your place and your tolerance for risk, and forgetting about what might be attractive if you were someone else.

Dealing with Friendly Advice

Listen to your friends on every other subject, but take their investment advice with a pinch of salt. Why? Because nine times out of ten your friends are going to see the world from their perspective as a doctor or miner or shopkeeper — they don't have a full view of the market.

Some time ago, a friend of James who had never invested in shares said he had bought some stock.

'Oh, really, what did you buy?' James asked.

'One.Tel, they're going great. My brother-in-law has a senior position with them and he says they're doing great', said the friend.

Why did he buy One.Tel instead of another telecom stock?

'Well, I've got some inside information. This guy is inside, you don't get to know someone like that very often', he answered.

Of course, James' friend never found out anything from his brother-in-law about One.Tel that he couldn't have read in the papers. The guy was an engineer not the chief financial officer!

At the end of the day only a handful of people at the very top really know everything that goes on in big companies. No doubt the One.Tel engineer sincerely believed in his company; that's why he worked there. But the recommendation was very poor investment advice — One.Tel collapsed a year later.

Lesson: Use expert opinion and your own good sense to determine investment advice — don't get your friends involved unless they really have expertise.

Avoiding Divorce Costs

Figuring out the cost of divorce on your wealth doesn't take a genius — splitting all your family assets in half (often in a hurry) is probably the worst thing you can do financially over your lifetime.

Avoiding the horrendous costs of divorce often isn't possible for many people but surely this cost is important enough for anyone in any relationship to consider very seriously.

Lesson: If avoiding the high cost of divorce makes everyone happier — including you — surely exploring every alternative is worth the effort. If divorce is unavoidable, then strive for an amicable split. The less time you spend in court or with divorce lawyers, the less the divorce will cost you financially and emotionally.

Dodging Those Dodgy High-Risk, High-Return Schemes

Ice-cream makes you fat. New Zealand gets a lot of rain. Paris is expensive. You know these things are true. You also know marketing ploys are out there to make you believe otherwise. The advertisements for ice-cream show slim models, the photographs of the Milford Sound get taken on sunny days and the travel brochures always say Paris is 'surprisingly good value'.

In the investment markets, the stakes get higher. You know high returns without high risk just don't exist. But the seductive attempts to change your mind never stop.

In 2008, a year of financial shocks and reversals of fortune, no fall from grace was more shocking than the unmasking of Wall Street hedge fund manager, Bernard Madoff, as a scamster.

Madoff ran one of the largest, and seemingly most successful, funds on Wall Street. His investors included a Who's Who of the American and European business and celebrity elite, attracted by Madoff's claims of annual 16 per cent returns over 15 years. Then, in 2008, when the financial music stopped, Madoff's fund was revealed for what it really was — a US$50 billion Ponzi scheme. A *Ponzi*, or *pyramid*, *scheme* involves paying returns to existing investors out of funds received from new investors. This works in booming markets when cash is pouring in, but comes to an abrupt halt when investors close their wallets.

The truly remarkable thing about the Madoff affair is that, in the three years leading up to Madoff's downfall, a number of people close to him had alerted the Securities and Exchange Commission — the US corporate watchdog — that Madoff's numbers didn't add up. The Securities and Exchange Commission had no excuses for its oversight, but many of the experienced investors caught up in Madoff's web should have understood that the returns he offered not only looked too good to be true, they *were* too good to be true. As the saying goes, it's only when the tide goes out that we see who was swimming naked.

Every week of the year, in Australia and around the globe, investment schemes that promise no risk and high returns get into trouble.

Lesson: Don't ever be fooled — high returns mean high risk, every time.

Toughing Out Your Good Investment Decisions

Your investing patterns are going to be quite similar to your overall personality but they need not be identical. Whatever way you live your life is up to you — but as an investor you have to be tough and efficient with your investment decisions.

Being tough and efficient doesn't mean you have to be unethical or socially irresponsible. In fact you can now find *ethical funds* (refer to Chapter 14 for more on these funds that choose to avoid investing in socially unacceptable areas like tobacco) or ethical superannuation options that may suit you best. But as an investor you must always be alert to opportunities or dangers in the market.

Successful investors take a long and unsentimental view. Never hang on to a stock because it rewarded you well in the past; the prospects must be good for the future. Likewise, don't sell out at the bottom of the market because you're simply fed up with waiting for the market to turn — tough it out and stay with good investments.

The question to ask yourself is this: Would I buy this investment at the current price? If the answer is no, then sell. If the answer is yes, then hold on and maybe even buy more.

Lesson: When you're playing golf or training your local football team, you can do whatever is best fun at the time. But, when you invest, concentrate on what matters — glamorous brands or luxurious locations mean absolutely nothing to investors. What matters is returns — get serious, get tough, get going!

Chapter 24

Ten Things Your Financial Adviser Never Says to You

*F*inancial advisers have a difficult role. If they were absolutely brilliant, they probably wouldn't need any clients because they'd be pretty rich already. Then again, financial advisers who clearly make a lot of money and spend it on fast cars and lavish lifestyles are often under suspicion for taking too much in fees.

Your financial adviser should be sensible but not a stick-in-the-mud. An adviser should be eager but not too enthusiastic. As you can see, the job's a pretty hard one.

Another potential problem is the fact that many people who dispense financial advice have poor qualifications: Sad to say, anyone who can spell their own name can put a sign on an office door and call themselves a financial adviser. The first question you should ask a potential adviser is, 'Are you licensed by the Australian Securities and Investments Commission?' If the answer is no, run a mile. If the answer is yes, then you can grill them on what they have to offer and how much they charge.

Like a doctor or a dentist, the first rule for any financial adviser must be to build a business and retain as many good clients as possible. As a result, an adviser can't really tell you everything. This chapter discusses some of the things you never hear them say.

'Go Somewhere Else'

Just imagine you go back to your financial adviser a year after your first meeting and she's sitting there in a tailor-made suit fiddling with her expensive mobile phone. She says: 'Everything I told you last year was wrong; I'm amazed you came back. You must never read the papers. Keep away from me; I just lose you money.'

Nope, this scenario isn't going to happen (unless your adviser has been sipping some very strong Irish whiskey before you arrived!).

The implicit deal between you and any financial adviser is that you're with them for better or worse — until you decide to leave. You have to make sure the adviser is doing the right thing by ensuring you're getting returns that are at least as good as if you were managing the money yourself.

You can always leave, but an adviser never reminds you about that option.

'You Get Me Commissions'

How come advisers still recommend certain finance houses even when the signs are clear that these companies are going downhill?

The answer is commissions. A growing number of advisers charge a fee for service, but many advisers still get commissions for recommending or sending over new clients to the major finance houses like AMP, BT, Macquarie or any of the major banks.

Advisers don't reveal these commissions to you unless they're pressed. If you have suspicions or you just want to 'clear the air', ask your adviser if the institutions he recommends pay him.

Don't be misled by financial planners who offer 'free' advice. Nobody in financial services does anything for nothing.

'Take a Risk'

At the back of every financial adviser's mind is the warning from Warren Buffett about the first rule of investing: 'Don't lose.'

If your adviser gets you to take risks and you lose money, you're probably likely to be much more dissatisfied than if you take almost no risk and make a reasonable return.

The dilemma for the adviser is that, if you lose money on his advice, then the possibility you may walk out the door increases dramatically.

If you're seeking higher returns, you have to make that aim clear to your adviser and accept that a higher risk exists that you can lose money.

If you want to take more risks than an adviser regards as reasonable, you must make that plan clear.

'You're a Mystery to Me'

You walk into your financial adviser's office and you remember the desk, the photos and the calendar on the wall. You only have one adviser. She looks across the desk and sees maybe the fourth person that morning. She has hundreds of clients.

You sit down and you have a very good idea of your financial situation. Your adviser glances at her files trying to remember who you are, what you do and the basic outline of your financial situation.

The adviser is never going to say: 'Well, I can't remember a thing about you. Let's start again.' But in reality that story is what happens every day in financial advisers' offices.

Make it easy. Remind the adviser who you are and what has occurred in the past. Refresh the adviser on your basic situation and recap on some of the issues you may have talked about the last time you met — family trusts, holiday homes or whatever issue is on the agenda in your life.

Don't expect the financial adviser to remember everything about you.

'You're Talking to an Adviser, Not a Wizard'

Financial advisers don't know everything, but they should know the basics about Australian investment markets and how the tax system works. However, this broad-spectrum knowledge doesn't mean they can answer questions on a devaluation of the yen or the latest tax ruling on thoroughbred foals.

An adviser is going to be a very honest professional indeed if he tells you 'I don't know' ten times in the course of a conversation about any subject.

Be realistic: The adviser is there to help you make decisions. If you're interested in very specific subjects, then you have to do a lot of work for yourself.

The best way to use a financial adviser is as a second opinion on your own financial plans.

'You Should Stay a Few More Minutes'

Often the best part of your meeting with a financial adviser is the last five minutes. The problem is that you can just begin talking in depth about your financial situation when the time's up.

An adviser knows that, if she covers the basic issues of tax returns and general investment advice, you're likely to be 90 per cent happy with the session. But you need to get the adviser to go those extra few yards to give you information that's of real value.

Get your adviser engaged with your situation. Book more time. Have an agenda of discussion items when you enter the office. If you can get the adviser to think about your plans a little more thoroughly, your visit will be that much more rewarding.

Book an extra half-hour with your adviser. This request signals you want to get some serious work done.

'We Need to Talk More about Overseas Markets'

Advisers know their local markets best of all. Your adviser in a suburban strip simply can't compete with mega-firms like J.P. Morgan or Macquarie Bank, where understanding overseas markets is a priority. Instead, many advisers simply ignore overseas markets.

You need to diversify your portfolio, which means putting some assets into international markets. The easiest way to diversify internationally is through some well-chosen managed funds.

At the very least, your adviser should be able to give you good advice on the best locally available 'international' managed funds. If you want to invest outside the realm of managed funds, you're going to have to do a lot more work.

Investing in overseas stocks and managed funds has become cheaper and easier thanks to online brokers. But the vast bulk of these services don't offer advice. If you want to invest in this direction you need either an adviser with first-hand overseas experience or an adviser within a global finance house.

You can't expect your local adviser to have the lowdown on international markets.

'You and I Should Invest Together'

Just because an adviser suggests you do certain things doesn't mean the adviser takes such a course himself.

Any adviser is going to balance what he thinks you should do with what the rest of the investment community sees as the safest thing to do. This strategy is why a huge number of people with managed funds are in just a handful of institutions like BT, Colonial and Perpetual.

Turning the tables on the adviser can bring additional useful information. Asking, 'What would you do if you were in my situation?' for example, can lead to some fresh perspectives from a tired or bored adviser. (Remember, like dentists or chiropractors, these guys have to deal with a lot of repetition.)

Never let an adviser offer you a single option — always make him explore all relevant options for your money.

'I Can't Answer that Because I Don't Understand the Tax System'

Our tax system is a huge, complex and contradictory mess. We sometimes wonder if anybody really understands how the whole complex system works, even those in the tax office.

Very few financial advisers fully understand the tax system, but they're sure as hell not going to make such an admission to you — after all, their job is to know more than you do.

Tax advice is a world within a world. If you get to the point that you feel you know as much as your financial adviser, then the time has come to consider using a specialist tax adviser as your financial adviser. This approach is taking the idea of using the adviser as a 'second opinion' to the limit but isn't so unusual among sophisticated investors.

Maybe all you need is tax advice.

'My Mother Wanted Me to Be an Accountant'

Who is your financial adviser? How did she get to be giving you advice? Qualifications are a big problem in financial advisory circles. The business is full of rogues who are discovering they can make a relatively easy living telling people elementary information they can easily find out if they read a few books (like this one).

So-called investment seminars where unqualified salespeople spruik property and 'risk-free' sharemarket stock-picking systems are still all too common. Unfortunately, the onus is on you to do some background checking before you trust your hard-earned cash with anyone who claims to be a financial expert.

Just to make life difficult, the demarcation lines between financial planners, accountants and even lawyers is becoming blurred. These days, large accounting firms and legal practices also have qualified financial planners on their staff. Whatever professional hat your adviser wears, the important issue is the quality of advice she gives.

The Financial Planning Association of Australia (www.fpa.asn.au), CPA Australia (www.cpaaustralia.com.au) and the Institute of Chartered Accountants in Australia (www.charteredaccountants.com.au) are all good places to start your search for a qualified financial adviser.

Don't assume you're talking to an expert until your adviser can prove to you he has the skills you need to hire.

Glossary

abnormals: Items of *revenue* and *expense* incurred during the ordinary business operations of a company, but considered abnormal by reason of their size and effect on the company's results during a particular *accounting period*.

accounting period: Interval of time in which the systematic recording, reporting and analysis of financial transactions of a business is undertaken.

actively managed bond funds: Funds that strive to get the best returns from the bond market.

All Ordinaries Accumulation Index: An *index* that measures movements in the price of the major *shares* listed on the *Australian Securities Exchange*, as well as *dividend* payments. All dividends are treated as if they are reinvested in the sharemarket. By comparison, the *All Ordinaries Index* measures price movements only; that is, capital gains or losses. Consequently, the Accumulation Index is regarded as a more accurate reflection of the total return on a sharemarket investment.

All Ordinaries Index (All Ords): A share price *index* measuring the market prices of the major *stocks* listed on the *Australian Securities Exchange*.

amortisation: A method of eliminating a *liability*, such as a *mortgage*, by periodic payments.

annual general meeting (AGM): The yearly meeting between the *directors* and *shareholders* of a *company*, at which shareholders are asked to elect the directors, discuss any shareholder resolutions and approve the operating and financial results.

annual report: A yearly record of a company's financial condition including a description of the firm's operations, its profit and loss accounts, balance sheet and statements of *cash flow*.

annual yield: The *profit* or *income* that an investment returns yearly. Similar to annual return.

appraisal: A professional opinion of the market value of a property.

appreciation: The increase of an asset's value.

ask: The price at which a broker is willing to sell. Also known as an *offer*.

asset: Any item of economic value owned by an individual or *company*.

asset allocation: The process of dividing investment funds among different kinds of *assets*, such as *stocks*, *bonds*, *real estate* and *cash*, to optimise the trade-off between risk and reward based on an individual's or institution's specific situation and goals.

asset backing: The value of a company's or trust's *assets* standing behind its issued *shares* or units. Expressed as an amount per share or per unit.

Association of Superannuation Funds of Australia (ASFA): The peak industry body reflecting all elements of the superannuation industry.

ASX: Abbreviation for the *Australian Securities Exchange*.

ASX code: The codes assigned by the *ASX* to each *security* on the stock exchange.

auction: A method for selling an *asset*, such as a house, to the highest bidder.

audit: An official examination and verification of financial accounts and records.

auditor: A person who undertakes an *audit*.

audit trail: A record of online transactions.

Australian real estate investment trust (A-REIT): See *real estate investment trust*.

Australian Securities and Investments Commission (ASIC): The body that regulates the *stock market* and financial advisers.

Australian Securities Exchange (ASX): The Australian national stock exchange, located in Sydney. Trading takes place from approximately 10 am to 4.05 pm, Monday through Friday, except on public holidays.

authorised capital: The maximum number of *shares* that a *company* is permitted to issue.

bad debts: Money that is owed to a company by a customer for products and services provided on *credit* that will likely remain uncollectable and will be written off.

balanced fund: A managed fund that offers investors a ready-mixed selection of all major asset classes and a balance between *income* and *capital growth*.

balance sheet: A key financial statement showing the nature and amount of a company's *assets*, *liabilities* and *capital* on a given date.

bear market: A market in which prices decline sharply against a background of widespread pessimism.

benchmark rate: The official *interest rate* for short-term cash investments set by central banks such as the Reserve Bank of Australia.

bid: (a) The highest price any buyer is willing to pay for a given *security* at a given time. (b) An offer of a specific amount of money in exchange for products and services, as in an *auction*.

blue chip: A big company with a reputation as a good investment in good times and bad times.

board of directors: Individuals elected by *shareholders* to oversee the management of a *company*. The members are paid, meet several times a year and assume legal responsibility for the company's activities.

bond: A legal contract in which an issuer promises to pay *bondholders* a specific rate (or a set formula for a rate) of *interest* and redeem (or buy back) the contract for the original price.

bond fund: A *managed fund* that invests in *bonds*, typically with the aim of providing stable income with minimal *capital risk*.

bondholder: The holder of *bonds* issued by government or a *company*.

bond market: The market for all types of *bonds*, whether on an exchange or over-the-counter.

bonus share: A share issued fully or partly paid to an existing *shareholder* in a *company*. Usually issued on a *pro rata* basis. Also known as a bonus issue.

book value: The value of an *asset* as it appears on a *balance sheet*, equal to cost minus accumulated *depreciation*.

broker: A person who buys and sells *stocks/shares*, insurance, *mortgages* and other financial products on behalf of clients.

brokerage: The *commission* that a *broker* charges on buying and/or selling investments or negotiating insurance for clients.

bull market: A period of buoyant trading during and immediately after a rise in share prices when traders are optimistic about the prospects of further price rises.

business cycle: A predictable long-term pattern of alternating periods of economic growth (*recovery*) and decline (slowdown or *recession*), characterised by changing employment, *asset* prices, industrial productivity, and *interest rates*.

business day: The part of a day when most businesses are operating, usually from 9 am to 5 pm, Monday through Friday.

buyback: See *share buyback*.

buyer's advocate: A person who acts on behalf of a buyer.

call option: An *option* contract that gives the holder the right, but not the obligation, to buy a certain quantity (usually 100 *shares*) of an underlying *security* from the writer of the option, at a specified price up to a specified date. Also known as a call.

call warrant: See *warrant*.

capex: Abbreviation for *capital expenditure*.

capital: The wealth (whether monetary or in assets) owned by an individual or *company*.

capital appreciation: The increase in the value of an *asset*.

capital expenditure: An addition to the value of a fixed *asset*.

capital gains tax (CGT): A tax on the profits arising from the increased value of *assets*.

capital growth: The increase in value of wealth owned by an individual or *company*.

capital stock: The number of *shares* authorised for sale by a company's charter.

cash: Money in hand or in the bank; investments made in short-term (up to 12 months) bank deposits or in the money markets.

cash flow: The net amount of money received by an individual or *company* in a certain period.

cash-management accounts: Accounts in which you leave funds that you may wish to use as cash — and withdraw within 24 hours — in a special account that pays a higher rate than is paid by ordinary cash accounts offered by banks.

cash-management trust (CMT): A form of *unit trust* that invests in the money market, generally for no longer than 12 months.

charge card: Any card with no pre-set spending limits that may be used repeatedly to borrow money or buy products and services on *credit*. You settle your account at the end of every month. If your account is paid late, you face a flat fee.

CHESS: Acronym for Clearing House Electronic Subregister System, which is an electronic transfer and settlement system used by the *Australian Securities Exchange*. Automatically issues updated holdings statements to the investor, and details of all share holdings on its register to the *stock* issuer.

class: A category of financial *assets*, such as *shares*, *property*, *fixed interest* and *cash*, which in turn can be broken down further to include domestic or international shares, domestic or international fixed interest, direct or indirect property investments, and so on.

closed-end fund: Where the *fund manager* issues a set number of units and then 'closes' the fund. No more units are ever issued and the fund has a limited lifespan, typically of five years.

closing transaction: A transaction in which the seller of an *option* terminates his/her obligation.

collateral: *Assets* such as *property* or *securities* provided by a borrower or guarantor as security for a loan.

commission: A fee payable as an incentive to a salesperson, usually based on the value of the goods or services sold.

commodity: A product that trades on a commodity exchange, including foreign currencies, metals and minerals, agricultural products and financial instruments and indices.

company: Any entity engaging in business, such as a proprietorship, partnership or *corporation*.

compliance listing: Putting a company's shares on the stock market without raising any money. See also *float*.

compound interest: Where your interest is rolled over into the following year's invested sum, creating an ever larger pool of money.

Consumer Price Index (CPI): A measure of the quarterly changes in the prices of a 'basket' of goods and services commonly purchased by metropolitan wage and salary earners. The most common method of measuring the rate of price inflation.

contingency: A condition that must be met in order for a *contract* to be legally binding.

contingent liability: A potential expense, which may or may not eventuate, but which may need to be provided for in a *company* or *superannuation* entity's accounts.

contract: A binding agreement between two or more parties for performing, or refraining from performing, some specified act(s) in exchange for lawful consideration.

contract for difference (CFD): A contract between an investor and a licensed provider that allows the investor to punt on the difference between the price of shares today and their price at some time in the future.

convertible notes: Investments that pay a set amount of interest for a set period before investors can convert them into ordinary shares; used by professional investors.

corporate bonds: *Bonds* issued by large companies in order to raise money for commercial projects.

corporation: Common form of business organisation, and one which is chartered by a state and given many legal rights as an entity separate from its owners. Characterised by the *limited liability* of its owners, the issuance of shares of easily transferable *stock* and existence as a going concern.

corporations law: Legislation regulating *corporations* and the *securities* and *futures* industry in Australia, administered by the *Australian Securities and Investments Commission*.

coupon: The *interest rate* on a *fixed-interest security*, determined upon issuance, and expressed as a percentage of the security's *par value*.

credit: (a) A contractual agreement in which a borrower receives something of value now and agrees to repay the *lender* at some later date. (b) The borrowing capacity of an individual or company.

credit card: Any card with a pre-set spending limit and pre-set minimum monthly repayment amount that may be used repeatedly to borrow money or buy products and services on credit. You pay interest-rate-based charges on any unpaid balance of the account after the due date.

credit rating: A published ranking, based on detailed financial analysis by a credit bureau, of your financial history, specifically as it relates to your ability to meet *debt* obligations. The highest rating is usually AAA, and the lowest is D. *Lenders* use this information to decide whether to approve a loan.

creditor: A person or organisation that extends *credit* to others.

currency market: The markets that deal in the movements in the *exchange rate* between different currencies.

current assets: The sum of all *assets*, including *cash* and *inventory*, that could be converted to cash in less than one year.

current liabilities: The sum of all money owed by a *company* or *corporation* and due within one year.

cyclicals: Stocks that are guaranteed to deliver a certain level of business regardless of economic conditions, such as in healthcare companies or electricity providers. Also known as defensive stocks.

daytrading: Buying or selling *stocks* in a single day, or a relatively brief timespan.

debenture: *Debt* backed only by the integrity of the borrower, not by *collateral*, and documented by an agreement called an *indenture*.

debt: A *liability* in the form of *bonds*, loan notes, or *mortgages*, owed to another person or persons and required to be paid by a specified date.

debt-to-equity ratio: The relative proportions of debt *securities* to *equities*.

debtors: An individual or *company* that owes *debt* to another individual or company (the *creditor*), as a result of borrowing or issuing *bonds*.

deed: The document that transfers *title* to real *property*.

delisted: Removed *shares* or *securities* that were once quoted on a stock exchange.

depreciation: The wear and tear and reducing value of *assets*.

deregulation: The scrapping of rules that stop foreign investors or companies from competing in Australia on an equal footing.

derivative: A financial instrument whose characteristics and value depend upon those of an underlying instrument or *asset*, typically a *commodity*, *bond*, *equity* or currency.

direct debit: Regular electronic debiting of funds from a nominated account.

director: One of several individuals elected by a corporation's *shareholders* to establish company policies, including selection of operating officers and payment of *dividends*.

discount: Anything selling below its normal price.

diversification: To vary *investments* and invest in a range of *assets* and *asset classes*, such as *bonds*, *shares* and so on.

dividend: A taxable payment declared by a company's *board of directors* and given to its *shareholders* out of the company's *earnings* (usually quarterly). Can take the form of cash (most common), stock or other property.

dividend cover: A ratio showing the number of times a company's *dividend* is covered by its *net profit*. Calculated by dividing net profit by dividend paid.

dividend imputation: A tax rule under which tax paid at the company level is credited to individual *shareholders*. Works by assessing shareholders on the total amount of the *dividend* and the *imputation credit*, and then allowing them to claim a *tax rebate* equal to the imputation credit.

dividend income: A cash payment made to *shareholders* from a company's *profits*. The main source of income from *share* investments.

dividend rate: The *dividend* shown as cents per *share*.

dividend-reinvestment plan (DRP):
A scheme that allows you to reinvest your *dividends* back into the company, usually at no extra cost and with no additional paperwork. *Shares* purchased this way are often offered at a *discount* to their current *market price.*

dividend type: The classification of a *dividend* as determined either by the *ASX* or by a *company*. Terms include interim, final and special.

dividend yield: The annual *dividend* expressed as a percentage of the last sale price for the *shares.*

doubtful debts: *Debts* on which it is considered likely that a loss will be incurred through payment not being received or not received in full.

dummy bidding: Where people pretend to bid at *auctions.*

earnings: (a) Money received for work. (b) The *cash flow* of an *asset*, such as a *bond* or *equity*, that is paid to the owner. (c) *Revenue* minus cost of sales, operating expenses and taxes, over a given period of time. Also called *income.*

earnings before interest and tax (EBIT): Similar to *net profit*, except that the effects of tax benefits, deductions and loans are factored out, providing a better measure of a company's performance.

earnings per share (EPS): A ratio calculated by dividing the after-tax profit by the number of *shares* on issue, which is used as an indicator of a *company's* performance.

economic entity: A group of entities comprising the parent entity and each of its subsidiaries.

EFTPOS: Acronym for electronic funds transfer at point of sale.

employee: A person engaged to perform certain duties, in return for wages or salary.

employee incentive scheme: A scheme for the issue or acquisition of *securities* to be held by, or for the benefit of, employees.

equities: *Shares* or any spin-off investments linked with public companies.

equity: The difference between the market value of a house and the amount the homeowner owes on it.

ethical funds: Funds that invest by pooling investor savings into entities such as environmental and socially positive activities like recycling, conservation, energy efficiency, preservation of endangered species, animal welfare and so on. Also referred to as socially responsible investment (SRI) funds.

ex-bonus, ex-bonus date: *Shares* that entitle the seller to retain the *bonus shares* being issued. The ex-bonus date occurs seven business days prior to and including the *record date.*

exchange rate: The rate at which one currency can be traded for another.

exchange-traded fund (ETF): A fund that tracks an *index*, but can be traded like a *stock.*

exchange-traded options (ETOs): *Options* that are bought and sold on the *options market* operated by the *ASX.*

ex-dividend: A *security* that no longer carries the right to the most recent *dividend*; or the period of time between the announcement of the dividend and the payment.

ex-dividend date: The first day of the ex-dividend period.

exercise price: The price at which the taker of an *option* may buy or sell the underlying *securities*. Also known as the strike price.

exit fee: A charge that may be levied when *assets* are withdrawn from a *managed fund* or *superannuation* fund.

expense: Any cost of doing business resulting from *revenue*-generating activities.

expiry, expiry date, expiration: The date on which all unexercised *options* or *warrants* in a particular series expire.

ex rights: Securities that entitle the seller to retain the right to participate in a 'new issue' then current.

extraordinary items: Items derived from very rare events or transactions that are distinct from the ordinary activities of the business and are not expected to recur frequently or regularly.

fair value: Fair value of a stock index *futures* contract is the current value of the underlying *shares* or *index*, plus an amount referred to as the 'cost of carry'. This amount reflects the cost of the money required to buy and hold the basket of stocks that make up the index, less the value of the *dividends* paid on those shares during the term of the futures contract.

financial institution: An entity that accepts money as savings or *investments* and in turn provides funds to borrowers.

financial lease: A lease that effectively transfers from the lessor to the lessee substantially all the risks and benefits incident to ownership of the leased *asset* without transferring legal ownership.

First Home Owner Grant (FHOG): Commonwealth Government grant to first-time buyers of a new or established house, home unit, flat or other type of self-contained fixed dwelling.

fixed asset: An *asset* such as plant, equipment or property.

fixed interest: A *security* where the return when held to maturity is fixed.

fixed-interest market: See *bond market*.

fixed-rate mortgage: A *mortgage* in which you lock into an *interest rate* for a specified period, such as one, two or three years.

float: The decision to put a *company's* *shares* on offer to the public.

foreign-registered trusts: Trusts that are overseas-based funds that you can buy inside Australia.

franked dividends: A *dividend* paid by a *company* out of *profits* on which the company has already paid tax. Franking credits, also called *imputation credits*, are a tax offset for Australian residents who receive dividend income from Australian-based companies.

franking rate: The company tax rate at which the *dividend* is franked. Dividends may be fully franked at the current Australian corporate tax rate of 30 per cent, or partially franked.

fundamental analysis: Analysis of *share* values based on factors such as sales, earnings and *assets* that are fundamental to a *company*.

fund manager: The individual or organisation in charge of managing investors' funds on behalf of a *financial institution*.

futures: A standardised, transferable, exchange-traded contract that requires delivery of a *commodity*, *bond*, currency, or stock *index*, at a specified price, on a specified future date.

futures exchange: A market in which *futures* and *options* on futures contracts are traded. In Australia, the Sydney Futures Exchange, operated by the Australian Securities Exchange, conducts futures trading.

futures option: An *option* (either *put* or *call*) on a futures contract, traded at the *futures exchange*.

Global Industry Classification Standard (GICS): A set of global industry definitions that serve to classify *companies* around the world according to the type of business operation they perform.

goods and services tax (GST): Federal value-added tax that is collected at all stages of the production and distribution process.

goodwill: An intangible *asset* of a *company*, reflecting the value of attributes such as customer loyalty and reputation.

government bonds: *Bonds* issued by federal and state governments. They carry an explicit government guarantee.

grossing up: Adding *imputation credits* (franking credits) to income received from *dividends*. The grossed-up dividend is then used to offset income tax payable on an individual's tax return.

hedge funds: *Managed funds* that primarily invest in *derivatives* like *options* and *futures* or any other *security* that 'derives' from ordinary *shares*.

home equity: The value of a homeowner's unencumbered interest in their property. *Equity* is the difference between the home's market value and the unpaid balance of the *mortgage* and any outstanding debt over the home. Equity increases as the mortgage is paid or as the property appreciates.

home loan: A loan whereby you pledge your home as the lender's *security* for repayment of your loan. The lender agrees to hold the *title* or *deed* to your property until you have paid back your loan plus *interest*.

house inspection: Where the overall condition of a property is examined.

imputation credit: A tax offset available to Australian residents who receive *franked dividends* from shareholdings in Australian-based companies.

income: (a) Money received for work. (b) The *cash flow* of an asset, such as a *bond* or *equity*, that is paid to the owner. (c) *Revenue* minus cost of sales, operating expenses and taxes, over a given period of time. Also called *earnings*.

indenture: A written agreement between the issuer of a *bond* and his/her bondholders, usually specifying *interest rate*, maturity date and so on.

index: A statistical indicator providing a representation of the price of the *securities* that constitute it.

indexed bonds: Funds that aim to achieve the exact same performance as a bond index.

index funds: Funds that mirror certain stock indices. Where managers 'track' (or copy and reproduce the performance of) an *index*.

industry sector: The general industry category into which a *company* is classified on a stock exchange.

insider trading: People using information on *stocks* to their advantage, before the information is disclosed to the stock exchange and made public.

insolvency: The inability to pay debts as they are due because of an excess of *liabilities* over *assets*.

instalment warrant: Investments that allow you to pay a deposit, or an instalment, on an *ordinary share* and pay the balance at a specified date in the future.

institutional investors: Managers of *superannuation funds* and other *managed funds* that invest in the market.

insurance bonds: Bonds issued by life insurance companies that aim to achieve regular income from a fund with *investments* in the *bond market*.

intangible assets: Resources owned by a *company*, fund or individual, including patents and *goodwill*.

Integrated Trading System (ITS): Since 2 October 2006, trading of *shares*, *warrants*, *fixed-interest securities* and company-issued *options* and *rights* has been conducted on the Click-XT system, also known as the Integrated Trading System. ITS replaced the older *SEATS (Stock Exchange Automated Trading System)*.

interest: (a) The *return* earned on funds that have been invested. (b) The amount a borrower pays to a *lender* for the use of his/her money.

interest cover: A measure of a *company's* ability to meet its *interest* obligations, calculated by dividing *income* by interest payments.

interest-only loan: A loan where only the *interest* is paid for an agreed term (usually a short period of one to five years) or during a construction period. The *principal* is then repaid over the remaining term of the loan by the conversion of repayments to principal and interest.

interest rate: The rate (as a percentage) charged by a *lender* on an amount borrowed.

interim dividend: A *dividend* that is distributed before the company's annual *earnings* have been calculated.

in-the-money option: A *call option* whose *exercise price* is below, or a *put option* whose exercise price is above, the current price of the *asset* on which the *option* is written.

intrinsic value: The perceived actual value of a *security*, based on fundamental indicators such as *assets*, *income* and *cash flow*, as opposed to its *market price*.

inventory: A *company's* merchandise, *raw materials*, and finished and unfinished products that have not yet been sold.

investment: An asset purchased with the aim of producing an *income* or capital gain.

investment adviser: A person (licensed) who advises individuals on suitable forms of *investment* for their *assets*, considering their tax position, *liabilities*, personal circumstances and so on.

investment bank: A bank that concentrates on deals between *corporations* and other large *investment* entities.

issued capital: That part of a *company's authorised capital* that has been issued in the form of *shares*.

joint venture: A contractual agreement joining together two or more parties for the purpose of executing a particular business undertaking. All parties agree to share in the *profits* and losses of the enterprise.

junk bond: A high-*risk*, non-investment-grade *bond* with a low *credit rating*; as a consequence, it usually has a high *yield*.

land tax: A state-based tax on the value of land (not buildings) held by you for *investment* purposes. Varies between states.

lease: A legal arrangement in which one party (the lessee) gains the right to use the *property* of another party (the lessor) for a stated period of time, in return for agreed periodical payments.

leasehold: *Property* held other than in absolute ownership.

leasehold improvements: Expenditures made by the lessee to alter or improve leased *property*.

lender: A private, public or institutional entity that makes funds available to others to borrow.

leverage: The degree of *gearing* or borrowing.

liability: A financial obligation, *debt*, claim or potential loss.

limited liability: Type of investment in which a partner or investor cannot lose more than the amount invested.

liquid assets: Assets that you can easily convert into cash, such as *shares* or *fixed-interest investments*.

liquidation: Process whereby *companies* and funds that are in the process of being *wound up*, with *assets* being sold and, as far as possible, *liabilities* settled.

liquidity: The ability to sell *investments* quickly.

listed company: A *company* that has agreed to abide by ASX listing rules so that its shares can be bought and sold on the *ASX*.

listed managed funds: *Managed funds* that can be bought and sold on the *stock market*.

listed stock: *Securities* that are approved for admission to a stock exchange.

listing: See *float; compliance listing*.

listing rules: An *ASX* set of rules that govern the procedures and behaviour of all ASX listed *companies* and listed *trusts*.

loan-to-valuation ratio (LVR): Measure used to determine the percentage of the *equity* in a *mortgage* or investment loan against the value of the *security*. If you own $50,000 worth of shares and borrow an additional $50,000 to invest in shares, you have an LVR of 50, or 50 per cent of the total value of your share portfolio.

lump sum repayments: Additional ad hoc repayments, made over and above your minimum repayment requirement.

managed funds: Pooled funds provided by thousands of individual investors devoted to particular *investments*.

management-expense ratio (MER): Total fees paid by the investor in an *investment* fund to the manager of the fund. Usually expressed as an annual percentage of the total amount invested.

margin: (a) The amount of *equity* required for an *investment* in *securities* purchased on *credit*. (b) The face value of a loan minus the value of the pledged *collateral*.

marginal rate of tax: The rate of tax that you pay on the portion of your salary that falls above a certain income threshold.

market capitalisation: The total market value of all *shares* of the *company* listed on the *stock market*, found by multiplying the number of shares on issue by the current *market price*.

market price: The prevailing price of *shares* traded on the *ASX*. May be the last price at which the shares traded, or the most recent price offered or bid for the shares.

master trust: An *investment* platform that provides administration under a single trustee and offers access to a wider range of investments and direct *shares* than other public-offer funds, with ownership held by a pool of investors. See also *wrap account*.

markets: Financial marketplaces such as the *stock market*, *bond market* and *currency market* that are key indicators to the health of the economy.

memorandum of association: The formal document subscribed by those wishing to form a *company* and giving details of the company.

merger: The combining of two or more *companies* into one, through an acquisition or a pooling of interests.

merging principle: A house where the value of the land is least affected by the condition of the house and has 'merged' with the land value — the ideal residential investment property.

middle-ring areas: Land within ten kilometres of a city centre.

minimum initial investment: Smallest amount that the promoter of an *investment* will accept.

minimum repayment required: The amount you are contractually obliged to repay each month, in order to repay your loan within the agreed term.

minority interest: The *equity* in a partly owned subsidiary that is not held by the parent *company* or its subsidiary companies.

mortgage: A charge over *property* given by the owner (borrower/*mortgagor*) to a lender (*mortgagee*) to secure repayment of a loan or to ensure satisfaction of a debt.

mortgage brokers: Agents who find you the best *mortgage* for a fee.

mortgagee: The lender of the funds.

mortgagor: The person(s) who owns the *property* offered in support of the loan.

mutual society: An organisation owned by its members, for the good of its members.

mutual fund: See *managed fund*.

negative gearing: Borrowing money to make an *investment*, where the return from the investment is less than the borrowing costs. Negative gearing is a popular strategy because it bestows certain tax benefits on the borrower.

net assets: Total *assets* minus total *liabilities*; proprietorship; owner's *equity*.

net asset value (NAV): The dollar value of a single unit in a *managed fund*, based on the value of the underlying *assets* of the fund minus its *liabilities*, divided by the number of units on issue. Calculated at the end of each business day.

net current assets: Current *assets* minus current *liabilities*; also called *working capital*.

net profit: The excess of all *revenues* and gains for a period over all *expenses* and losses of the period.

net tangible asset backing: The net physical assets owned by *shareholders* of a *company* at balance date.

net tangible assets (NTA): An indication of what each share in a *company* is worth if all the *assets* were liquidated, all the *debts* were paid and the residual was distributed to the ordinary *shareholders* on a per-share basis.

no-liability company: A public *company* whose *shareholders* are not liable for the *debts* of the company. Restricted to mining companies.

no-load funds: Funds that don't charge an entry fee.

offer: Price at which a *broker* is willing to sell. Also known as the *ask*.

official list: Names of *securities* permitted to trade on the *ASX*.

open-ended funds: Where a fund is always capable of expanding the number of units on issue. As the fund grows the *fund manager* continually issues more units. An open-ended fund is the most common structure for *managed funds*.

operating profit (loss): The *profit* (loss) for the relevant period resulting from the operations of a *company*.

opportunity cost: The price of not investing in better *investments*.

option: A contract that gives the holder the right, but not the obligation, to buy or sell a *commodity* or *security* during a given timeframe. See also *call option*, *put option*.

ordinary share: A class of *company share* that has no special rights attached. Holders of ordinary shares are entitled to voting rights and *dividends* as declared. Also called ordinary fully paid shares.

out-of-the-money: An *option* that has been made valueless by market movements.

par value: Not applicable in Australia. Elsewhere, the par value of a *company's shares* is the price at which they were issued, as distinct from the current *market price*.

parent company: A *company* that owns enough *stock* in another firm to control management and operations by influencing or electing its *board of directors*.

pari passu (of equal step): Indicates that one series of *equity* will have the same rights and privileges as another series of equity.

participating dividend: *Dividend* paid on participating preferred *stock*.

participating preference shares: Preference shares that, in addition to a regular *dividend*, pay an additional dividend (the *participating dividend*) when common stock dividends exceed a specified amount.

pay as you go (PAYG) income tax withholding variation: A tax law enabling you to claim deductions in advance for *interest* on *investment* loans that falls due over the following 12 months.

pay as you go (PAYG) withholding tax: A legal requirement to withhold a certain amount of income for income tax purposes.

penny stocks: Cheap *stocks* that offer the prospect of big gains.

personal loan: An arrangement in which a *lender* gives money or *property* to a borrower, and the borrower agrees to return the property or repay the money, usually along with *interest*, at some future point(s) in time.

placement: The selling of new *shares* to select *shareholders*, especially *institutional investors*, through a special arrangement.

pooled investment: An *investment* in which a number of individuals give money to a professional manager, who manages the *assets* as a pool. Includes *superannuation funds*, *unit trusts*, *cash-management trusts* and generally available *managed funds*.

preference shares: *Capital stock* that provides a specific *dividend* that is paid before any dividends are paid to common *shareholders*, and that takes precedence over common stock in the event of a *liquidation*.

prepayment: The payment of all or part of a *debt* prior to its due date.

preservation age: The age at which you can withdraw your *superannuation*.

price-to-earnings (PE) ratio: A measure of how expensive a *stock* is. Equal to a stock's *market capitalisation* divided by its after-tax *earnings* over a 12-month period, usually the previous financial year but occasionally the current or next financial year.

principal: (a) The amount borrowed, or the part of the amount borrowed that remains unpaid (excluding *interest*). (b) The part of a monthly payment that reduces the outstanding balance of a *mortgage*. (c) The original *investment*.

principal and interest loan: A loan in which both the *principal* and *interest* are repaid, during the agreed term of the loan.

private equity: *Investment* in private (unlisted) *companies*.

private-equity funds: *Managed funds* that invest in start-up *companies*.

privatisation: When governments sell state *assets* on the *stock market*.

profit: The positive gain from an *investment* or business operation after subtracting all *expenses*.

profit and loss statement: Formal document published by a *company* showing all *revenue* and *expenses* relating to a specific period, generally six months and one year. Also called an earnings report.

pro-forma: Description of *financial statements* that have one or more assumptions or hypothetical conditions built into the data.

promissory note: A document signed by a borrower promising to repay a loan under agreed-upon terms.

property: That which is legally owned by an individual or entity.

property trust: See *real estate investment trust*.

pro rata: In proportion to, as determined by a specific factor.

prospectus: A legal document offering *securities* or *managed fund* units for sale.

proxy: (a) A written authorisation given by a *shareholder* for someone else, usually the company's management, to cast his/her vote at a shareholder meeting or at another time. (b) A person who represents another person.

put option: An *option* contract that gives the holder the right, but not the obligation, to sell a certain quantity of an underlying *security* to the writer of the option, at a specified price by a specified date.

put warrant: See *warrant*.

quotation: The highest *bid* or lowest *ask* price available on a *security* at any given time.

raw materials: Unfinished goods consumed by a manufacturer in providing *finished goods*. Classified as *inventory*.

real estate: A piece of land, including the air above it and the ground below it, and any buildings or structures on it.

real estate agent: A licensed salesperson who sells *real estate*.

real estate investment trust (REIT): A *managed fund* that specialises in investment property.

re-amortise: To recalculate the minimum repayment required to repay the outstanding balance of your loan over the remaining period (particularly where the loan balance has substantially increased or decreased from the original amount).

receivables: Amounts owed.

receiver: A professional administrator appointed either by a court or by creditors, if an organisation or person is unable to pay its *debts*.

recession: Two consecutive quarters, three-month periods, where the economy doesn't grow.

record date: The date on which a *company* closes its books to determine which *shareholders* are registered to receive *dividends* or *bonus shares*.

redraw facility: The component of your *variable-rate* loan into which you can make extra repayments when you can afford to, and later draw on these funds if you need to.

rental guarantee: The promised rate of return on an *investment* offered by a property developer.

rental yield: The annual rate of rental return on an investment property against its purchase price or current value.

reserves: The proportion of a *company's profit* not distributed to *shareholders* as *dividends*.

retail investor: Individual investor, not an extremely wealthy individual, professional investor, *company* or *corporation*.

retained earnings: *Earnings* not paid out as *dividends* but instead reinvested in the core business or used to pay off *debt*.

retirement savings account (RSA): A form of retail *superannuation fund* offered by banks to protect part-time workers and low-income earners.

return: The amount of money received annually from an *investment*, usually expressed as a percentage.

return on assets: A measure of a company's *profitability*.

return on equity: A measure of how well a *company* used reinvested *earnings* to generate additional earnings.

return on investment: The *income* that an *investment* provides in a year.

revenue: The total dollar amount collected for goods and services provided.

rights issue: An offer to existing *shareholders* to purchase additional *shares* in the company, in proportion to their holding, usually at a lower price than the current *market price*.

risk: The quantifiable likelihood of loss or less-than-expected *returns*.

risk–reward ratio: The level of reward you expect from a given level of *risk*. The higher the risk, the higher the potential reward (and losses).

rollover: Transfer of an eligible termination payment to a rollover fund or to another *superannuation* fund.

salary sacrifice: Where you place some of your pre-tax salary directly into *superannuation*. Salary sacrifice attracts significant tax benefits.

SEATS: Acronym for *Stock Exchange Automated Trading System*. See *Integrated Trading System (ITS)*.

security: (a) A financial *investment*, such as a *share* or *bond*, that is tradeable on financial markets. (b) Documentation held by the *lender* (or *mortgagee*) regarding *property* supporting the loan.

semi-government bonds: *Bonds* issued by government-funded agencies or statutory bodies.

settlement: Finalising of the sale of a *property*, as its *title* is transferred from the seller to the buyer.

share buyback: When a company buys back its own *shares*, and then cancels them, in order to boost the value of the remaining shares.

share certificate: A formal declaration of ownership of a specific number of *shares* in a *company*.

shareholder: A person who owns *shares* in a *corporation* or *company*.

shares: Also known as *stocks*. A slice of ownership in a company that's publicly traded on the *stock market*.

short selling: The sale of *securities* that are not yet owned, in the expectation that the price will fall and they can be bought back later at a *profit*.

simple interest: The *interest* calculated on a *principal* sum, not compounded on earned interest.

small caps: *Shares* in smaller *companies*; that is, companies with a *market capitalisation* of less than $150 million.

socially responsible investment (SRI) funds: See *ethical funds*.

stamp duty: A state government tax assessed on the selling price of the property. Each state has different rules and calculations.

stock market: The organised trading of *stocks* through exchanges and over-the-counter.

stocks: Also known as *shares*. A slice of ownership in a *company* that's publicly traded on the *stock market*.

straight-through processing (STP): The ability to process transactions instantly, offered by online stockbrokers.

strata title: The most common *title* associated with townhouses and home units; evidence of ownership of a unit, which is called a 'lot', in a strata plan. Individuals each own a small portion (such as a unit or townhouse) of a larger property, but where there is common property (external walls, windows, roof, driveways, foyers, fences, lawns and gardens) that all owners share.

strike price: See *exercise price*.

subscribers: The initial purchasers of the *warrants* in the primary issue.

subsidiary: A *company* for which a majority of the voting *stock* is owned by a holding company.

substantial shareholder: A *shareholder* who holds a substantial number of *shares* in a *company*.

superannuation: A long-term savings vehicle for investment *assets* that operates primarily to provide income for retirement.

superannuation fund: A fund established primarily to provide benefits for members on their retirement, or alternatively, on their resignation, death, disablement or other specified event. Usually a *trust fund* governed by a *trust deed* and administered by trustees.

takeover: The acquisition by one *company* of *shares* in another company so as to gain a controlling interest.

takeover premium: The extra strength in a *company share* price attributed to the possibility of the company being taken over by another.

taxable income: assessable income minus any allowable deductions, calculated for the purpose of assessing gross tax payable.

tax deductible: Payments that people may deduct against federal and state *taxable income*.

tax file number (TFN): A number allocated to taxpayers by the Australian Taxation Office.

tax rebate: A reduction in tax liability allowed in certain circumstances. Often described as a percentage.

technical analysis: An approach to the analysis of *stock* and *futures markets* and their future trends that examines price patterns without reference to fundamental share valuations.

term: The duration of a loan or a specific period within that loan. Usually written in months.

term deposit: Money invested for a fixed period of time at a specified rate of *interest*, which applies for the length of the deposit.

termination benefit: The benefit payable to a member/holder from a fund on termination of the member's service or that which is entitled if the fund is terminated.

time value: The balance of an *option* premium not represented by the option's intrinsic value.

title deed: Legal document disclosing the legal description and ownership of a *property*.

trading: The buying and selling of *securities* or *commodities* on a short-term basis.

trading halt: A temporary stoppage of *trading* in a particular *security* for a specific reason, such as a pending news announcement.

trust deed: An agreement spelling out the methods of receipt, *investment* and disbursement of funds under a *superannuation* plan, *unit trust*, charitable trust and so on.

trust fund: A fund whose *assets* are managed by a trustee or a board of trustees for the benefit of another party or parties.

turnover: For a *company*, the ratio of annual sales to *inventory*; or the fraction of a year that an average item remains in inventory. For a *managed fund*, the number of times per year that an average dollar of *assets* is reinvested.

underlying instrument, underlying security: The *asset* that the holder has the right to buy or sell, or against which a cash payment is made on exercise of an *option* or *warrant*.

undervalued: An *investment* that is trading at a price less than its real worth.

underwriter: A *broker* or bank that arranges the sale of an issue of *securities* on behalf of a client.

unit trust: A form of *pooled investment*, where a number of smaller investors buy units in a trust that is promoted and managed by professional investment managers. Governed by a *trust deed*, and has trustees and a management company.

unitholder: A person who owns units in a *managed fund*, or *unit trust*.

unlisted funds: Funds that are not listed on the *stock market*.

valuation: A report detailing a professional opinion of a *property's* value.

variable-rate mortgage: An *interest rate* that goes up or down depending on movements in money-market interest rates.

vendor: A seller of an *asset*. In *real estate* transactions, the vendor is the person disposing of the *property*.

volatility: The extent of fluctuation in share prices, *exchange rates*, *interest rates* and so on. The higher the volatility, the less certain an *investor* is of return, and therefore volatility is one measure of *risk*.

warrant: A financial instrument issued by a bank or other financial institution that is traded on the *ASX*. Warrants may be issued over *securities* such as *shares* in a company, a currency, an *index* or a *commodity*. Call warrants give the purchaser the right to buy securities in the future and put warrants give the purchaser the right to sell securities. See also *instalment warrant*.

weighting: The relative proportion of each of a group of *securities* or *asset* classes within a single *investment* portfolio.

winding-up: The stopping of a business operation with the realising of *assets*, discharging of *liabilities* and so on.

working capital: *Current assets* minus *current liabilities*.

wrap account: An *investment* platform that provides administration under a single trustee and offers access to a wider range of investments and direct *shares* than other public-offer funds, with ownership held by the investor. See also *master trust*.

write down (up): To reduce (or increase) the recorded value of an *asset*.

write off: To charge an *asset* amount to expense or loss, in order to reduce the value of that asset and a person's earnings.

yield: The *profit* or *income* that an *investment* returns; usually expressed as an annual percentage of the initial investment. See also *rental yield*.

Index

• N •

Notes

Notes

Notes

FOR DUMMIES®

Business & Investment

Starting an Online Business

0-7314-0991-4
$39.95

Business Plans

1-74031-124-8
$39.95

Investing for Australians

0-7314-0838-1
$54.95

Superannuation

0-7314-0715-6
$39.95

Buying & Selling Your Home

1-74031-166-3
$39.95

Investing in Real Estate

0-7314-0724-5
$39.95

Online Share Investing

0-7314-0940-X
$39.95

Charting

0-7314-0710-5
$39.95

Leadership

0-7314-0787-3
$39.95

Freelancing for Australians

0-7314-0762-8
$39.95

Australian Resumes

1-74031-091-8
$39.95

Sorting Out Your Finances

0-7314-0746-6
$29.95

FOR DUMMIES®

Reference

Work / Life Balance

0-7314-0723-7
$34.95

World Poverty

0-7314-0699-0
$34.95

Sustainable Living

1-74031-157-4
$39.95

Wedding Planning

0-7314-0721-0
$34.95

Gardening

1-74031-007-1
$39.95

Australia's Dangerous Creatures

0-7314-0722-9
$29.95

Sustainable Australian Travel

0-7314-0784-9
$34.95

English Grammar

0-7314-0752-0
$34.95

Technology

The Internet

0-7314-0985-X
$39.95

QuickBooks QB

0-7314-0761-X
$39.95

MYOB Software

0-7314-0941-8
$39.95

eBay

1-74031-159-0
$39.95

FOR DUMMIES®

Health & Fitness

Breast Cancer
1-74031-143-4
$39.95

Menopause
1-74031-140-X
$39.95

Food & Nutrition
0-7314-0596-X
$34.95

Diabetes
1-74031-094-2
$39.95

Fitness
1-74031-009-8
$39.95

Weight Training
1-74031-044-6
$39.95

Yoga
1-74031-059-4
$39.95

Pilates
1-74031-074-8
$39.95

Golf
1-74031-011-X
$39.95

Cricket
1-74031-173-6
$39.95

Aussie Rules
0-7314-0595-1
$34.95

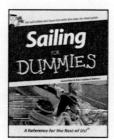

Sailing
0-7314-0644-3
$39.95

Printed in Australia
03 Feb 2025
LP040932